QUICK AND POPULAR
READS FOR TEENS

Edited by Pam Spencer Holley
for the Young Adult Library Services Association

American Library Association
Chicago   2009

Pam Spencer Holley is a former school librarian and retired coordinator of school libraries for Fairfax County (Virginia) Public Schools. She is the author of *What Do Children and Young Adults Read Next?* volumes 1–6, and now contributes to the online version called Books and Authors. Holley originated and wrote the "Audiobooks It Is!" column for *Voice of Youth Advocates,* 2003–2007, and is a former chair of Best Books for Young Adults and the 2004 Printz Award and a past president of the Young Adult Library Services Association.

Library of Congress Cataloging-in-Publication Data
Quick and popular reads for teens / edited by Pam Spencer Holley for the Young Adult
   Library Services Association.
      p. cm.
   Includes bibliographical references and index.
   ISBN 978-0-8389-3577-4 (alk. paper)
      1. Teenagers—Books and reading—United States. 2. Reading promotion—United
States. 3. Young Adult Library Services Association. 4. Young adults' libraries—
United States—Book lists. 5. Young adult literature—Bibliography.   I. Holley, Pam
Spencer, 1944–
Z1037.A1Q53 2009
028.5'5—dc22
                                                            2008049691

ISBN-13: 978-0-8389-3577-4

Printed in the United States of America
13 12 11 10 09   5 4 3 2 1

CONTENTS

WEB Additional material can be found on the book's companion website at
www.ala.org/editions/extras/holley35774.

PREFACE

For more than fifty years, the Young Adult Library Services Association (YALSA) has been the leader in book selection for all types of readers. The Best Books for Young Adults list is the oldest of the division's lists, but more selection lists have been added to respond to observed needs and changes in teen interests. For example, there are now selection lists featuring graphic novels, audiobooks, films, debut works, and nonfiction.

With the recognition and acceptance that not all teens like to read, members of the Young Adult Services Division (YASD), YALSA's predecessor, first presented the idea for a High Interest/Low Literacy Committee in the mid-1970s. By the early 1980s, YASD had formed a committee to select titles of a lower reading level that were of interest to teens. From that initial committee came the list first titled Recommended Books for the Reluctant Young Adult Reader, which is now known as Quick Picks for Reluctant Young Adult Readers (QP). The yearly QP list consists of titles published in the previous year which, according to the professional opinion of librarians and input from teens, are surefire hits with teens.

The Popular Paperbacks for Young Adults (PPYA) Committee was established after a trial in which YALSA and Baker and Taylor developed genre lists of paperbacks to fill display dumps. Although Baker and Taylor eventually ended its partnership with YALSA, it was obvious that these thematic lists were popular with teens and librarians, and YALSA needed to continue offering them. The PPYA committee now selects four themes each year, and then, with no limitation on copyright dates, chooses paperbacks popular with teens to fit those themes.

In this book, you will first find an introductory chapter about teen readers and then two chapters reviewing the origin, history, and selection processes for both the QP and PPYA committees, as written by former committee members. A chapter on programming, also by a former QP committee member, offers suggestions for using the lists in your library, as well as further readings. The next two chapters, covering fiction and nonfiction, contain the annotated listings of the titles selected by the QP and PPYA committees from 1999 to 2008—a decade's worth of titles for each list. The annotations have all been rewritten to offer more descriptive help for librarians as they provide readers' advisory service to teens or develop their collections. The original annotations, written by committee members with the teen reader in mind, are available at www.ala.org/yalsa/booklists/. In addition, a collection of thematically organized booklists in the final chapter will help with developing displays, producing bookmarks, and selecting titles to share with teens.

The purpose of this work is to provide school and public librarians, teachers, professors, authors, students, or anyone else interested in literature for teens a reference to "quick and popular" titles. It is hoped that users will not stop with the lists available here but add to them on the basis of their own library collections and the interests of the teens they serve. If users attend an ALA midwinter meeting or annual conference, they can stop and observe a QP or PPYA meeting to hear the level of discussion, learn about many new titles, and perhaps even volunteer to serve on one of the committees.

ACKNOWLEDGMENTS

Several knowledgeable YALSA members contributed chapters to this book, and their experience on the committee for either Quick Picks for Reluctant Readers or Popular Paperbacks for Young Adults added that touch of insider information to their writings: Paula Brehm-Heeger served on the PPYA committee for the 2004, 2005, and 2006 lists; Stacy Creel was a member of the QP committee for the 2005, 2006, and 2007 lists; and Jamie Watson was a member of the QP committee for the 2004, 2005, and 2006 lists, chair for the 2006 list, and administrative assistant for the 2007 list. In addition to their committee experience, these authors bring to their chapters insight garnered from their careers as librarians working with teens to understand and promote their reading interests.

Thanks to Louisa Storer, a former graduate assistant at Queens College, for preparing some of the annotations for recent QP lists. In the YALSA office, Stevie Kuenn was invaluable in jump-starting this project and then keeping us on task. People I had never met in ALA Editions kindly answered all my questions about bibliographic details and other rookie questions: I am grateful for the help I received from Eugenia Chun and Christine Schwab. Though I was saddened when my good friend Stephanie Zvirin left *Booklist,* what a treat to discover we were working together on this project. Thanks also to Beth Yoke, executive director of YALSA, who conceived the idea for this book and then submitted an application for a Carnegie Grant. When YALSA received the grant, the funding needed to hire an editor and contributors was available and writing began. A large share of the acknowledgments must go to the teens, both those who read avidly and those who read reluctantly, for it is their comments, enthusiasm, and suggestions that ultimately determine which books land on selection lists and which committees YALSA creates to help both librarians and teens.

CHAPTER 1

INTRODUCTION
YALSA, Teens, and Reading
Paula Brehm-Heeger and Stacy Creel

The mission of the Young Adult Library Services Association (YALSA) is to advocate, promote, and strengthen service to young adults as part of the continuum of total library service and to support those who provide service to this population. YALSA has identified several activities and concerns as essential in fulfilling this vital mission. Among this list of compelling concerns, none ranks higher than evaluating and promoting materials of interest to adolescents through special services, programs, and publications. The annual Quick Picks for Reluctant Young Adult Readers (QP) and Popular Paperbacks for Young Adults (PPYA) lists clearly fall under the "evaluating and promoting materials of interest to adolescents" umbrella. But why is the selection of titles for these lists, put together by dedicated and knowledgeable library professionals, such an essential activity for YALSA? Why should all librarians, educators, and adults concerned with the health and well-being of teenagers spend their valuable and increasingly limited time, resources, and energy learning about and utilizing the QP and PPYA lists for the benefit of the teenagers with whom they work? A brief examination of reading habits among teenagers ages 12–18, both past and present, provides insight into just why these lists are vital for strengthening service to all young adults in the nation's libraries.

Today's librarians face many challenges, including getting teens not only into their libraries but also into reading. This concern is widely acknowledged,

---

Paula Brehm-Heeger is manager of the Central Region for the Public Library of Cincinnati and Hamilton County. A past president of YALSA, she is the author of *Serving Urban Teens* (Libraries Unlimited, 2008). **Stacy Creel** is assistant professor in the Division of Library and Information Science at St. John's University, Queens, New York. She is a former editor of *Voice of Youth Advocates*.

but opinions differ on why these challenges exist and also on the state of teens and reading in America. Are teens reading or not? Which teens are reading more, and which teens are reading less? Are they reading what they say they are reading? And what counts as reading (Aronson 2006; Gardner and Dillon 2005; National Endowment for the Arts 2007)? The pendulum of public opinion swings between the idea that young adults are not reading at all and what Aronson calls "hand-wringing over what a concerned parent fears they might be reading too avidly" (Aronson 2005). So what is the reality behind these seemingly contradictory ideas regarding teens and reading?

A good place to start unraveling the mystery about teens and their reading habits is with a look at the origins of the concept of *reluctant readers*. A common, long-standing perception about why teens are not reading or are reluctant to read is associated with reading skill. When reading is difficult for them, they do not like to do it. This belief about why teens are reluctant readers is not a new concept. In 1952, the Executive Committee of Capital Area School Development Association recognized the needs of low-level teen readers and produced *Fare for the Reluctant Reader*—an annotated listed of teen-tested titles divided by grade level and category (Bush and Dunn 1952). The idea that teens do not read because they lack the skills to do so has remained popular over the years and has led to such ideas as connecting teens to reading through hi/lo books—books deemed to have high interest but requiring low reading skills (LiBretto 1985; Williams 1987).

As the concept was developed more fully, the reasons some teens fall into this category became more complex. The thought that teens are not reading simply because they lack the skill gave way to more nuanced discussions. By 1969, the term *reluctant reader* had expanded to include readers "who have the ability to read without mechanical problems but have little or no inclination to read except what is required for work or normal everyday life" (Chambers 1969, 4). This view included a list of reasons that youth ages 11–17 were not reading—a list that probably sounds familiar to many of today's librarians: the dislike of stories, the lack of time, the fact that teens like group activities, and the influx of technology replacing reading as a leisure time activity. In her 1996 *School Library Journal* article "No Time, No Interest, No Way: The 3 Voices of Aliteracy," Kylene Beers demonstrates the further evolution of the reluctant teen reader concept, with reluctant readers now classified into three categories: dormant, uncommitted, and unmotivated. The dormant reader has a positive view of reading but does not commit the time to read or lacks the free time for pleasure reading. The uncommitted reader views reading as a skill but does not have necessarily negative feelings about the skill. The unmotivated reader has a negative view of reading and readers. Stacy Creel, who worked with youth for ten years in a public library setting and spent three years on the QP committee, formulated the following categories:

> *The A+ Student.* This group of teens reads frequently for school assignments but not for pleasure. If it is not important for their college application,

they may not have time, or see the need, to read. They have so much academic reading that even pleasure reading can seem like a chore or an assignment.

The Athlete. These teens may struggle with academics or reading, but not necessarily. Often their lack of recreational reading comes from their hectic schedule; practices, pep rallies, games, and studying to keep their grades up may not leave much time for recreational reading. Additionally, the stereotypical image of the athlete puts pressure on this group to look and act a certain way, an image that may not include being a reader.

The Average Joe/Jane. These teens can take reading or leave it. They may be enticed to read when presented with the "right" book but do not seek out reading on their own. They may come in for assigned open-choice reading, get a book, read it and enjoy it, but not check out another book until the next semester.

The English as Second Language. This group of teens may or may not participate in recreational reading in their native language if materials are available. Reading in English may be a struggle, and finding high-interest recreational books at the appropriate level can be a challenge that keeps them from reading. Additionally, they may perceive that there is a stigma to carrying around a "baby" book or books below level.

The "I Only Read . . ." This is a controversial category. If teens read only one type of book, are they "reluctant"? Some librarians may say, "No, they're reading on their own for pleasure," and others may say, "Yes, if they have read all the vampire fiction in the library and won't read anything else, then they aren't reading."

The Incarcerated. This group of teens may be most closely related to the historical version of the reluctant reader. They often have diagnosed learning or emotional disabilities (34 percent) and have a poor academic record including low achievement, low literacy skills, truancies, being held back, and suspensions (Harris et al. 2006).

The Low Skill Level. This group of teens fits the historical view of reluctant readers who are "poor readers or those teenagers unable to read materials written for their grade level" (Nelson 1998).

The Popular. These teens may be leaders in their schools; they are on the prom committee, in clubs, and have large social groups of friends. Socially accepted, they have many outside interests. Recreational reading may not be an accepted part of their image and may not fit into their schedule of activities.

The Outsiders. This group includes goths, skateboarders, and many other teens who consider themselves alternative. These teens may frequent the library to use technology but may not be aware that libraries have books that would interest them, or they may feel that reading does not fit their image.

The Turned Off. These teens most likely had a negative reading experience somewhere along their educational journey. They may have struggled with reading in class or found an assigned reading to be painful or boring; they then associate that negative experience with reading in general.

What about those teens who really do (or would) like to read but are in desperate need of help in discovering books and literature they actually would enjoy—yes, *enjoy*—reading? Recent reports such as the NEA's "Reading at Risk" and the 2006 Yankelovich Scholastic survey certainly paint a picture of declining leisure reading among teenagers, with the Scholastic survey stating that only 16 percent of 15–17-year-olds read for pleasure every day (Cart 2007). Many teens do not seem to have the slightest idea where to find "fun" books or, more likely, do not know that such books even exist. This lack of awareness of enticing books designed specifically for teens, the very audience to which these books are targeted, has not been helped by the fact that "years of bad marketing have made it difficult to convince teens that there are young adult titles worth reading" (Morris and Eaton 1999).

But convince them we must. If teens are to develop a lifelong reading habit, the importance of pleasure reading during the teen years cannot be underestimated. These days there is a "growing recognition that reading skills need to be nurtured well into adolescence" (McGrath 2005). Combine this with a new perspective from the publishing world on marketing and publishing for teenagers indicating that "YA publishing [has never] been healthier" (McGrath 2005), and it is clear that this is the perfect moment for librarians, teachers, and parents to grab the reins and lead teens straight to the entertaining, popular fare that can help them appreciate the enjoyment that comes from reading. There has never been a better time to convince teens that reading for pleasure is more than okay—it can actually be a heck of a good time!

This brings us to the two reading lists created by committees of YALSA that are the focus of this book. These lists are essential tools for successfully meeting the challenge of encouraging all teens to read for pleasure. These are not only especially appropriate lists for use with reluctant readers but also valuable for leading any teen to a book he or she might like. Before now, these two helpful resources had not been available in one book.

The first is the Quick Picks for Reluctant Young Adult Readers. The list was inaugurated by a committed that started in 1982, the High Interest/Low Literacy Level Materials Evaluation Committee. The committee produced an annual list titled High-Interest Low Reading Level Booklist. In 1988, the list came to be known as Recommended Books for the Reluctant Young Adult Reader, and in 1995 the committee and its list became Quick Picks for Reluctant Young

Adult Readers (QP). The QP charge is "to prepare an annual annotated list of recommended books appropriate for reluctant young adult readers" with the purpose of reaching "young adults (ages 12–18) who, for whatever reasons, do not like to read. The purpose of this list is to identify titles for recreational reading, not for curricular or remedial use" (www.ala.org/yalsa/booklists/quick picks/).

The second is the Popular Paperbacks for Young Adults (PPYA), born out of collaboration with YALSA and Baker and Taylor in the late 1980s. Originally, the list focused on five genres, with corresponding paperback dumps sold to fit the books and the theme. When Baker and Taylor stopped supporting the project in 1995, a new committee formed to "annually prepare one to five annotated list(s) of at least ten and no more than twenty-five recommended paperback titles, selected from popular genres, topics or themes." The purpose of the PPYA list is "to encourage young adults to read for pleasure by presenting to them lists of popular or topical titles that are widely available in paperback and represent a broad variety of accessible themes and genres" (www.ala.org/yalsa/booklists/poppaper/).

This book highlights a decade's worth of these two annual lists' recommendations, books that can be used with young adults who are not avid readers. Although the lists are not new, librarians and other practitioners may not remember them as first options when doing readers' advisory or looking for themes. This book is most appropriate for young adult librarians, library media specialists working in middle and high schools, English teachers, and students and faculty in graduate schools of library and information science, but teens, non-youth librarians, parents, and others who work with young adults may also find it useful.

REFERENCES

Aronson, Marc. 2005. "Getting Over the Rainbow Party." *Publishers Weekly* 252 (32): 66.

———. 2006. "Don't Buy the Hype." *School Library Journal* 52 (6): 36.

Beers, G. Kylene. 1996. "No Time, No Interest, No Way: The 3 Voices of Aliteracy." *School Library Journal* 42 (2): 30–33.

Bush, Bernice C., and Anita Elizabeth Dunn. 1952. *Fare for the Reluctant Reader.* Albany: State University of New York, New York State College for Teachers. *Editor's Note: It is important to note that this edition, a follow-up to* Fare for the Reluctant Reader: Magazines and Audio-Visual Aids for the Slow Learner in Grades 7–10 *(1951), excludes titles in the earlier book that were not successful when tested with teens.*

Cart, Michael. 2007. "Teens and the Future of Reading." *American Libraries* 30 (9): 52–53.

Chambers, Aidan. 1969. *The Reluctant Reader.* Oxford: Pergamon Press.

Gardner, C. A., and Cy Dillon. 2005. "The Future of Books." *Virginia Libraries* 51 (1): 2–3.

Harris, Pamela J., et al. 2006. "Integration of Culture in Reading Studies for Youth in Corrections: A Literature Review." *Education and Treatment of Children* 20 (4): 749–79.

LiBretto, Ellen. 1985. *High/Low Handbook: Books, Materials, and Services for the Problem Reader.* 2nd ed. New Providence, NJ: Bowker.

McGrath, Ann. 2005. "A New Read on Teen Literacy." *U.S. News and World Report* 138 (7): 68.

Morris, Holly J., and Nicole Eaton. 1999. "Why Johnny Can't Stop Reading Books." *U.S. News and World Report* 127 (6): 66.

National Endowment for the Arts. 2007. "Reading at Risk: 10 Key Findings." http://www.nea.gov/about/NEARTS/2004_v2/neaARTS_2004_v2.pdf (accessed February 26, 2009).

Nelson, Judy. 1998. "Quick Picks: A Committee Struggles." *Journal of Youth Services in Libraries* 11 (4): 388–90.

Williams, Helen. 1987. "Characterizations in High-Interest/Low-Vocabulary Level Fiction." *School Library Journal* 42 (2): 30–33.

ADDITIONAL READING

Grillo, Thomas. 2005. "Reaching Teens: Back to the Future." *NEA Today* 23 (5): 26.

Hardy, Lawrence. 2005. "Forgetting How to Read or Just Re-Locating It?" *Education Digest* 70 (6): 33–41.

Jones, Patrick, Maureen L. Hartman, and Patricia P. Taylor. 2006. *Connecting with Reluctant Teen Readers: Tips, Titles, and Tools.* New York: Neal-Schuman.

LiBretto, Ellen, and Catherine Barr. 2002. *High/Low Handbook: Best Books and Websites for Reluctant Teen Readers.* 4th ed. Westport, CT: Libraries Unlimited.

Milliot, Jim. 2007. "New NEA Report Finds More Reading Declines." *Publishers Weekly* 254 (46): 4.

Mize, Jessica. 2006. "Teens' Recommendations for Reluctant Readers." *Young Adult Library Services* 5 (1): 9.

Picker, Lauren. 2005. "Girls' Night Out Gets Smart." *Newsweek* 145 (12): 54.

"Picking the Quick Picks." 2006. *Young Adult Library Services* 4 (2): 7–9.

"Popular Paperbacks for Young Adults." 2008. *Young Adult Library Services* 6 (3): 23–35.

"Quick Picks for Reluctant Young Adult Readers." 2008. *Young Adult Library Services* 6 (3): 26–28.

Reynolds, Marilyn. 2004. *I Won't Read and You Can't Make Me: Reaching Reluctant Teen Readers.* Portsmouth, NH: Heinemann.

Snowball, Clare. 2005. "Teenage Reluctant Readers and Graphic Novels." *Young Adult Library Services* 3 (4): 43–45.

"Top Ten Quick Picks for Reluctant Readers." 2007. *Voice of Youth Advocates* 30 (1): 7.

Watson, Jamie, and Jennifer Stencel. 2005. "Reaching Reluctant Readers with Nonfiction." *Young Adult Library Services* 4 (1): 8.

Williams, Bronwyn T. 2005. "Leading Double Lives: Literacy and Technology in and out of School." *Journal of Adolescent and Adult Literacy* 48 (4): 702–6.

CHAPTER 2

QUICK PICKS FOR RELUCTANT READERS
Origin, History, and Committee Processes

Jamie Watson

I n 1930, the Young Adult Services Division (YASD, YALSA's predecessor) began the first selection list for young adults. Although originally focusing on adult books for teens, the list went through various versions until 1966, when it became Best Books for Young Adults, better known as BBYA. For the next ten years, BBYA was the recognized selection tool for librarians to use for collection development or readers' advisory work with teens. The BBYA list was formulated on the premise that teens wanted and liked to read and that a list of best books was all the stimulus and direction they needed to enjoy reading. In the mid-1970s, however, librarians acknowledged that not all teens enjoyed reading; many teens associated it with schoolwork or tasks to be done. With the growth of the two-income family, many more teens became latchkey kids who spent after-school hours in the library because it was a safe place. Realizing that many of these teens were not interested in reading, librarians searched for ways to reach out to this segment of their users.

PHASE I: THE HIGH INTEREST/LOW LITERACY LEVEL COMMITTEE

In 1976, conversations between staff at *Booklist,* the review journal of the American Library Association, and YASD produced a new committee, the High Interest/Low Literacy Level Committee, chaired by Ellen LiBretto. The committee was charged with exploring the possibility of having a High/Low

---

Jamie Watson is assistant materials manager at Harford County Public Library, near Baltimore. She also serves as the young adult literature specialist and blogger for www.adlit.org, a project of WETA-TV in Washington, D.C.

My Reluctant Reader's Story, by Stacy Creel

I grew up in a house where my parents did everything right to create readers. My dad read the Sunday funnies to us and both parents read us stories at night. We saw them reading and my mom took us to the library. My older sister was an avid reader, but my brother and I were reluctant, to say the least. In first grade, I remember being in the low group in reading and, even though they called us the daisies, we knew that we were the "bad" readers struggling through *Dick and Jane* while the other flower groups read much more exciting things about going to the park and sailing. Through all of elementary and middle school, I remember finishing only one book; it was something I chose to read for a book report about a girl in Ireland during the potato famine. Thank goodness my teachers read the classics out loud, or I would have never been exposed to *Freckle Juice, Tales of a Fourth Grade Nothing, Treasure Island,* or *Where the Red Fern Grows.*

My hatred of reading grew as I struggled through assigned classics like *The Red Badge of Courage,* which held little appeal for me, and I quickly labeled reading a geek activity. I started high school still not reading for pleasure and hardly ever for school. In ninth grade, I had to do an oral report on a classic. I picked my book the way any good reluctant reader does—by the skinny size. I read *Of Mice and Men* and was so moved by the book that I cried and became hysterical during my oral report. I was, of course, horrified and actually had to leave the room, but it was a turning point. I began reading some of the other assigned books (but not all) instead of just reading the first, middle, and last chapters or the Cliffs Notes, and I actually began to read some books for pleasure, even though I hid it from my friends. For a couple of years, my leisure reading consisted only of Harlequin romances, but my parents were just glad I was reading and didn't push me; eventually, I did move on to other genres and a PhD in library and information science.

Whatever happened to my brother—the other reluctant reader? He still isn't a reader and openly detests reading. Throughout high school and college, he hid our books, causing my mother to have to pay for numerous library books and fines. He made it through high school and college without ever reading an entire book, which is one of his favorite things to torture me and my sister (another PhD) with. At 28, he read his first book for pleasure in its entirety—a John Grisham title—while working at a dry cleaning business that had a box of used books for sale. Although he has never to my knowledge read another book for pleasure, he has a son who is wild about reading, so he reads lots of board books and other children's stories. I can only hope that he'll discover the children's and teens' classics he missed and other wonderful books that come as his son finds them.

preconference at the 1978 ALA annual conference and determining how the committee could work with *Booklist* to publish quarterly booklists of hi/lo materials, which could also be sold as pamphlets.

During initial conversations, the preconference convenors assumed that teens' low reading levels made them reluctant to attempt reading. Thus, the committee decided that any books considered for a hi/lo list had to rank below a sixth-grade reading level on a readability test and were to be of general, rather than curricular, interest. For these initial tests, the Fry Readability Scale was used. The directions for "Frying" a book are as follows:

- Select three 100-word passages from near the beginning, middle, and end of the book.

- Skip all proper nouns.

- Count the number of sentences in each 100-word passage, estimating to the nearest tenth of a sentence.

- Count the total number of syllables in each 100-word sample. It may be most convenient to count every syllable over one in each word and add 100. Average the number of syllables for the three samples.

- Plot the average number of syllables and sentences on a graph. Where the plots fall on the graph determines the readability. (Download the Fry readability graph from http://school .discoveryeducation.com/schrockguide/fry/fry2.html.)

Though librarians could determine reading level using such tedious methods, there was no formula to measure teen taste in books. Even as the committee developed criteria, Timothy Standal's article in the March 1978 *Reading Teacher* stated that reading levels were great starting points but that

> not all the factors that should be weighed can be weighed, and the ones that can be weighed don't always provide the most useful information. Therefore, readability formulas don't—can't really—include some factors that are potentially powerful predictors. That is why teachers occasionally find a child with a strong interest in some area who can read about that topic in materials that nearly any readability formula would suggest are beyond his or her level. . . . And, of course, a total lack of experience with or interest in some subject on the part of one child may render material about that subject unreadable even though the child should, according to the formula used, breeze through it. . . . A teacher who regards the formulas as guides and who is aware of the experiences, interests, and aspirations of the various children in her/his charge almost automatically overcomes the previously stated deficits of readability formulas. The various formulas cannot take interest and previous experience into consideration, but the teacher can—and should.

Thankfully, the High/Low Committee attempted to take other criteria into consideration besides Fry Readability, as shown by these samples from their initial evaluative criteria:

- Is the appearance of the book suitable to the age intended?

- Is the book awkward in shape (e.g., square) or using glossy paper, which sets it apart from other books geared to this age group?

- Does the writing style assume that young people reading on this level are dumb?

- Does the subject have teenage appeal? Is the topic current or of immediate interest to teenagers?

- Can you see this title as a bridge to something more difficult?

- Overall is the book readable?

The committee identified subgenres in both fiction and nonfiction. For fiction, the committee highlighted areas such as adventure, automotive, legend-folklore, mystery, social problems, and sports; in nonfiction, they saw such topics as automotive, biography, career, health, history, science, sports, and travel as important. Teen interest in these subgenres has changed little in the past thirty years, though legend-folklore has likely been replaced by fantasy and the supernatural.

The first committee was guided by this function statement: "To evaluate written and audiovisual materials for young adults with low literacy levels. To select, annotate, and prepare for publication a list of significant titles of high-interest, easy reading or understanding level." To select books for the list, the six committee members reviewed and considered only books that the publisher designated as hi/lo titles. Over time the selection of audiovisual materials became the responsibility of another YALSA committee.

The initial list of forty-eight titles from 1982 contains genres that will be familiar to those who work with reluctant readers, including problem novels, adventure stories, and mysteries. Many series titles peppered the nonfiction list, such as the Picture Life series from Franklin Watts, with titles featuring Jimmy Carter, Muhammad Ali, Stevie Wonder, Reggie Jackson, and O. J. Simpson. A Crestwood series highlighted such monsters as Bigfoot, Dracula, Godzilla, and King Kong. Longtime librarians may recognize these titles as being considered juvenile for most teens today.

Further lists in the 1980s stayed small, averaging thirty titles, and featured more of the same type of hi/lo material. Limitations of the list criteria soon became apparent. The number of publishers calling their books hi/lo stagnated, at best, or actually shrank. The look of hi/lo books made it obvious that they were published for remedial readers, so teens, always sensitive to peer pressure and appearances, avoided them to keep from being labeled as special or different.

Finally, because only books that had been designated hi/lo could be considered, some undesignated titles that appealed to reluctant readers could not be included on the list. William Sleator's *Interstellar Pig*, for example, appeared on the 1985 BBYA list but not on the Reluctant Readers list. Ironically, the first title to appear on both the BBYA and the Reluctant Readers lists did so that same year, with Eve Bunting's *If I Asked You, Would You Stay?*

The early committee meetings were largely spent reading and completing the Fry test. Committee members were not required to read all the books, since they were only trying to reach consensus on which titles to include on their lists. Members had often not even seen, much less read, most of the books until they arrived at conference, where single copies were available for their use.

As the High/Low Committee matured, many of its limitations were addressed. In 1986, list criteria expanded to include titles that not only scored below the sixth-grade level but also met high-appeal criteria, regardless of whether they were specifically published or marketed for the hi/lo reader. The committee also began to consider book format more closely, avoiding those that appeared juvenile. The definition of a reluctant reader began to expand. As former chair Barbara Lynn wrote in a letter to publisher William Morrow, the reason for reluctance in reading could be a teen "lacking skills, lacking motivation, or having emotional problems. Our list is NOT geared strictly to the severely disadvantaged reader even though some of the titles chosen might be used with them."

PHASE 2: RECOMMENDED BOOKS FOR THE RELUCTANT YA READER COMMITTEE

Once the criteria expanded, a name change became necessary. Starting in 1987, the list was retitled Recommended Books for the Reluctant YA Reader. The name change "reflect[s] a committee's charge more accurately: to choose a list of outstanding titles that will stimulate the interest of teenagers who are reluctant readers. Though the list is not intended for the severely disabled reader, some of the titles . . . may be appropriate for them" (YASD 1989, 1282). The first list under the new name and criteria included forty-one titles, thirty-five of which were fiction.

The late 1980s saw another change as the nomination system was altered. From the inception of the committee until 1989, each book had required a completed evaluation form and a Fry test. A book could not be received and rejected without paperwork that provided the reason for its rejection. The list of received titles in 1987 numbered nearly four hundred, each of which had to be evaluated by at least one committee member with the paperwork sent to the chair. Once a committee member rejected a book, no one else was required to read it unless another committee member spoke up in its favor.

To manage the large number of books received, the chair assigned each committee member a publisher, and the members were responsible for reviewing that publisher's titles. Though the committee asked publishers to send their releases to the entire committee, if that proved difficult they were encouraged to at least send their titles to the committee member assigned to their publishing house, in addition to sending one copy of each title to the YASD office. The committee found itself having to route books, for committee members were not receiving the entire year's output of titles from all publishers.

The old system worked reasonably well when the committee considered only officially designated hi/lo books, but once the eligible titles expanded to include all YA publishing and submitted titles numbered more than four hundred, the amount of paperwork that had to be managed by the chair became overwhelming.

As the committee and its criteria evolved, many practices were modeled after those of the BBYA Committee. In 1989, a *Booklist* consultant joined the Recommended Books committee to help maintain consistency for a group that was, by necessity, constantly changing. The committee had become "more viable . . . with an emphasis on what will appeal to young adults rather than the Fry readability," wrote Selection Committee Task Force chair Pam Spencer to YASD director Anne Weeks. During this time, the size of the committee grew from six members to eleven.

The selection lists continued to be published as brochures, with the annotations more teen-focused and with no mention of low reading level. YASD used the title Quick Picks for Great Reading for the 1990 list. An introduction to the 1993 list begins, "Are you looking for a good book to read—only reading's not your thing?" This statement best summarizes what the committee was attempting to accomplish: find good books to appeal to the reluctant reader.

When new guidelines were established in 1993, the YALSA board eliminated the requirement of a low Fry score. Five current and past members of the committee prepared a manual reflecting the new guidelines, which emphasized that reluctant readers were not unskilled but instead belonged to one of the following reading categories:

"dormant"—those who do not generally read but who do not have anything against it; they just have other priorities.

"uncommitted"—they do not think reading is fun and tend to read magazines and informative nonfiction.

"unmotivated"—those who hate to read but can be convinced with songs and poetry magazines.

As the manual summarizes, "Students do not ask for books that contain words of one syllable or sentences of two or three words. And none say they want dull materials with static illustrations. What is right for reluctant YA readers is something that appeals but is not inferior to another kind of its genre."

Continuing with the switch from consensus to nominations, the manual states

> Committee members are responsible for reading all nominated books no matter how boring or distasteful the books may

appear. Members can participate in discussion and vote on books only after reading the entire book. . . . Final selection of the list is based on thoughtful voting that is not limited to concerns about a balanced list or other non-criteria selection. . . . Any questions about how to shelve, catalog or use the book are extraneous: books on the list are to appeal to reluctant YA readers. Members should focus on the audience, understanding that this is a nation-wide list and is intended to address the needs of a diverse cross-section of young adults. Books are not to be excluded solely because of their controversial nature. (YALSA 1994, based on Carter 1993)

PHASE 3: THE CURRENT INCARNATION—QUICK PICKS FOR RELUCTANT YOUNG ADULT READERS

In 1995, YALSA officially changed the committee name to Quick Picks for Reluctant Young Adult Readers. Chair Sue Rosenzweig initiated the final major change in committee criteria, that of gathering teenagers' opinions to select the final list of titles. Comments from hundreds of reluctant-to-read teens were added to the professional opinions of the eleven committee members. Despite several demographic variables, ranging from location to age to economic status, the reluctant teens tended to agree more than disagree, often to the amazement of the adults who nominated the titles.

Adding teen input produced many unexpected results. Who would have predicted that, in the first year that teen comments were considered so seriously, one of the top ten Quick Picks would be Bruce Coville's retelling of Shakespeare's *A Midsummer Night's Dream*? An e-mail from Rosenzweig to the YALSA office in February 1997 included teen comments such as "It is nice drawing and it [is] neat story and I liked it" and "I never knew how good his books were. The pictures are magnificent." This was also the first year the list included more nonfiction than fiction. Committee members recognized that nonfiction held great appeal for reluctant readers, but it took the impact of teen opinions for the number of nonfiction titles to increase.

In 1996, Kylene Beers published her groundbreaking *School Library Journal* article about reluctant readers and elaborated the concepts of dormant, uncommitted, and unmotivated reluctant readers mentioned in the committee manual —a working definition that reinforces the idea that reluctance is more likely to stem from social or cultural issues than from poor reading skills.

In the committee's early years, growth and change were frequent as the charge was rewritten to represent the reluctant teen reader more accurately. In the 1970s and 1980s, the Fry Readability test was the principal criterion for a book's inclusion on the list. Beginning in the 1990s, the Fry test was dropped and teen input was included in committee discussions. In the 2000s, the importance of teen feedback increased and helped determine the final list.

In 2001, administrative assistant John Sexton responded to a publisher query about how titles are selected by writing:

> How do we find the "right" book? Among our most important criteria for selecting books for the Quick Picks list are the appeal of the cover, the accessibility of the text, and the ability of the story to hook the reader in the first several pages. In the end, however, the most important factor in evaluating a Quick Pick title is the feedback we receive from the reluctant teen readers in our own areas. Teen input from reluctant readers is an essential aspect of the committee's selection process.

THE MAKEUP OF THE LIST

The YALSA Reluctant Reader list has nearly doubled in size since its inception (see table 1). Although this is partly explained by the inclusion of only hi/lo

Chronology of Significant Changes for the High/Low—Reluctant Reader—Quick Picks YALSA Committee

1976:   High Interest/Low Literacy Level Committee organizes preconference and possibility of working with *Booklist* to produce appropriate selection brochures.

1982:   First list selected and published as High-Interest Low Reading Level; Ellin Chu first chair.

1987:   Selection list renamed Recommended Books for the Reluctant Young Adult Reader.

1989:   Selection method changed from consensus to nomination.

1990:   New list renamed Quick Picks for Great Reading.

1993:   Fry Readability scoring eliminated as selection criterion.

1994:   Manual for Quick Picks written.

1995:   Committee renamed Quick Picks for Reluctant Young Adult Readers; teen opinion included as selection criterion.

1996:   Quick Picks selection list first published online on the YALSA website.

2000s: Emphasis on teen opinion increased for selection to final list.

Year	No. Titles	Fiction	%	Nonfiction	%
1982	48	28	58.3	20	41.6
1983	30	17	56.6	13	46.4
1985*	30	17	56.6	13	46.4
1986	39	24	61.5	15	38.5
1987	41	35	85.4	6	14.6
1988	61	56	98.8	5	8.2
1989	37	33	89.2	4	10.8
1990	44	32	72.7	12	27.3
1991	36	23	63.9	13	36.1
1992	56	27	48.2	29	51.8
1993	65	36	55.4	29	44.6
1994	63	42	66.6	21	33.3
1995	110	57	51.8	53	48.2
1996	77	44	57.1	33	42.9
1997	77	27	35.1	50	64.9
1998	68	32	47.1	36	52.9
1999	74	46	62.2	28	37.8
2000	78	43	55.2	35	44.8
2001	79	36	45.6	43	54.4
2002	61	27	44.3	34	55.7
2003	78	30	38.4	48	68.6
2004	79	30	38.0	49	62.0
2005	80	47	58.8	33	41.2
2006	91	45	49.5	46	50.5
2007	76	46	60.5	30	39.5
2008	107	69	64.5	38	35.5

**TABLE 1
Number of fiction and nonfiction titles on YALSA reluctant reader lists**

* The list years were changed in 1985 to conform to the standard set by the Newbery and Caldecott Awards, so the 1985 list consists of titles published in 1984. From then on, years indicate when the list was voted on and completed and include titles published the previous year.

titles in the early years, there are other factors: more books for teens have been published every year, and as various types of reluctant readers are recognized, so are the types of books that interest them. Committee members now search widely, from review journals to bookstores, to find titles that will appeal to reluctant readers, rather than relying solely on a finite group of books submitted by publishers.

As can be seen from the table, once the committee eliminated the Fry test and ushered in a broader definition and understanding of reluctant readers, the size of the list exploded. To ensure that the list represented the best of titles for reluctant readers, the number of "yes" votes required for a book to make the list was raised from six to seven. From 1982 until 1994, the list total averaged forty-six titles. In 1995, when teen opinions were introduced, the number soared to 110; since then the list has averaged eighty-one titles.

The percentage of nonfiction titles has certainly increased since the list's inception, and they have taken the greater share in nine different years. From lows of 8.2 percent and 10.8 percent in 1988 and 1989, the number of nonfiction titles has steadily increased, a fact that distinguishes the Reluctant Readers list from the BBYA list; in the past seven years, only 20 percent of the titles on the BBYA list have been nonfiction (Koelling 2007).

In 1996, YALSA began publishing the lists online, a practice that continues today at www.ala.org/yalsa/booklists/quickpicks/. The list annotations have always been written as short, snappy come-ons to interest teens in reading the book. The annotations in this volume have been largely rewritten to provide librarians with a better sense of the book so they can decide whether to add it to their collection, make it part of a display, or include it in booklists. The original annotations remain on the YALSA website.

THE CHANGING ROLE OF THE COMMITTEE

In the earliest years of the committee, the majority of reading, evaluating, and annotating was done by the members at conference. Though some publishers submitted titles directly to committee members, the majority of the books were sent to the YASD office, which sent them to conference, where the committee members used the Fry test to evaluate them. As the number of submissions grew, publishers were asked to submit books directly to committee members. Until the late 1980s, however, committee members were still assigned specific publishers, and other committee members looked at these publishers' offerings only if more votes were needed to make a final selection.

Once the 1994 manual was put into place, however, members were expected to read widely. Today, members have to read all nominated titles to vote for them. In addition to reading and evaluating, committee members are also responsible for searching other avenues for possible nominations. In addition to traditional bookstores, members often locate potential titles in teen-oriented stores such as Hot Topic and Urban Outfitters, publishers' catalogs, teen magazines, or direct suggestions from teens. It is often these hidden gems that might not receive any reviews that make Quick Picks such a unique and teen-focused list.

In the mid-1990s, the work of the committee expanded as gathering teen feedback on nominated titles became a matter of routine. This could be time consuming, for librarians often worked with several groups of reluctant teen readers to obtain a wide range of opinions. Thus began the precedent of minimizing the librarian's opinion and maximizing teen recommendations for inclusion of a title on the list. At conference, committee members voice the opinions of the reluctant readers as well as their own.

During conference, nominated books are available for committee members to read and for audience members to examine. During discussions, each book is reviewed, with the nominator presenting the title, followed by comments from audience members. The rest of the committee members then add their views, with the chair speaking last.

After the committee discusses each title, members vote in a straw poll, "yes," "no," or "undecided" by a simple show of hands. Committee members who have not read a nominated book must vote "undecided." Though this vote is not binding, it indicates to the committee those titles certain to be included and those that lack a sufficient number of committee readers, which usually initiates a flurry of additional reading. The final morning of conference, members often speak for or against titles about which they feel strongly. After this last opportunity to speak, the final vote is taken, with a necessary seven of the eleven members approving for a book to be added to the list.

After tabulating the final vote and completing the list, the committee finalizes the annotations. This is always an entertaining but stressful time; committee members are tired after a long weekend of reading and discussing book titles but also relieved to see their task so near completion. Because Quick Pick annotations are generally fun to read and write, the committee's punchiness often works to the advantage of the annotations.

A YALSA member's first year on the committee is spent in a probationary phase as he or she learns to pace reading time, obtain teen input, respond to correspondence from the chair, and contribute to the discussion at conferences. At the end of the year, the chair and the YALSA president-elect discuss each first-year member to determine who should be reappointed for two more years. Those members who have read, nominated, shared books, collected teen comments, and participated in discussions throughout the year are generally reappointed for the remaining two years of a three-year term. If committee members are unable to keep up with their charge, the chair recommends that their appointment not be renewed and their service ends. Selection committees are in-demand appointments, with no lack of replacements, so the onus is on the appointee to keep up with committee responsibilities.

THE ROLE OF THE CHAIR

Oh, how the Internet has simplified the job of the chair. In the High/Low years, the chair's task included sending letters to publishers to explain the role of the committee, soliciting books to be sent to the YASD office or to members, running the meetings at conferences, and submitting the final list to the office and to *Booklist*.

As the committee expanded beyond hi/lo titles, the number of books increased, as did the volume of paperwork. Until 1989, committee members filled out two copies of an evaluation form for each book, keeping one for their records and sending one on to the chair on a weekly basis. The chair then compiled the evaluations and sent each committee member a list of recommended titles, as well as titles that did not make the cut. In these pre-Internet days, this involved a lot of typing, copying, and mailing or faxing, whereas now the chair can send a group e-mail with attachments. In 1989, when committee members received more than four hundred titles from publishers, the chair stressed the need for a nomination process rather than a paper-centered evaluation of huge numbers of books.

Though the electronic age has simplified the role of the chair, the job is by no means easy. Chairing responsibilities begin as soon as the previous year's list is finalized at the midwinter conference. Publishers are aware of the importance of the selection lists to their sales and are ready to send their new books to committee members. The first task of the chair is to contact the publishers and provide them with an overview of the committee function along with an updated roster of members and addresses. In addition, new members require an orientation and returning members benefit from a reminder about committee rules and deadlines.

Nominations usually open in February. All nominations are submitted electronically via YALSA's Quick Picks web page (www.ala.org/yalsa/book lists/quickpicks/) and are delivered electronically to the in-box of the chair, the administrative assistant (a nonvoting committee member), and the YALSA staff liaison. After checking eligibility and verifying bibliographic information, the chair contacts the committee with a list of nominated titles, sent either immediately or in small batches every few days; before the advent of the Internet, the chair sent nominations only once a month. Meanwhile, the administrative assistant notifies the publishers of any nominated titles and, if necessary, requests that a copy of the title be sent to committee members.

Other chair responsibilities include setting the agenda for conferences, contacting both the YALSA office and committee members about sending or bringing books to conference, working with the YALSA office to make room and meeting arrangements, and setting up the room at conference. Once the meetings begin, the chair runs the meeting, which includes introducing members who

Quick Picks Chairs

YALSA members who have chaired the High/Low, Reluctant Readers, or Quick Picks Committee:

Elizabeth Acerra	Maureen Hartman	Nancy Reich
Lora Bruggeman	Diane Tixier Herald	Sue Rosenzweig
Ty Burns	Mary Long	John Sexton
Peter Butts	Barbara A. Lynn	Helen Tallman
Jane Chandra	Jack Martin	Nel Ward
Ellin Chu	Joy Millam	Jamie Watson
Sarah Couri	Judy Nelson	
Judy Druse	Melanie Rapp-Weiss	

may have met only virtually, explaining the charge and committee procedures, and facilitating the book discussions. The chair also serves as YALSA host and representative to audience members, who are often publisher representatives. Finally, there are conference reports to complete and issues or concerns to discuss with the YALSA board liaison.

Either the chair or the administrative assistant maintains a digital list of nominations and posts it on various websites, which not only aids the committee members as they plan their reading but allows others the opportunity to read and discuss nominated titles. Responsibility for the discussion list available to observers at conference belongs to the YALSA office, which prints the list and sends it to conference. Immediately after conference discussion ends, the chair finalizes the list, double-checks the bibliographic information and annotations, and provides the YALSA office with an electronic copy of the annotated list, along with a press release. The chair's final tasks are to write letters to supervisors of committee members acknowledging their work on the Quick Picks Committee, fill out final reports, and serve as a mentor to the incoming chair.

These are the scheduled tasks, but throughout the year the chair is also called upon to answer many questions from committee members, other YALSA members, publishers, and occasionally even the press. Chairs serve as constant cheerleaders to motivate and encourage their committee members. Chairing a YALSA selection committee is a real, and valuable, procedural lesson in leadership.

SUMMARY

In the nearly thirty years that this committee has been in existence, it has changed and grown in response to shifts in the publishing field as well as to studies that redefine teens and their reading. This is a testament to the committee members and to YALSA as both continue to observe and learn more about reluctant readers, teenage readers, and the culture at large. The committee will continue to evolve, but always maintaining its awareness that the purpose of the list is to find and promote those books of interest to reluctant readers.

REFERENCES

Beers, G. Kylene. 1996. "No Time, No Interest, No Way: The 3 Voices of Aliteracy." *School Library Journal* 42 (2): 30–33.

Carter, Betty. 1993. "What Is a Reluctant Reader?" Paper presented at the annual conference of the American Library Association, New Orleans, LA, June 29.

Koelling, Holly. 2007. *Best Books for Young Adults,* 3rd ed. Chicago: American Library Association.

Standal, Timothy C. 1978. "Readability Formulas: What's Out, What's In?" *Reading Teacher* 31 (6): 643.

YALSA Quick Picks Task Force. 1994. *Manual for Quick Picks.* Chicago: American Library Association.

YASD. 1989. "Recommended Books for the Reluctant Young Adult Reader, 1989." *Booklist* 86 (3): 1282–86.

ADDITIONAL READING

Caywood, Carolyn. 1993. "Judge a Book by Its Cover." *School Library Journal* 39 (8): 58.

Jones, Patrick. 2004. *Connecting Young Adults and Libraries: A How-to-Do-It Manual for Librarians.* New York: Neal-Schuman.

LaPlante, Joseph R. 1996. "'Reluctant' Readers Get School 694 Books." *Providence Journal-Bulletin*, January 24.

Rosenzweig, Susan. 1996. "Books That Hooked 'Em: Reluctant Readers Shine as Critics." *American Libraries* 27 (6): 74.

Ward, Nel. 1973. "Quick Picks: Recommended Books for the Reluctant Young Adult Reader." *ALAN Review* 1 (Spring): 56–61.

Zadora, Amanda. 2002. "Wrestling with Reading." *Teaching PreK–8* 32 (7): 58.

CHAPTER 3

POPULAR PAPERBACKS FOR YOUNG ADULTS
Origin, History, and Committee Processes

Paula Brehm-Heeger

Determining which books will grab young adults' attention and become popular with them is an age-old challenge. This challenge is complicated when a teen is asking for or interested in reading about a particular subject or within a particular genre, oftentimes a genre with which a librarian is not familiar. What if the teen is a reluctant reader—someone who, either by choice or because of ability, does not view reading as a priority? Or, what if a teenager has decided he or she does indeed enjoy reading and now is looking to broaden his or her reading tastes? In situations like these, the skill of even the best readers' advisor is tested, yet librarians face these readers' advisory scenarios every day. Browse through the daily posts on YALSA's heavily used electronic list yalsa-bk (http://lists.ala.org/sympa/info/yalsa-bk/) and you are sure to find desperate requests for booklists or suggested titles in a particular genre or on a particular topic.

In response to such teen reading requests, teen sections in many libraries are stocked with bookmarks and recommended reading lists, often grouped by genre and theme. Among these lists YALSA's Popular Paperbacks for Young Adults (PPYA) has found a place as an invaluable resource that must be included in the toolbox of every librarian working with teens. The origins of this essential list resulted from a variety of trends, including the increasing popularity of the paperback, changing purchasing patterns in libraries, and usefulness of genre-focused lists to help librarians best serve the entire spectrum of teen customers, from the most reluctant to the most voracious readers.

In preparing this chapter in 2007, I was assisted by previous PPYA chairs and YALSA directors Mary Arnold, Diane Colson, Pam Spencer Holley, Sally Leahey, Walter Mayes, Mike Pawuk, Dawn Rutherford, Francis W. Stack, Deb Taylor, and Marin Younker, from whose personal communications I quote directly.

THE INFLUENCE OF THE PAPERBACK FORMAT

The first book in the Sweet Valley High series, *Double Love* (Bantam), was published as an original paperback in 1984. More than fifteen years after its initial publication, the popularity of the first title in this long-running series remained evident, with *Double Love* coming in at an impressive number 184 on a 2001 *Publishers Weekly* ranking of the top two hundred best-selling children's paperbacks of all time (Roback and Britton 2001). However, at the same time that *Double Love* was busy introducing teens to the suburb of Sweet Valley, California, via the paperback format in the mid-1980s, libraries were not necessarily including paperbacks of any kind in their collections.

For many years hardbacks had been the reigning format of choice for both school and public libraries, with paperbacks occupying a distinct second-class status—if they were purchased at all. In a 1994 speech delivered at a YALSA-sponsored ALA annual conference program, noted YA literature expert Michael Cart acknowledged "the traditional library resistance to buying the format [original paperbacks]" and also a "certain prejudice against the impermanence of the form" (Cart 1995). By the mid-1990s, however, the resistance by many libraries to collecting paperbacks was beginning to erode.

One reason for this change was that the popularity of paperbacks for young people was becoming hard to ignore. In 1993, sales of hardcover books for children were 8 percent below 1992 sales, but sales of paperbacks for the same target audience during the same period increased by nearly 16 percent (Lodge 1994). These figures group both children's and young adult book sales under the general term "children's books." Regardless of this general grouping, publishers understood the implications of the figures for the young adult paperback market. They were beginning to feel that "paperback is clearly the format of choice" for middle school students and young adults (Lodge 1994).

Another reason many libraries were changing their opinion about the value of purchasing paperbacks was funding. In the 1980s, school and public library budgets suffered severe cuts. When their budgets turned into what Cart referred to as "the incredible shrinking man," libraries were inclined to "eschew a hardcover for a paperback edition of a book" (Cart 1995; Lodge 1994). Where previously a library might always choose to purchase the hardback edition of a book, even when titles were released simultaneously in both paperback and hardback formats, with budgets tightening, more and more libraries were opting to collect titles in paperback. Some libraries suffering budget crunches began to skip purchasing hardbacks at all and instead waited for the paperback release. A major benefit of this change was that it allowed for more copies to be purchased, though this shift often meant waiting a year or longer for the paperback release date to acquire a particular title.

Whether it was because of the need to alter purchasing patterns in response to smaller budgets or a desire to actively offer teens reading material in the format they seemed to prefer, the change in attitude of librarians and their libraries toward collecting paperbacks set the stage for YALSA to explore the potential of this emerging format.

ORIGINS OF THE POPULAR PAPERBACKS LIST

During the same era that publishers and booksellers were becoming particularly eager to capitalize on the growing popularity of paperbacks targeted to young adults, YALSA teamed up with book distribution company Baker and Taylor to work on a paperback-related marketing idea. Baker and Taylor was interested in stuffing "book dumps" with young adult paperbacks. Book dumps, once common in both school and public libraries, are small cardboard stands or display racks that stand alone or sit atop a table and typically hold mass-market or trade paperbacks for face-out display. As YALSA past president Pam Spencer Holley recalls, Baker and Taylor "came to YALSA (known at that time as YASD) for ideas. Or maybe it was the other way around," about how to fill these cardboard book dumps.

In 1988, Holley and YASD executive secretary Evelyn Shaevel worked to establish five genre committees charged with creating paperback lists of romance, horror, science fiction, sports, and mystery titles. Baker and Taylor agreed to help with the marketing of these lists. The selected genre paperbacks were highlighted through book dump displays sold by Baker and Taylor. A grant from the Carnegie Reading List Fund was used to support efforts to develop the genre booklists as well as bookmarks and tip sheets. By 1989, two more genre committees were created, for fantasy and humor. A historical fiction genre committee was added in 1991 (Fine 1992).

In addition to the production of the lists, bookmarks, and tip sheets, YALSA focused on creating unique ways to support and publicize the idea of genre paperbacks. Efforts included a 1991 "Genrecon" preconference. Attendees enjoyed a day and a half of author presentations, panels, discussion groups, and even a costume event. "I'll never forget Suzanne Manczuk, who led the romance discussion," recalls Holley, "all dressed up in a beautiful, long, antique linen nightgown—very romantic looking."

Baker and Taylor abandoned the sale and marketing of genre book dumps in the early 1990s and in 1994 discontinued their support for publication of the paperback genre lists (Leahey 2005). But the positive response from librarians and YALSA members to the collaboration and subsequent genre paperback lists kept the idea of creating and marketing paperback-only genre lists alive. Displaying genre paperbacks in visually appealing book dumps was having an impact on sales, and booksellers and distributors were taking note. A 1994 *Publishers Weekly* article cited book dumps as another "development that is driving library purchases of paperbacks" (Lodge 1994). Evidence that librarians across the country also enthusiastically embraced this genre display option is seen in an October 1993 exchange from the Publib electronic discussion list, in which one librarian stated that her library "enjoyed the genre dumps we purchased from ALA Graphics (developed by YALSA)" and asked for ideas on where she might purchase a new book dump because ALA had, by that time, discontinued selling the units (Caywood 1993). One respondent agreed that the dumps were "great" and that this type of display made it easy for young adults to "find the books in the genre they want" (Patterson 1993).

The original genre paperback-only lists project ceased when the collaboration between YALSA and Baker and Taylor ended. But in the mid-1990s, the concept of formally promoting paperbacks through specific genre lists gained momentum. In 1995, the creation of the new Popular Reading Committee was approved by the YALSA board of directors. The guidelines were formally renamed "policies and procedures" and returned by the board to the developing committee in October 1996, accompanied by a set of responses to questions raised in the committee's report. The first meeting of the new committee was held at the annual ALA conference in 1996, and the first list was published in 1997 (Leahey 2005), the same year that YALSA sponsored a preconference focused on popular teen reading: "Popular Reading: What Young Adults Really Read and Why" (see Bernier et al.'s 2007 chronology).

This first list included a brief explanation of the genesis of the Popular Reading/Popular Paperbacks list concept by explaining that "Popular Paperbacks is a reincarnation of the topic committees, but broader in scope. Since the topic booklists were still current, the committee decided to tackle five topics of interest to a variety of teens in lieu of any specific topic" (YALSA 1997). The name of the committee was changed from Popular Reading to Popular Paperbacks for Young Adults (PPYA) by a board vote at the 1997 midwinter meeting. Revisions to the policies and procedures for PPYA occurred in 1998 and again in 2002.

EVOLUTION AND CHANGES IN PPYA

Former PPYA committee chair Francis William Stack offers his impression about the motivation behind the creation of the new list by saying, "They (YALSA) wanted a list that was teen-tested unlike BBYA [Best Books for Young Adults]. Older books that the teens loved to read or subjects that teens were into now, rather than the Best Books published this year." By the time PPYA joined YALSA's family of booklists and awards, both the Best Books for Young Adults and Quick Picks for Reluctant Young Adult Readers lists had existed for decades. PPYA, although related to these other well-known lists, was created to fill a clearly different need.

The original purpose of the list, stated in an October 1996 correspondence between then YALSA deputy director Linda Waddle and president Deb Taylor, was "to encourage young adults to read for pleasure by presenting to them lists of popular or topical titles which are widely available in paperback and which represent a broad variety of accessible themes and genres." This purpose remained a formal element in the policies and procedures from the creation of the committee until a 2002 revision removed the statement. The committee charge, to "annually prepare one to five annotated list(s) of at least ten and no more than twenty-five recommended paperback titles, selected from popular genres, topics or themes," has endured through several revisions.

Another unique element of the recommendations made by YALSA's Executive Committee in 1996 to members of the original Popular Reading Committee was that publishers *not* be solicited to send paperbacks for committee members to consider. One primary reason for this response, according to Taylor, was that the "Popular Reading List is not a duplication of Best Books and Quick Picks, nor is the committee." Clearly, from the initial days of the PPYA list there was a focus on making this list very different from other existing YALSA lists.

The original recommendations from the YALSA Executive Committee emphasized that the new list focus on teen appeal and accessibility. The issue of currency was also discussed, but even in the early discussions it was clear that books on this list must, above all else, be "popular." Indeed, one of the original criteria that remains on the list today is that "popularity is more important than literary quality." Other original criteria listed by Taylor included these:

- Titles must be in print and available in paperback.

- Both young adult and adult titles may be considered.

- Both fiction and nonfiction may be considered.

- Copyright dates are not a consideration.

- A book that has appeared on a previous Popular Reading list cannot be selected.

- Nominations from publishers for their own titles are not eligible.

- Each committee will have the latitude to select its own topics (this will ensure the inclusion of timely topics, currently fashionable subjects, and fads), but as a matter of course certain perennially popular genres, topics, or themes should be considered.

Not all of the original criteria and recommendations have remained in place over the course of PPYA's ten-year existence. The first notable change involved the PPYA committee soliciting paperbacks from publishers. An August 2000 e-mail exchange between YALSA president Mary Arnold and the Popular Paperbacks Committee indicates a change in thinking on the part of YALSA's leadership. Arnold stated, "The chair can now contact publishers to let them know what subject lists this year's committee is looking for books on; if publishers want to send review copies, they can be given the sub-committee chair contact info." These instructions do, however, emphasize that "mostly" committee members are responsible for finding their own nominations.

A second revision to the criteria resulted in a significant change in options available to committee members for future nominations to the PPYA lists. Originally, any book that had appeared at any time on a PPYA list could not appear on any future PPYA list. This selection criterion had been a source of frustration for committee members over the years, as is illustrated by an August 2003 e-mail exchange between PPYA committee chair Mike Pawuk and the PPYA committee's liaison to the YALSA board of directors. Pawuk stated that "both new and older committee members have expressed interest in revising the PPYA Policies and Procedures. . . . The chief concern, as it was last year, was a strong desire to lift the ban on including titles that were on a previous list." Pawuk went on to recommend a shorter ban on books appearing on the list of either two or five years and suggested that strong consideration be given to "lift the ban totally." This particular criterion was subsequently revised for the 2005 list and now reads, "A book that appeared on a previous Popular Paperbacks list can be selected after 5 years have passed since it last appeared on the list." Although the change impacts PPYA lists in a variety of ways by permitting books that had appeared on a genre list one year to appear again on either a similar or completely differently themed genre list at a later point, the most significant and long-term impact will be seen on lists with themes that are likely contenders for repeating or updating, such as "Lesbian/Gay Tales" published in 1997 and the related list "GLTBQ" published in 2006.

Repeat Book Titles on the PPYA List

Since the 2005 change of policies and procedures that allowed books previously selected for a PPYA list to be selected again after five years, only the ten titles listed below have been selected for more than one list.

Bauer, Cat. *Harley, like a Person.* PPYA 2002; PPYA 2008.

Bauer, Joan. *Thwonk.* PPYA 1999; PPYA 2007.

Cormier, Robert. *Tenderness.* PPYA 1999; PPYA 2005.

Gaiman, Neil. *Neverwhere.* PPYA 1999; PPYA 2008.

Klause, Annette Curtis. *Blood and Chocolate.* PPYA 2000; PPYA 2008.

Moore, Terry. *Strangers in Paradise: High School.* PPYA 2002; PPYA 2005; PPYA 2006.

Napoli, Donna Jo. *Zel.* PPYA 2000; PPYA 2005.

Shetterly, Will. *Elsewhere.* PPYA 1999; PPYA 2005.

Wallace, Rich. *Wrestling Sturbridge.* PPYA 1999; PPYA 2008.

Yamanaka, Lois-Ann. *Name Me Nobody.* PPYA 2003; PPYA 2005.

HOW THE COMMITTEE WORKS

Unlike other YALSA selection lists such as BBYA and QP, for which committee members select from books published in the list year, PPYA committee members must annually set a direction for their nominations by determining what subjects, genres, and themes will be the focus of that year's lists. The first order of business for PPYA committee members at the midwinter conference is determining the number and focus of lists the committee will produce, something that must be established before nominations of any kind can be considered. The committee has a great deal of latitude in deciding the subjects, genres, and themes for its lists and also has the freedom to decide the final number of annotated lists to produce. The current policies and procedures dictate simply that the committee prepare "one to five annotated list(s) of at least ten and no more than twenty-five recommended paperback titles, selected from popular genres, topics, or themes."

When asked how their committees determined the focus of the lists, many former PPYA chairs noted that committee members engaged in an intense and passionate—but good-natured—brainstorming session to decide the genres and themes for the coming year's lists. "We made a long list of possible categories, keeping patron demand in mind, and then discussed and voted for those for which we felt there was the greatest need," was how 2006 committee chair Walter Mayes described this process. Sally Leahey, 2005 committee chair, noted that "this was always one of the most fun discussions of all," and 2007 committee chair Diane Colson commented that "these always seemed like intense discussions to me!" Marin Younker, 2008 committee chair, emphasized that the committee examined past lists to ensure they were not duplicating efforts but also to update lists "that continue to be popular."

Additionally, themes suggested but not selected from previous years are communicated to incoming chairs so that they can be considered for the following year. This tradition of passing suggestions from one year to the next not only ensures that important themes and topics receive the consideration they deserve but also helps the incoming committee focus on the task at hand. This also means that tricky topics discussed and passed on by one year's committee continue to come up for discussion. Mayes cited the creation of the "Books That Don't Make You Blush" list as a great example of how the process of multiple committees from different years discussing the possibility of a subject can lead to a very valuable list. Mayes explained:

> Every year I was on PPYA [the discussion] started with "we get a lot of requests for Christian fiction list." Each committee tried hard to deal with this issue. . . . When I became chair, I had a goal in mind of not shying away from the responsibility to meet the obvious patron demand for a Christian fiction list and announced, "one way or another we will have a list that meets this patron demand." Books That Don't Make You Blush was

PPYA Themes through the Years

1999 (89 titles)
- Good Sports—23 titles
- Teen Culture—22 titles
- Changing Dimensions—25 titles
- Different Drummers—19 titles

2000 (91 titles)
- Short Takes—24 titles
- Page Turners: Adult Novels for Teens—25 titles
- Romance: Passion and Heartbreak—22 titles
- Self-Help—20 titles

2001 (84 titles)
- Humor—25 titles
- Paranormal—16 titles
- Poetry—22 titles
- Western—21 titles

2002 (96 titles)
- Relationships: Friends and Families—24 titles
- War: Conflict and Consequences—23 titles
- Tales of the Cities—24 titles
- Graphic Novels: Superheroes and Beyond—25 titles

2003 (97 titles)
- Lock It, Lick It, Click It: Diaries, Letters and Email—25 titles
- Flights of Fantasy: Beyond Harry and Frodo—25 titles
- This Small World: A Glimpse of Many Cultures—22 titles
- I've Got a Secret—25 titles

2004 (96 titles)
- If It Weren't for Them: Heroes—23 titles
- On That Note: Music and Musicians—23 titles
- Guess Again: Mystery and Suspense—25 titles
- Simply Science Fiction—25 titles

2005 (89 titles)
- Read 'Em and Weep—23 titles
- Own Your Freak—25 titles
- Gateway to Faerie—21 titles
- All Kinds of Creepy—20 titles

2006 (97 titles)
- Books That Don't Make You Blush: No Dirty Laundry Here—24 titles
- Criminal Elements—25 titles
- What Ails You?—25 titles
- GLBTQ—23 titles

2007 (98 titles)
- Get Creative—25 titles
- Religion: Relationship with the Divine—23 titles
- What's So Funny?—25 titles
- I'm Not Making This Up: Addictive Nonfiction—25 titles

2008 (86 titles)
- Sex Is . . .—20 titles
- What Makes a Family?—23 titles
- Magic in the Real World—21 titles
- Anyone Can Play—22 titles

born, an accomplishment of which our entire committee was particularly proud.

The guidance of the committee chair as well as more senior committee members is essential at this stage of the process to ensure that the final topics selected are not based solely on strong interest from individual committee members and that these final topics offer the committee reasonable opportunities to find ten to twenty-five high-quality titles to populate each list. Diane Colson emphasized that "committee members, in their enthusiasm, could sometimes latch on to a topic that immediately calls to mind several great choices, but then on reflection seems weak as a topic for a list of twenty titles." Some genres and themes tend to come up in some form year after year, such as science fiction and fantasy, but as 2001 committee chair Francis William Stack commented, "Popular culture and current topics or fads were foremost in our goal." Walter Mayes noted that "some choices were no-brainers, dictated by current events or trends." Once the number of lists and themes of each of these lists have been decided, the committee must make the next decision outlined in the PPYA policies and procedures and determine whether the committee will "operate as a committee of the whole" collectively discussing all topics and lists under consideration or (after deciding to produce more than one themed list) "subdivide so that each subcommittee deals with only one genre, topic, or theme." The tradition for the past several years has been in favor of the subcommittee organization, with one member of the committee being selected as a subchair for each list on which the various subcommittees are focusing. With only fifteen members on this committee, all, including subcommittee chairs, are frequently assigned to work on two or (less commonly) three lists.

These important questions of organization and focus, unique to PPYA and faced by each year's committee members, are decided annually at the ALA midwinter meeting. Because committee member appointments to all YALSA award and selection committees, including PPYA, begin immediately *after* the midwinter meeting, decisions about list topics, the number of lists to be produced, and the organization of the committee are actually decided by the previous year's committee members. This is necessary for each year's committee to be able to complete its work during the required time frame. Committee members are, however, appointed to a two-year term, so at the beginning of committee members' second year they do have the opportunity to be actively involved in decisions about the upcoming year's lists and committee work.

NOMINATIONS

The process of nominating titles for the various PPYA lists begins immediately after the midwinter meeting. Because the committee is no longer discouraged from interacting with publishers, the list topics for that year are communicated to various publishers likely to be interested in submitting paperbacks for consideration. This part of the PPYA process is not unlike the process used by the BBYA and QP committees. The task of contacting publishers is left to the committee chair, who usually works closely with the administrative assistant if the chair has elected to name someone to this position. The administrative assistant may be a current, voting member of the committee, or the chair may select someone from outside the committee. If the latter choice is made, the administrative assistant attends all committee meetings but is a nonvoting member.

The PPYA push for nominations does not stop once communications are sent out to publishers. On the contrary, PPYA cannot count on publisher submissions to provide the bulk of titles to be considered and instead must rely heavily on committee members to find good nominations. PPYA policies and procedures recommend that committee members identify titles "by reading the paperback section of 'Forecasts' in *Publishers Weekly* and by exploring the paperback shelves of bookstores at regular intervals."

Another unique part of the PPYA nomination process is the committee's need to "shape the list" and focus on the essence of the general topic, theme, or genre each list is to cover. The role of each subcommittee's chairperson is an essential element in helping each list become a cohesive, logical group of titles. Still, it is the chair of the overall committee who is perhaps the most integral part of this process. Frequently not assigned to any specific subcommittee, the committee chair often attempts to read nearly every book nominated for each list. This requires a near Herculean effort, with many reading hundreds more titles than any other single committee member. But this effort is not without great benefits, for the chair is then in a position to offer valuable perspective and guidance in helping the subcommittee chairs focus their lists.

DEFINING POPULARITY

No discussion of the PPYA process would be complete without discussing the role of teen opinion and input in determining both nominations and the final makeup of the list. Soliciting teen opinions and input begins as soon as nominations start, and these teen opinions play a significant—the most significant—role in committee members' decisions about what titles make the final list. As former chair Sally Leahey noted, "Now that I'm serving on Quick Picks, I see a real difference in the way the two committees are viewed by the outside world, and I just don't get why this is since they both focus so much on teen opinion." Past chairs Mayes and Stack echoed Leahey's sentiments: "We worked hard to keep it [popularity] utmost in our minds as we did our work," explained Mayes. Stack noted that "popularity was our main goal. To select topics and books the teens would want to read." Former committee chair Dawn Rutherford believes that "part of what keeps the list vibrant is striving to always find what it is that teens enjoy." Both Mayes and Colson emphasized the need for committee members to rely on professional judgment when it came to determining the popularity of lesser-known books, which, as Colson explained, "do become popular once you start recommending [them]."

The central question on the minds of PPYA committee members, often voiced during discussions about the list, is "what is popular?" The initial question about popularity leads to several other challenging questions, such as who defines popularity—librarians or teens? Does it differ from city to city and school to school? The question of popularity is also complicated because the answer does not depend on whether a book will appeal to a particular type of reader. Teens who are reluctant to read are certainly more likely to read a popular book, but teens who are not considered reluctant readers are equally likely to pick up a popular title. Defining popularity is not easy. Committee members use several factors when making this judgment, including whether or not a book circulates, if teens frequently request a particular title, and how teens respond when committee members ask them directly about a title.

Another important question for PPYA committee members is whether or not quality of the nominations should be considered. As former chair Leahey put it, "How bad does the book have to be quality-wise before we can't stomach having it on a list?" In a perfect world, all books would be both popular with teens and considered to be of high quality by librarians. But such titles are rare, and no one knows this better than those who have served as PPYA committee members. The 2005 PPYA committee summed up its feelings about the issue with a T-shirt that clearly weighed in on one side of the issue: "It's all about the popular!" Many committee members, including Leahey, report that it is a

---

Lists So Nice, They Came Up Twice (or More)

Some themes and ideas are so perpetually popular that they turn up in one form or another in different lists from different years. Although each list is clearly unique, related lists include the following:

Flights of Fantasy (2003) / Gateway to Faerie (2005)

Changing Dimensions (1999) / Paranormal (2001) / Simply Science Fiction (2004)

Different Drummers (1999) / Own Your Freak (2005)

Adult Mysteries for Teens (1998) / I've Got a Secret (2003) / Guess Again: Mystery and Suspense (2004)

Romance: Passion and Heartbreak (2000) / Read 'Em and Weep (2005)

relief to let the literary merit question go and "just focus on what kids really like." Committee chairs encourage members to use teen opinions as the primary driver in deciding what is popular and thus what is the best fit for the PPYA list and, as Marin Younker explained, "to be sure committee members are correct in our assessment of popularity." All the same, in the end, as Mayes noted, "we also were not against using our professional expertise." Sometimes committee members have difficulty remaining focused on the supremacy of popularity when making the final determination about makeup of the final list. But in the end it is popularity that counts the most. "Several times committee members had to swallow their bile for titles that they personally detested but fit the list," reported Mayes.

NUTS AND BOLTS

In addition to discussing popularity and quality, shaping the list, and gathering the all-important teen input, the PPYA committee also must be certain to adhere to a specific time line of tasks outlined in the committee polices and procedures. A discussion list of titles must be assembled prior to each ALA annual conference, and so members submit nominations to the chair by May 1. The chair then creates a ballot for distribution to the full committee by May 15, and completed ballots are returned to the chair by June 1. Only titles receiving "yes" votes from a majority of committee members remain on the list for discussion at the annual conference.

Committee members familiarize themselves with nominated titles (if the committee has divided into subcommittees, members concentrate on the titles on their respective subcommittee nomination lists) to ensure a productive discussion. At least two discussion meetings at the annual conference are scheduled by the chair. These sessions not only focus on individual nominations but also provide additional time to shape the list and get to the essence of what kinds of titles address the year's particular topics. At the final meeting a ballot is taken and titles not receiving the required number of votes (typically a simple majority) are eliminated from the working list.

The period from the annual conference to November 1 is used by committee members for further reading and evaluation of possible nominations. Additional nominations are submitted to the committee chair no later than November 1, with the chair creating a final list of nominations for distribution to the committee by December 1. Completed ballots are returned to the chair by December 15. The resulting list of nominations is then distributed to committee members no later than the end of the first week in January. Three discussion meetings are scheduled for the midwinter meeting by the chair, and a final list (or lists) is assembled by ballot at the conclusion of the third meeting. The committee determines its own voting procedure for deciding the titles to be included on the final list.

Both the subcommittee chairs and the general committee chair are important during the midwinter meetings. First, because one or more of the nominated titles may have an older copyright date or in some way may be difficult for all committee members to obtain prior to the conference, the committee chair (often working with the subcommittee chairs) makes certain that a copy of every nominated title is available during the conference. Committee members are then able to read any titles they may not have had access to previously. The second vital role the committee chair and subcommittee chairs play is to be sure that committee members listen to each other during the passionate final deliberations. Often subcommittee chairs lead the discussion of their respective list's nominations, with the general committee chair offering additional comments and support in moderating the discussion when necessary—particularly in engaging and soliciting opinions from less outspoken committee members.

After titles have been selected, the committee prepares an annotated list (or lists) of selected titles. According to committee policies and procedures, these annotations are "written in a style that will capture the interest of the target audience—young adults aged twelve to eighteen." Over the years these annotations have evolved to be short, breezy, and, when appropriate, humorous. Another element of the final annotated list that has evolved is the inclusion of summary comments, not only from the committee chair but also from subcommittee chairs; these subcommittee chair comments first appeared on the 2002 list.

THE PAPERBACK FORMAT TODAY

The original concept for a popular-reading genre-themed list populated by paperbacks evolved during an era when many booksellers, publishers, and eventually librarians were beginning to think that the vast majority of teens preferred books in paperback format to hardcover. It is easy to see why. As mentioned earlier, data indicated rising sales of young adult paperbacks. Additionally, in the late 1980s and early 1990s, increased attention was being paid to cover art differences—both in design and target market—between hardcover and paperback releases. A 1987 *Publishers Weekly* article emphasized that hardcover jacket art, designed with institutions like libraries in mind, and paperback covers, focused on direct appeal to teenagers, "demand two radically different marketing approaches" (Evans 1987). The article goes on to reveal that, because of the strong sales of young adult paperbacks at the time, artists working on hardcover jacket art received a flat fee ranging typically from $400 to $1,000, whereas artists working on paperbacks received fees in the $1,200–$3,000 range, with additional funds for props and other expenses.

But whether paperbacks, particularly paperback cover designs, are really more appealing to most teenagers is not entirely clear. As Ed Sullivan (2000) reiterated in a *VOYA* article focused on the young adult hardcover versus paperback debate, it is always important to remember that "teens are unpredictable." In his direct research and surveys of teens, despite his own assumptions that teens would prefer paperback art, Sullivan discovered that "hardcover jacket designs are often preferred among many, if not a majority, of the targeted paperback audience."

There is more to the paperback format than cover art, of course. Teens may prefer paperbacks for a variety of practical reasons such as their being smaller, lighter, and easier to carry or slip into a backpack or bag for a bus ride home. But PPYA is a relatively new list when compared to other long-standing YALSA-sponsored lists including BBYA and QP, and it is always possible that this list may evolve yet again as a better understanding of teen reading tastes is gained. As former chair Sally Leahey commented, "I'm thinking it might make more sense to have popular themed lists, regardless of binding."

SUMMARY

The Popular Paperbacks for Young Adults list has changed over the years, emerging from a short-term collaboration between YALSA and Baker and Taylor to become one of the most useful and unusual lists available today. Beyond the important role the list plays in helping librarians connect teens with books and reading, PPYA also holds a distinct place on YALSA's spectrum of lists, often functioning as a bridge that leads teens from the Quick Picks for Reluctant Young Adult Readers list to Best Books for Young Adults and finally to YALSA's most literary titles of all, those earning the Michael L. Printz Award for Excellence in Young Adult Literature.

REFERENCES

Bernier, Anthony, et al. 2007. "Two Hundred Years of Young Adult Library Service History: A Chronology." http://pdfs.voya.com/VO/YA2/VOYA200708chronology_long.pdf (accessed November 11, 2007).

Cart, Michael. 1995. "Of Risk and Revelation: The Current State of Young Adult Literature." *Journal of Youth Services in Libraries* 8 (Winter): 151–64.

Caywood, Carolyn. 1993. Comment on "Generic Paperback Dumps," Publib, comment posted October 28. http://lists.webjunction.org/wjlists/publib/1993-October/063678.html.

Evans, Dilys. 1987. "The YA Cover Story." *Publishers Weekly* 232:112–15.

Fine, Jana R. 1992. "YASD: A Narrative History from 1976 to 1992." Young Adult Library Services Association, www.ala.org/ala/mgrps/divs/yalsa/aboutyalsa/yasdnarrative.cfm (accessed November 11, 2007).

Leahey, Sally. 2005. "Popular Paperbacks Tenth Anniversary." *Young Adult Library Services* 3 (3): 31–33.

Lodge, Sally. 1994. "Paperbacks: A Silver Lining?" *Publishers Weekly* 241:30–33.

Patterson, Jill. 1993. Comment on "Generic Paperback Dumps," Publib, comment posted October 28, http://lists.webjunction.org/wjlists/publib/1993-October/063678.html.

Roback, Diane, and Jason Britton. 2001. "All-Time Best Selling Children's Books." *Publishers Weekly* 248. www.publishersweekly.com/index.asp?layout=article&articleid=ca186995 (accessed November 11, 2007).

Sullivan, Ed. 2000. "Judging Books by Their Covers, Part II: Hardcover vs. Paperback." *Voice of Youth Advocates* 23 (October): 245–48.

YALSA. "Popular Paperbacks for Young Adults." 1997. www.ala.org/ala/mgrps/divs/yalsa/booklistsawards/popularpaperback/1997popularpaperbacks.cfm (accessed November 11, 2007).

CHAPTER 4

PROGRAMMING, DISPLAYS, AND READERS' ADVISORY

Stacy Creel

Programming for teens can be a rewarding yet challenging experience; it can be even more challenging when trying to reach out to reluctant young adult readers who are not typical library customers. The good news is that there are plenty of resources to use, from tried-and-true programs by professionals in the field to websites from systems across the country displaying their exciting offerings. But remember that not every program is the right program for every place and every teen. This chapter highlights some resources and some things that you can do to reach out to your reluctant readers.

STEP 1: WHAT DO TEENS IN YOUR COMMUNITY LIKE?

When trying to draw reluctant readers into the library, the first step you as a professional can take is to get to know what has captured the interest of teens in your community, and reluctant teens in particular. Take some time to think about and observe what teens spend their time doing. Are they listening to their iPods or MP3 players, playing video games, hanging out with friends, watching television or movies, attending sporting events or concerts? These are some obvious things that many teens like, so the next step is to discover how to relate them to your library.

The Harris County (Texas) Public Library, for example, tied together popular movie and book combinations. For *The Sisterhood of the Traveling Pants,* one hands-on activity involved decorating a pair of jeans: the jeans started out at one branch, then were sent on to the next branch, where the decorating continued. Celebrating the *Napoleon Dynamite* movie, the library linked it with *Napoleon Dynamite: The Complete Quote Book* and hosted a party that included such prizes as bobblehead dolls and personalized lip balm (www.hcpl.net/teens/).

Television shows such as *CSI, Monster Garage,* and *Fear Factor* naturally link with books like *Crime Scene: The Ultimate Guide to Forensic Science, Monster Garage: How to Customize Damn Near Anything,* and *The Fear Factor Cookbook.* These books lead to programs that can have special appeal to the elusive male reluctant reader.

Libraries across the country have used the draw of teens to music to entice nontraditional library users into the library (Kan 2006). From battles of the bands to teen choice awards to karaoke, all have helped bring teens into libraries. It is great that there is a connection between teens and music, but how do you figure out what to do? Here is one example of how the process may lead to a punk concert.

The Punk Concert

This example is based on a program with more than three hundred attendees that was held on the plaza of the Central Library of the Houston Public Library (www.hpl.lib.tx.us). First, prepare a sound rationale for the program containing the following:

- why this program should take place

- the benefits and risks

- the costs

- the support you will need, including personnel (custodial, security, supervision) and building support

- examples of other successful, similar programs

- book tie-ins

Next, take this information to your administration and gain their support.

The third step is to determine which local bands teens are interested in hearing. There are two ways that you can accomplish this: ask the teens or ask a local club that caters to teens or sponsors a teen night. The local club can also be a good source of information about sound technicians and a place to advertise.

Then consider the best day and time for teens to attend a punk concert; surely it would be more fun on a Friday night at dusk than on a Saturday afternoon. An early Friday night, as long as it is not during football season, allows the band to perform for the library (maybe at a reduced rate) and still make a later gig, makes parents feel better about a concert that ends at a decent hour, and provides teens with enough time to do something else that night, like get coffee or a meal with their friends. Picking the best day and time for teen programs of any type may take a while to figure out, so observe teen traffic in and around the library, check the local school district website for events and schedules, and do not forget to ask teens you see in and out of the library.

After you have established a day and time, pick your location. Before you begin advertising, seek out and apply for any needed permits. Book the band and begin advertising at schools, your library and nearby branches, and nontraditional venues. For example, fliers (small for taking and larger for posting) can be dropped off at local clubs and stores teens may frequent, like Hot Topic. Make sure to include a map to the event's location, because the target audience are not regular library users. Send out press releases to the local newspaper and radio or television shows and add a copy of it to your library's website. Approach a local store or vendor about supplying water, drinks, or snacks, depending on your library's policies.

A week prior to the concert, remind important staff (like facilities and the manager on duty) of the event. Set up a related book display so that anyone heading to the bathroom will see the display; using the bathroom may be the only time some teens ever enter the library, so it is your one chance to grab their attention. Related books or books of interest could be titles like the following:

- books on current bands or old favorites (*So What? The Good, the Mad and the Ugly*)

- graphic novels or manga (I Luv Halloween series)

- extreme sports and skateboarding (*Skate and Destroy: The First 25 Years of "Thrasher" Magazine*)

- alternative lifestyles or body art (*Body Type: Intimate Messages Etched in Flesh*)

- how to play an instrument like bass or drums, and making it in a band (*The Musician's Handbook: A Practical Guide to Understanding the Music*)

- website/blog–inspired books (*PostSecret: Extraordinary Confessions from Ordinary Lives*)

- edgy fiction (*Nick and Norah's Infinite Playlist*)

See if the band will give away goodies (such as stickers with their name on them) or if a local store will donate freebies.

Now you are ready to enjoy the concert. One last note of advice is to be sure that you have some positive responses ready if adult bypassers have negative comments about the concert or program. Most likely, they will not understand the lyrics but may complain about the noise.

If you do not feel up to the live concert challenge or have fewer hours to work with (before and after school), think about attempting some of Kevin A. R. King's (2006) more subtle music programs, like music discussion groups or music-themed book discussion groups.

STEP 2: THINK CREATIVELY

Reluctant teen readers may not be drawn into your library for typically successful programs, although you can never underestimate the power of female teens to draw male teens into some less-than-obvious programs, like making a decorative Valentine's Day box to stuff with candy. Thinking outside the box can be a little harrowing as you try to navigate the system in which you are working. It is always important to have a sense of your administrative team and garner their support. Doing a simple Internet search of library and teen programs will quickly show you that libraries now offer activities and programs such as game days, creating graphic novels, anime clubs, and much more. To reach the reluctant reader, and probable non–library user, these outstanding programs cannot be promoted in the traditional library manner, such as on the website or with fliers in the library. Think instead of where graphic novel, comic book, and manga readers go and advertise there. Post fliers in game stores and teen centers. If you find that teens in your community are not interested in graphic novels or comic books but are interested in other topics such as tattoos or online social networks, then try to find a way to do a program about those topics. If your library is in an urban area, try brief booktalks on some of the growing body of urban fiction for teens. Book and movie tie-ins are always popular, or you can try your own version of "Rapping with the Stars."

Display: Advice and Reality

Ask CosmoGirl! about Guys

Ask CosmoGirl! about Your Body

Banks, Tyra. *Tyra's Beauty Inside and Out*

CosmoGirl! Words to Live By

Daldry, Jeremy. *The Teenage Guy's Survival Guide*

Drill, Esther, et al. *Deal with It! A Whole New Approach to Your Body, Brain and Life as a gURL*

Leslie, Jeremy, and David Roberts. *Pick Me Up*

Pletka, Bob, ed. *My So-Called Digital Life: 2,000 Teenagers, 300 Cameras, and 30 Days to Document Their World*

St. Stephen's Community House. *The Little Black Book for Girlz: A Book on Healthy Sexuality*

Warren, Frank. *PostSecret: Extraordinary Confessions from Ordinary Lives*
Possible realia tie-ins: used disposable camera, postcards, mirror, empty heart-shaped box, glasses

The Tattoo Info Session

This controversial workshop also took place at the Houston Public Library's Central Branch and was developed because many teens are interested in tattoos (see the "Body Adornment" list in chapter 7). The workshop presented the pros and cons of tattooing, featuring a local tattoo artist, a health official, and an anti-gang task force officer as speakers. The original live demonstration of tattooing was not included in the final performance because of pressure from the city council, but the workshop was still well received.

STEP 3: ASK THE TEENS

The first chapter of this book mentions many different types of reluctant readers; some of those types will use your library system and some will not. You cannot depend on traditional in-house library surveys to assess how you are doing and what types of programs and activities reluctant teen readers will attend. Instead, you must go where they are. It is not always easy to do this without seeming like a stalker, but it can be done. As reported in "Early Adolescents' Reading Habits" (Creel 2007), teens were surveyed at libraries, schools, shopping malls, churches, and even on the street. Start by immediately saying that "I'm _____ from _____ library, and I'm talking to teens about the library." You will be

---

Display: Fairies and Fairy Tales

Black, Holly. *Tithe: A Modern Faerie Tale*

——. *Valiant: A Modern Tale of Faerie*

Dokey, Cameron. *Beauty Sleep*

Haddix, Margaret Peterson. *Just Ella*

Lynn, Tracy. *Snow*

McKinley, Robin. *Spindle's End*

Napoli, Donna Jo. *Beast*

Scalora, Suza. *Fairies: Photographic Evidence of the Existence of Another World*

Vande Velde, Vivian. *The Rumpelstiltskin Problem*

> Possible realia tie-ins: fairy wings, fairy dolls, wands, maps with the names changed to magical names, goblets, red rose, plastic slipper

surprised how willing they are to share their opinions. Be sure to follow your system's rules for interviewing prior to and during information gathering.

Once you have information on what your teens are interested in doing at the library, make it happen. Either establish a teen advisory group or work with an existing one to gain insight and help you plan programs. Even if they are not reluctant readers, they may have friends who are. If they help with a program like a poetry slam and prepare the publicity, select the prizes, and set up the library for the event, they will be more committed to coming and bringing in friends to expand your audience. Specific groups of reluctant readers can be targeted with special programs designed just for them. If "the A+ Student" reluctant reader is singled out, then an SAT study group might be organized. If a program for "the Athlete" is being considered, bringing in a local athlete to talk about getting into the profession would be a draw.

Reaching Out to GLBTQ Teens

The Houston Public Library worked closely with Houston Area Teen Coalition of Homosexuals (HATCH) to ensure that GLBTQ teens felt welcome in the library. In addition to receiving a grant for gay and lesbian teen books and audiovisual

---

Display: Graphic Novels, Comics, and Drawing

Bancroft, Tom. *Creating Characters with Personality*

Benton, Jim. *It's Happy Bunny: Life. Get One.*

Blattberg, Julie, and Wendi Koontz. *Backstage with Beth and Trina: A Scratch and Sniff Adventure*

Caldwell, Ben. *Fantasy! Cartooning*

Ganz, Nicholas. *Graffiti World: Street Art from Five Continents*

Hosler, Jay. *Clan Apis*

Lee, Lela. *Angry Little Girls*

Medley, Linda. *Castle Waiting: The Lucky Road*

Millar, Mark. *The Tomorrow People*

Miller, Steve, and Bryan Baugh. *Scared! How to Draw Fantastic Horror Comic Characters*

Sugiyama, Rika. *Comics Artists—Asia: Manga Manhwa Manhua*

Possible realia tie-ins: Colored pencils, Sharpies, tracing paper, figurines

materials, they hosted an exhibit of photographs from Adam Mastoon's *The Shared Heart: Portraits and Stories Celebrating Lesbian, Gay, and Bisexual Young People.* A perfect follow-up activity would have been to have the teens of HATCH and others write their own story or do their own portrait with the option to share or not.

STEP 4: MAKE A SPACE AND PLACE FOR THEM

Getting teens into your school or public library may be more easily accomplished if you have gone out of your way to create a place that is inviting and interesting to them. Are the staff welcoming? Have they been trained to have realistic expectations, like the need for teens to socialize and use technology? Does the space appeal to their tastes and needs; is there varied seating? Not every library has the budget to do major renovations, and many libraries have done programs similar to the show *Trading Spaces* to redesign on a dime and show that a huge budget is not necessary to make a huge impact. *VOYA*'s "YA Spaces of Your Dreams" column and YALSA materials provide many resources to guide you in making your space one that is truly for teens.

STEP 5: WHAT'S IN IT FOR ME? WHAT'S IN IT FOR THEM?

Another thing to ask yourself when you are doing displays and programs for teens, especially reluctant teen readers, is what is in it for them? They need incentives to attend your program or check out books. Incentives may include any of the following:

- food
- prizes (e.g., random winners assigned to the records of certain rotating titles)
- meeting a school requirement (e.g., a book discussion group on required summer reading, including a free copy of the book)
- academic reward (e.g., some grade incentive or extra credit in advance for participation in a book discussion group or program)
- recognition (e.g., extra time on the computer or a coupon to be turned in for up to $1 in overdue fines)

Regular outreach programs and activities such as book discussion groups and booktalking can also be modified to reach reluctant readers. Try brief booktalks (no more than two minutes) of books recommended by YALSA, other organizations, or teens. Booktalking for reluctant readers should include such nontraditional materials as audiobooks, DVDs, graphic novels, and magazines.

Successful booktalking strategies and tips can be found in *Connecting Young Adults and Libraries* (Jones 1992). Successful programs cannot be judged by the same criteria used to evaluate children's programs—attendance, for example. It is much easier to fill a room with forty toddlers (brought by their parents) than to fill a room with forty teens, especially reluctant readers. Know first what you expect the participants to get from the program, whether it be gaining a skill or changing an attitude. If five teens come and have a positive experience, then the library program was successful. Library systems traditionally depend on numbers as a measure of success; since your numbers may be small, especially when dealing with reluctant readers, obtain anecdotal evidence (verbal feedback) that can be recorded and shared.

The additional reading at the end of this chapter offers some titles to help in planning programs to entice reluctant readers into your library. Another suggestion is to find out what the current library systems of active members of YALSA and AASL are doing. For example, by going to www.ala.org/yalsa/ and clicking on "Selection List Contacts," you can find the addresses for the committee members currently serving on selection committees. Take some time to find their library system's or school's web page to see their programs and displays. Visit YALSA's website, www.ala.org/yalsa/, to find resources and ideas. Additional information is available to YALSA members through *YAttitudes,* the division's quarterly e-mail newsletter.

Although some reluctant readers may never set foot in your school or public library, others will come to hang out with friends, grab some technology time, attend an especially appealing program, or research school assignments. These visits to the library present the opportunity for exposing reluctant readers to books through attention-grabbing displays. There are several ways to do this, depending on your relationship and comfort level with the teens. Jack Martin, former QP chair, would put stacks of free books out on tables in Teen Central at the New York Public Library with a sign asking teens to tell him if any of them should be ordered.

One method for providing readers' advisory service is to approach individuals or small groups with easy-to-sell, "grab their attention" titles. Placing a small stack of books on the table and giving a two- to three-sentence booktalk on several might entice the teens to flip through one. This is an especially good way to highlight some of your more attractive nonfiction books that might never be discovered on the shelves. Other nontraditional displays like the old "Box of Good Books" and its counterpart "Box of Bad Books" still appeal to many teens.

These methods of displaying short stacks of books may not be your style, but every library can emulate the traditional bookstore type of display. First, if it has been a while since you stopped by your local bookstore or chain, take some time to do so. You can also look at pictures of displays found on www.flickr .com/groups/bookdisplays/ or do a simple Internet search of library displays to boost your creativity. Next, take advantage of some of the ready-made resources available if you are too busy to come up with themes or feel like you are in a creative slump. Look over the annotated titles from YALSA's QP and PPYA lists in chapters 5 and 6 or the booklists in chapter 7 for ready-made displays. Since the PPYA lists are organized by theme, you can search out ones that might be popular in your community with all kinds of readers. The QP lists contain titles that have been tested with various types of reluctant readers across the country, so in many cases they should have sure selling power. YALSA also creates many other themed and award lists containing titles of interest to reluctant readers, like the Great Graphic Novels list (www.ala.org/yalsa/ggnt/) and Teens' Top Ten (www.ala.org/teenstopten/). Additionally, several of the review journals, such as *Booklist* and *VOYA,* offer thematic lists. Many libraries create lists and post them on their websites; there are also customer- or user-created lists on many retail websites. In addition to these online lists and professional resources, take advantage of the knowledge available from staff and teens in your library or library system.

One way to make the displays more meaningful to your individual library is to ask teen volunteers, teen advisory groups, or teens in the library to help you come up with a theme and suggested titles. Work with the teens at the beginning of the project to ensure that staff and teens are in agreement about the theme of the display and its interpretation. Using staff picks and teen picks is another good way to add variety to your displays. Simply create cards similar to the one shown here and have the circulation desk hand them out and place them in the teen areas. As the cards are collected, they can be sorted by genre and then either used to develop book displays, compiled into a bookmark, or posted on a bulletin board for others to read.

SUMMARY

Teen librarians have a wealth of information available to them as they establish a program of library service that encourages teens not only to use the library but also to become part of a group that helps decide the components of that program. If that first step is hard to take, subscribe to YALSA's ya-yaac electronic

_____ recommends:
(First name, last initial)

Title: _____

Author: _____

Why: _____

_____

_____

discussion list (http://lists.ala.org/wws/info/ya-yaac/) to interact with and receive advice from other librarians about working with teens. Young adult librarians routinely offer details on their programs that could range from objects made from duct tape to Harry Potter–themed food or Twilight saga parties. Once you plan and experience your first program, you will be eager to try more. If a program turns out to be a bust, there will be lots of sympathetic listeners on ya-yaac to bolster your spirits with tales of their flops.

Make use of the lists in this book to set up displays for teens or add titles to your collection, review the committee information to begin your own teen selection committee, and check out YALSA's website for its other selection and award lists (www.ala.org/yalsa/).

REFERENCES

Creel, S. L. 2007. "Early Adolescents' Reading Habits." *Young Adult Library Services* 5 (4): 46–49.

Jones, Patrick. 1992. *Connecting Young Adults and Libraries: A How-to-Do-It Manual.* New York: Neal-Schuman.

Kan, Katharine. 2006. *Sizzling Summer Reading Programs for Young Adults.* Chicago: American Library Association.

King, Kevin A. R. 2006. "Get with the Program: Add Mix and Stir." *Voice of Youth Advocates* 29 (5): 410.

ADDITIONAL READING

Alessio, Amy. 2008. *Excellence in Library Service to Young Adults,* 5th ed. Chicago: Young Adult Library Services Association.

Alessio, Amy J., and Kimberly A. Patton. 2007. *A Year of Programs for Teens.* Chicago: American Library Association.

Anderson, Sheila B. 2005. *Extreme Teens: Library Service to Nontraditional Young Adults.* Westport, CT: Libraries Unlimited.

Dickerson, Constance B. 2004. *Teen Book Discussion Groups @ the Library.* Teens @ the Library series. New York: Neal-Schuman.

Edwards, Kirsten. 2002. *Teen Library Events: A Month-by-Month Guide.* Greenwood Professional Guides for Young Adult Librarians. Westport, CT: Greenwood Press.

Honnold, RoseMary. 2003. *101+ Teen Programs That Work.* Teens @ the Library series. New York: Neal-Schuman.

———. 2005. *More Teen Programs That Work.* Teens @ the Library series. New York: Neal-Schuman.

———. 2007. *Get Connected: Tech Programs for Teens.* New York: Neal-Schuman and the Young Adult Library Services Association.

Jones, Patrick Jones. 2004. "Reaching Out to Young Adults in Jail." *Young Adult Library Services* 3 (1): 16–19.

Ott, Valerie A. 2006. *Teen Programs with Punch: A Month-by-Month Guide.* Libraries Unlimited Professional Guides for Young Adult Librarians. Westport, CT: Libraries Unlimited.

CHAPTER 5

NONFICTION ANNOTATIONS
Quick Picks for Reluctant Readers and Popular Paperbacks for Young Adults, 1999–2008

Pam Spencer Holley

The original annotations, written with the teen reader in mind, are available on the YALSA booklists website (www.ala.org/yalsa/booklists/). The annotations in this chapter have been rewritten to provide librarians with more descriptive information to aid them in collection development, readers' advisory service, and creation of displays, booklists, or pathfinders.

50 Cent. *50 x 50: 50 Cent in His Own Words.* Simon & Schuster, 2007. QP 2008.
Handwritten song lyrics, original stage passes, personal essays, and family photos reveal the life of this entertainer from Queens whose fame goes beyond the music industry.

———. *From Pieces to Weight: Once upon a Time in Southside Queens.* Pocket, 2006. QP 2006.
In this literate, honest memoir, the rap superstar from Jamaica, Queens, chronicles his personal history from orphan to drug kingpin, felon, and finally music legend.

Aaseng, Nathan. *Navajo Code Talkers.* Walker, 1994. PPYA 2002 (War).
Messages communicated in the native language of the Navajo soldiers confused the enemy, who could not decipher "the code," and helped the Allies during World War II.

Abadie, M. J. (Marie-Jeanne). *The Everything Tarot Book: Discover Your Past, Present, and Future: It's in the Cards.* Everything series. Adams Media, 1999. PPYA 2001 (Paranormal).
Beginning with the history of tarot cards, instructions enable the reader to interpret the images on the cards and conduct tarot card readings to learn about the future.

Abrams, Judith Z. *The Secret World of Kabbalah.* Kar-Ben, 2006. PPYA 2007 (Religion).
This guide to making God part of one's everyday life contains excerpts from Jewish texts to help along this spiritual journey.

Adelman, Penina, Ali Feldman, and Shulamit Reinharz. *The JGirl's Guide: The Young Jewish Woman's Handbook for Coming of Age.* Jewish Lights, 2005. PPYA 2007 (Religion).
A combination of Jewish text, psychology, and advice from Jewish women and teens clarifies both teen and Jewish issues.

Adoff, Arnold. *The Basket Counts.* Illustrated by Michael Weaver. Simon & Schuster, 2000. QP 2001.
Swish! That magical sound when the ball hits "nothing but net" is but one of the many excitements of basketball captured in Adoff's rhymes and Weaver's illustrations.

————, ed. *I Am the Darker Brother: An Anthology of Modern Poems by African Americans.* Illustrated by Benny Andrews. Aladdin, 1997. PPYA 2001 (Poetry).
First published in 1968, this updated title includes the works of 19 new writers and gives readers a mix of classic and contemporary works by black poets.

Ahmedi, Farah, with Tamim Ansary. *The Other Side of the Sky: A Memoir.* Simon Spotlight, 2006. PPYA 2007 (I'm Not Making This Up).
Crippled after stepping on a land mine while on her way to school, Farah and her mother eventually flee Afghanistan for America after family members are killed.

Alabiso, Vincent, Kelly Smith Tunney, and Chuck Zoeller, eds. *Flash! The Associated Press Covers the World.* Abrams, 1998. QP 1999.
The major historic people and events of the 20th century are portrayed in 150 photographs and essays from Associated Press staff.

Allen, Judy. *Unexplained: An Encyclopedia of Curious Phenomena, Strange Superstitions and Ancient Mysteries.* Kingfisher, 2006. QP 2007.
Both black-and-white and color illustrations accent baffling mysteries, ranging from crop circles to frog showers, premonitions, disappearances, and hauntings.

Alvarado, Melissa, Hope Meng, and Melissa Rannels. *Subversive Seamster: Transform Thrift Store Threads into Street Couture.* With photographs by Matthew Carden. Tauton, 2007. QP 2008.
Three talented seamstresses supply basic sewing instructions for 30 projects that will restyle thrift shop finds into inexpensive, personalized fashion garments.

Amend, Bill. *Welcome to Jasorassic Park: A FoxTrot Collection.* Andrews McMeel, 1998. PPYA 1999 (Teen Culture).
Life in the 1990s for the Fox family—Jason, Paige, Peter, Andy, and Roger—is collected in this FoxTrot edition.

Anderson, Joan. *Rookie: Tamika Whitmore's First Year in the WNBA.* With photographs by Michelle V. Agins. Dutton, 2000. QP 2001.
This pictorial biography of 6'2" center Tamika records her early life growing up in Tupelo, MS, her candid comments, and her practice routine for the WNBA's New York Liberty team.

Anglesey, Zoe, ed. *Listen Up! Spoken Word Poetry.* Ballantine, 1999. PPYA 2001 (Poetry).
Photographed at some of their award-winning poetry slams, nine up-and-coming spoken-word artists contribute suggestions for writing poetry and performing onstage.

————. *Word Up! Hope for Youth Poetry from El Centro de la Raza*. El Centro de la Raza, 1992. PPYA 2001 (Poetry).
Poems written by the participants in the Hope for Youth Poetry Workshop illustrate the importance of building community, which in turn builds power.

Aranzo, Aronzi. *The Bad Book*. Translated by Anne Ishii. Vertical, 2007. QP 2008.
Making stuffed felt figures of the "bad" creatures of manga, such as the Liar, the Thief, or the Kidnapper, are easy when you follow these instructions.

Armstrong, Lance, and Sally Jenkins. *It's Not about the Bike: My Journey Back to Life*. Penguin, 2001. PPYA 2006 (What Ails You?).
Cycling up mountains is arduous enough, but Armstrong's struggle against invasive testicular cancer is a true story of courage and determination.

Arnoldi, Katherine. *The Amazing True Story of a Teenage Single Mom*. Hyperion, 1998. QP 1999.
The struggles of a teen mother to support and educate herself are accented by black-and-white cartoons.

Ash, Russell. *Firefly's World of Facts*. Firefly, 2007. QP 2008.
A subject arrangement of wide-ranging topics, enlivened by illustrations, charts, and graphs, combines the best of almanacs, atlases, encyclopedias, and websites.

————. *The Top 10 of Everything 1998*. DK, 1999. QP 1999.
Filled with lists, photos, and illustrations is this informative work ranging from the trivial to the factual about TV, music, sports, books, and travel.

Ashanti. *Foolish/Unfoolish: Reflections on Love*. Hyperion, 2002. QP 2004.
Famed hip-hop artist Ashanti shares love poems written during her teen years, each accompanied by a backstory.

Atkin, S. Beth. *Voices from the Fields: Children of Migrant Farm Workers Tell Their Stories*. Little, Brown, 2000. PPYA 2003 (This Small World).
Through interviews, photographs, and poems, nine children of migrant workers reveal their life stories and desire for an education to keep their generation out of the fields.

Ballard, Robert D., and Rick Archbold. *Ghost Liners: Exploring the World's Greatest Lost Ships*. Little, Brown, 1998. QP 1999.
Archival and contemporary photographs, along with diagrams and illustrations, describe five sunken ships, including the *Titanic, Andrea Doria,* and *Lusitania*.

Baltin, Steve. *From the Inside: Linkin Park's Meteora*. With photographs by Greg Waterman. Bradson, 2004. QP 2006.
The alt-metal Linkin Park's world tour to promote their CD *Meteora* is captured here in full-color photos and comments from band members.

Bancroft, Tom. *Creating Characters with Personality: For Film, TV, Animation, Video Games, and Graphic Novels*. Watson-Guptill, 2006. QP 2007.
Techniques for drawing characters to establish a personality before any words are spoken are explored in this book by the creator of the dragon Mushu in Disney's *Mulan*.

Bang, Molly. *Picture This: How Pictures Work*. SeaStar, 2000. PPYA 2007 (Get Creative).
Referring to Little Red Riding Hood, Bang

explains how shapes, such as circles or triangles, and colors evoke certain feelings to create the whole piece of art.

Banks, Tyra. *Tyra's Beauty Inside and Out.* HarperPerennial, 1998. PPYA 2000 (Self-Help).
A successful model, Tyra shares not only life lessons about relationships but also tips on makeup, hairdos, fashion styles, skin care, exercise, and healthy eating.

Barry, Lynda. *One Hundred Demons.* Sasquatch, 2005. PPYA 2007 (Get Creative).
Barry uses her distinctive, stylized drawing to defeat the demons from her past, whether they be a cruel comment about her dancing or the memory of a smell from someone's house.

Baseball's Best Shots: The Greatest Baseball Photography of All Time. DK, 2000. QP 2001.
Every decade of baseball's 130-year history has photo reminders, including Babe Ruth's farewell, game action, and shots of fans, players, coaches, and stadiums.

Basketball's Best Shots. DK, 2002. QP 2003.
More than 300 action photos of well-known basketball players, on court and off, capture both the athletics of the sport and the cultural changes throughout its history.

Baskin, Julia, et al. *The Notebook Girls: Four Friends, One Diary, Real Life.* Warner, 2006. PPYA 2007 (I'm Not Making This Up).
Meeting at Stuyvesant High School just before September 11, the four authors start a joint diary in a composition notebook of the everyday events of their school, home, and social life.

Beals, Melba Pattillo. *Warriors Don't Cry: A Searing Memoir of the Battle to Integrate Little Rock's Central High.* Washington Square, 1994. PPYA 2004 (If It Weren't for Them).
One of nine black students chosen to integrate Little Rock Central High School in 1957, Melba daily faced screaming segregationists, the National Guard, and U.S. soldiers, plus her homework.

Beatty, Scott. *Batman: The Ultimate Guide to the Dark Knight.* DK, 2001. QP 2002.
Using the archives of DC Comics, this overview of all things Batman, from his suit to the Batmobile and the weapons in his utility belt, is well illustrated.

———. *JLA: The Ultimate Guide to the Justice League of America.* DK, 2002. QP 2004.
Facts and figures about the interplanetary group of superheroes are found in this comprehensive, colorful work, which includes a time line and chapter of biographies.

Beil, Karen Magnuson. *Fire in Their Eyes: Wildfires and the People Who Fight Them.* Harcourt Brace, 1999. QP 2000.
Dramatic photos not only explain the tasks of firefighters, their tools, and training but also show the power and intensity of various fires.

Bell, Janet Chatman, and Lucille Usher Freeman, eds. *Stretch Your Wings: Famous Black Quotations for Teens.* Little, Brown, 1999. QP 2000.
Organized in topical chapters, more than 400 quotes are gathered from athletes, writers, musicians, comics, and politicians, each of whom has a brief biography in the index.

Bell, Ruth. *Changing Bodies, Changing Lives: A Book for Teens on Sex and Relationships,* 3rd ed. Times Books, 1998. PPYA 2000 (Self-Help).
Cartoons, photographs, line drawings, and teen quotes explain the mental and physical workings of the human body.

Benton, Jim. *It's Happy Bunny: Life. Get One.* Scholastic, 2005. QP 2006.
The most charming bunny in pop culture imparts his favorite inspirational words of wisdom.

————. *It's Happy Bunny: Love Bites.* Scholastic, 2005. QP 2006.
Happy Bunny's first book is filled with advice for romance, though illustrations indicate he is rather unlucky in love.

————. *It's Happy Bunny: What's Your Sign?* Scholastic, 2005. QP 2007.
In this popular series, Happy Bunny explores the inner workings of astrology through an assortment of quizzes and games.

Berman, David. *Actual Air.* Open City, 1999. PPYA 2001 (Poetry).
From a member of the alternative rock band the Silver Jews, storytelling lyrics show a regard for history and a sense of Americana.

Bernstein, Anne D. *The Daria Diaries.* MTV, 1998. PPYA 1999 (Teen Culture).
Based on the television series *Daria,* sarcastic, often abrasive Daria Morgendorffer shares her take on high school life, nonathletic friends, and family problems.

Best Shots: The Greatest NFL Photographs of the Century. DK, 1999. QP 2000.
Great moments in football are depicted in photos that freeze the action, both on the field and off, as players celebrate wins, catch touchdown passes, or sit dejectedly after a loss.

Bey, Dawoud. *Class Pictures.* Aperture, 2007. QP 2008.
Noted photographer Bey's informal portraits of students, accompanied by their autobiographical statements, present a powerful look at a generation.

Bissinger, H. G. *Friday Night Lights: A Town, a Team, and a Dream.* HarperPerennial, 1991. PPYA 1999 (Good Sports).
A winning season for the Permian High School Panthers football team, which routinely pulls in 20,000 fans on a Friday night, has a far-reaching effect on its hometown of Odessa, TX.

Blais, Madeleine. *In These Girls, Hope Is a Muscle.* Grand Central, 1996. PPYA 1999 (Good Sports).
A group of genteel, middle-class white girls from Amherst, MA, manage to toughen up and win their state's high school basketball championship.

Blakeney, Faith, Justina Blakeney, and Ellen Schultz. *99 Ways to Cut, Sew, and Deck Out Your Denim.* Crown, 2007. QP 2008.
Though basic instructions and a pattern are provided, some knowledge of sewing is assumed for these projects, which include a sundress, banana bag, and iPod case.

Blattberg, Julie. *Backstage with Beth and Trina: A Scratch and Sniff Adventure.* Illustrated by Wendi Koontz. Abrams, 2006. QP 2007.
Scratch and sniff all the expected scents, from cigarettes to stale beer, as rock groupies Beth and Trina score a backstage tour of their favorite musical group.

Blink-182 with Anne Hoppus. *Blink-182: Tales from Beneath Your Mom.* Pocket, 2001. QP 2002.
A band member's sister shares the behind-the-scenes, sophomoric hijinks of these touring musicians, along with never-before-published photos.

Block, Francesca Lia, and Hillary Carlip. *Zine Scene: The Do-It-Yourself Guide to Zines.* Girl Press, 1998. PPYA 1999 (Teen Culture).
For teens who want to be published in magazine format, this work provides a how-to section along with zine samples from a wide variety of expressive authors.

Boards: The Art and Design of the Skateboard. Universe, 2003. QP 2004.
Hundreds of color photos of the popular graphics emblazoned on skateboard decks populate this work, and interviews with talented skateboarders are a bonus.

Boese, Alex. *Hippo Eats Dwarf: A Field Guide to Hoaxes and Other B.S.* Harvest, 2006. PPYA 2007 (I'm Not Making This Up).
In this era of Internet misinformation, here is help for ferreting out the fake virus warnings, doctored photos, and other scams.

Boitano, Brian, and Suzanne Harper. *Boitano's Edge: Inside the Real World of Figure Skating.* Simon & Schuster, 1997. QP 1999.
Using personal stories and photographs, noted skater Boitano explains what is required to compete internationally in figure skating, including costume price and rink etiquette.

Bonnell, Jennifer. *D.I.Y. Girl: The Real Girl's Guide to Making Everything from Lip Gloss to Lamps.* Puffin, 2003. QP 2004.
Inexpensive, easy-to-make crafts enable teens to decorate lamps, create gift items such as soaps or bracelets, and recycle old jeans while giving each item a personal touch.

Boyer, David, ed. *Kings and Queens: Queers at the Prom.* Soft Skull, 2004. PPYA 2006 (GLBTQ).
Attending any high school prom can be a nightmare for the GLBTQ students, as revealed by these photos and stories from the past 70 years.

Boylan, Jennifer Finney. *She's Not There: A Life in Two Genders.* Broadway, 2004. PPYA 2006 (GLBTQ).
After childhood, marriage, fatherhood, and life as a novelist and college professor, Boylan accepts that he is female and writes movingly about being transgendered.

Bradley, James, and Ron Powers. *Flags of Our Fathers: Heroes of Iwo Jima.* Bantam, 2001. PPYA 2004 (If It Weren't for Them).
Son of one of the flag raisers from the famous World War II photo, Bradley researched all six men of Easy Company to learn more about the momentous event.

Bressler, Karen W., and Susan Redstone. *D.I.Y. Beauty.* Alloy, 2000. QP 2001.
Responding to questions sent by teens to Alloy.com, beauty experts advise about hair and skin care; interviews with makeup artists and a history of beauty practices are included.

Brewster, Hugh, and Laurie Coulter. *882½ Amazing Answers to Your Questions about the* Titanic. Scholastic, 1999. QP 2000.
Diagrams, illustrations, and archival images supplement the answers to questions about the passengers on board the *Titanic,* its construction, and its launching.

Brisick, Jamie. *Have Board, Will Travel: The Definitive History of Surf, Skate and Snow.* HarperCollins, 2004. QP 2005.
Maps, accompanied by historical and contemporary photographs, enrich this complete history of the intertwined surfing, skateboarding, and snowboarding cultures.

Brooke, Michael. *The Concrete Wave: The History of Skateboarding.* Warwick House, 1999. QP 2000.
This complete history of the sport includes inventors, investors, stars, and media plus anecdotes from Brooke's Skategeezer home page.

Brous, Elizabeth. *How to Be Gorgeous: The Ultimate Beauty Guide to Hair, Makeup and More.* Seventeen series. HarperCollins, 2000. QP 2001.
Teen magazine *Seventeen* helps makeup divas, as well as those who sport the natural look, with tips on skin care, nails, makeup, and hair.

Brown, Bobbi, and Annemarie Iverson. *Bobbi Brown Teenage Beauty: Everything You Need to Know to Look Pretty, Natural, Sexy and Awesome.* HarperCollins, 2000. QP 2001.
Beauty editor of NBC's *Today* show, Brown hopes each teen will recognize her own natural beauty and enhance it with makeup and healthy living.

Brown, Dee. *Bury My Heart at Wounded Knee: An Indian History of the American West.* Holt, 2001. PPYA 2002 (War).
Making use of primary sources, Brown lets the words of the Indian chiefs describe how their land was lost to Anglo-Americans.

Brunvand, Jan Harold. *Be Afraid, Be Very Afraid: The Book of Scary Urban Legends.* Norton, 2004. PPYA 2005 (All Kinds of Creepy).
From spiders hidden in hairdos to menacing men with hooks for hands or rum flavored by a dead man's body, new and old legends are collected and analyzed.

Buckley, James, Jr. *Scholastic Book of Firsts: More Than 1000 of the Coolest, Biggest, and Most Exciting First Facts You'll Ever Read.* Scholastic, 2005. QP 2006.
Do you know when the first zipper was invented, or the first dog flew in space, or the first sneaker was produced? Answers to these, and more, are found in this "firsts" book.

Burgess-Wise, David. *The Ultimate Race Car Book.* DK, 1999. QP 2000.
Superb color photos of competitive racing cars of the past century accompany information about the tracks, races, and driver personalities in this history of auto racing.

Caldwell, Ben. *Fantasy! Cartooning.* Sterling, 2005. QP 2006.
A young cartooning artist shares his techniques for drawing characters that combine modern Disney, animator Don Bluth's dragons, and the Cartoon Network.

Canfield, Jack, Mark Victor Hansen, and Kimberly Kirberger. *Chicken Soup for the Teenage Soul Letters: Letters of Life, Love and Learning.* Health Communications, 2000. QP 2002.
In response to *Chicken Soup for the Teenage Soul,* letters written by teens, parents, and teachers offer thanks or share similar experiences.

———. *Chicken Soup for the Teenage Soul II: 101 More Stories of Life, Love and Learning.* Health Communications, 1998. PPYA 2000 (Short Takes).

Arranged thematically in eight sections, these stories by teens help others to continue on life's journey, attend school, work, date, and prepare for the future.

Capote, Truman. *In Cold Blood.* Vintage, 1994. PPYA 2007 (I'm Not Making This Up).
Well researched, this work reports in journalistic fashion the 1950s crime that shocked America when two men shotgunned a Kansas family of four for no apparent reason.

Caprio, Robert. *Are We There Yet? Tales from the Never-Ending Travels of WWE Superstars.* Pocket, 2005. QP 2006.
Photos accompany vignettes of everyday life on the road for wrestlers and divas as they encounter tourist traps, rental car problems, and strip clubs.

Capuzzo, Michael. *Close to Shore: The Terrifying Shark Attacks of 1916.* Broadway, 2002. PPYA 2007 (I'm Not Making This Up).
This inspiration for *Jaws* recounts the summer a great white shark terrorized bathers along the New Jersey shore, just as more Americans were turning to ocean swimming.

Carle, Megan, and Jill Carle. *Teens Cook: How to Cook What You Want to Eat.* Ten Speed, 2004. PPYA 2007 (Get Creative).
Sisters, one a vegetarian and one not, one who follows directions and one who doesn't, share their favorite recipes for teen cooks.

Carlowicz, Michael. *The Moon.* Abrams, 2007. QP 2008.
From its fiery birth billions of years ago to its role in mythology and religion and its effect on the tides, the Earth's moon is documented in spectacular images.

Carlson, Lori M., ed. *Cool Salsa: Bilingual Poems on Growing Up Latino in the United States.* Fawcett, 1995. PPYA 2001 (Poetry).
Mixing language, translations, and subject matter leads to a potpourri of poems representative of Latino culture.

————. *Red Hot Salsa: Bilingual Poems on Being Young and Latino in the United States.* Holt, 2005. QP 2006.
Available in both Spanish and English, the writings of famous poets join with student poets to reveal thoughts on family life, language, and identity.

Carroll, Rebecca. *Sugar in the Raw: Voices of Young Black Girls in America.* Three Rivers, 1997. PPYA 2000 (Short Takes).
In a series of interviews with 15 young women, their spirit, determination, and plans for the future are clearly heard.

Catalano, Grace. *Meet the Stars of Dawson's Creek.* Laurel-Leaf, 1998. PPYA 1999 (Teen Culture).
This book features the stars—who were relatively unknown when filming began—of this television show popular from 1998 to 2003.

Chang, Pang-Mei. *Bound Feet and Western Dress: A Memoir.* Anchor, 1997. PPYA 2003 (This Small World).
Born to a respected Chinese family, Chang refuses to have her feet bound, marries and divorces, then works in a bank for women, eventually moving up to vice president.

Charles S. Anderson Design Co. and Michael Nelson. *Happy Kitty Bunny Pony: A Saccharine Mouthful of Super Cute.* Abrams, 2005. QP 2006.
America's obsession with cuteness, seen in images of kittens, chipmunks, panda cubs, and other animals from CSA Design, is tempered by Nelson's witty captions.

Christe, Ian. *Sound of the Beast: The Complete Headbanging History of Heavy Metal.* HarperCollins, 2003. QP 2004.
Quotes and photos add to the history of heavy metal bands such as Metallica, Black Sabbath, and Iron Maiden and such musicians as Ozzy Osbourne and Alice Cooper.

Chryssicas, Mary Kaye. *Breathe: Yoga for Teens.* DK, 2007. QP 2008.
Guidance through both challenging and relaxing yoga poses gives teens an outlet from stress and the opportunity to learn something new.

Clark, Jerome. *Unexplained! Strange Sightings, Incredible Occurrences and Puzzling Physical Phenomena.* Visible Ink, 1998. PPYA 2001 (Paranormal).
Fans of the supernatural will devour this work, which examines both hoaxes and strange phenomena such as crop circles, UFOs, Bigfoot, and Martians.

Clarkson, Mark. *Battlebots: The Official Guide.* McGraw-Hill, 2002. QP 2003.
Look behind the scenes at the popular destructive sport of robotic competitions waged by bots and seen on Comedy Central.

Cobain, Kurt. *Journals.* Riverhead, 2002. QP 2003.
From the dozens of notebooks written by Cobain, eight survived his suicide and are reproduced here, filled with thoughts that range from the mundane to the morbid.

Coker, Cheo Hodari. *Unbelievable: The Life, Death and Afterlife of the Notorious B.I.G.* Three Rivers, 2003. QP 2005.
Family interviews and photos add a personal touch to this celebration of the hip-hop rapper Christopher Wallace, aka Biggie Smalls, aka the Notorious B.I.G.

Coleman, Loren, and Jerome Clark. *Cryptozoology A to Z: The Encyclopedia of Loch Ness Monsters, Sasquatch, Chupacabras, and Other Authentic Mysteries of Nature.* Fireside, 1999. PPYA 2001 (Paranormal).
Cryptozoology is the study of "hidden animals," a new science that has emerged following increased sightings of Bigfoot, the Loch Ness monster, and other legendary creatures.

Collier-Thompson, Kristi. *The Girls' Guide to Dreams.* Illustrated by Sandie Turchyn. Sterling, 2003. QP 2004.
To help teenage girls understand their unsettled lives, a dictionary arrangement from "acne" to "zoo" explains the symbolism and images of their dreams.

Colton, Larry. *Counting Coup: A True Story of Basketball and Honor on the Little Big Horn.* Grand Central, 2001. PPYA 2008 (Anyone Can Play).
Though Sharon LaFarge is a talented basketball player, her quest for a college scholarship is derailed by family members and friends on the reservation.

Columbia University's Health Education Program, ed. *The "Go Ask Alice" Book of Answers: A Guide to Good Physical, Sexual, and Emotional Health.* Holt, 1998. PPYA 2000 (Self-Help).
Selected from the Go Ask Alice website are these unbiased answers to teen questions about hangover survival, nose piercing, lesbianism, and dietary problems, among others.

Conniff, Richard. *Rats! The Good, the Bad, and the Ugly.* Crown, 2002. QP 2003.
This natural history author not only demystifies rats but also reveals their impact on humans.

Cooke, Kaz. *Real Gorgeous: The Truth about Body and Beauty.* Norton, 1996. PPYA 2000 (Self-Help).
Shattering the myths about dieting, cosmetics, and their promotional advertisements, here's sensible, humorous advice for learning to live with your body.

Coombs, Davey, and the editors of Racer X Illustrated. *MX: The Way of the Motocrosser.* Abrams, 2003. QP 2004.
Photographs of this popular extreme motorcycle sport will lure teens into reading the text as they learn about some of its stars and sense the power and thrill of a motocross.

Cooper, Robbie. *Alter Ego: Digital Avatars and Their Creators.* Chris Boot, 2007. QP 2008.
Seventy gamers and their avatars are profiled, accompanied by a glossary of gaming terms.

Corbett, Sara. *Venus to the Hoop: A Gold Medal Year in Women's Basketball.* Anchor, 1998. PPYA 1999 (Good Sports).
Twelve women come together for a year to form the 1996 U.S. women's Olympic basketball team and go for the gold.

CosmoGirl, ed. *Ask CosmoGirl! about Guys: All the Answers to Your Most Asked Questions about Love and Relationships.* Sterling, 2006. QP 2007.
Thoughtful yet entertaining answers are provided to wide-ranging questions about dating, friendship, and boyfriends, with references to other sources for additional help.

———. *Ask CosmoGirl! about Your Body: All the Answers to Your Most Intimate Questions.* Sterling, 2006. QP 2007.
Included in this self-help book are well-researched answers to all those embarrassing girl questions, from covering up zits or hickeys to fighting depression.

———. *CosmoGirl! Make It Yourself: 50 Fun and Funky Projects.* Sterling, 2007. QP 2008.
Teens can add to their personal style with these varied projects, including a ribbon-front halter top, necklaces, decorated ballet flats, and spa treatments.

———. *CosmoGirl! Quiz Book: All about You.* Sterling, 2004. QP 2005.
Who are you? Answering the multiple-choice quizzes from CosmoGirl helps you figure out whether you're "friendly vanilla," "creative chocolate," or "intense coffee."

———. *CosmoGirl! Quiz Book: Discover Your Personality.* Sterling, 2005. QP 2006.
This collection of 26 fun and insightful quizzes helps you determine the type of CosmoGirl you are.

———. *CosmoGirl! Words to Live By.* Sterling, 2006. QP 2007.
Drawn from authors, athletes, magazine readers, and the editors of *CosmoGirl,* 500 insightful quotes help teens with their family, friends, relationships, school, and life.

Covey, Sean. *The 7 Habits of Highly Effective Teens: The Ultimate Teenage Success Guide.* Simon & Schuster, 1998. PPYA 2000 (Self-Help).
Based on Covey's adult model, this step-by-step guide allows young adults to make the most of their teen years, from developing relationships to resisting peer pressure.

Crawford, Saffi, and Geraldine Sullivan. *The Power of Birthdays, Stars, and Numbers: The Complete Personology*

Reference Guide. Ballantine, 1998. PPYA 1999 (Teen Culture).

Information on the zodiac, fixed stars, and numerology is available in a day-by-day listing that reveals personal traits and one's position in the universe.

Crisp, Terri. *Out of Harm's Way: The Extraordinary True Story of One Woman's Lifelong Devotion to Animals.* Simon & Schuster, 1997. PPYA 2004 (If It Weren't for Them).

Driven to rescue animals from natural and man-made disasters, Crisp has not only saved thousands but also set up a nationwide animal rescue plan.

Csillag, Andre. *Backstreet Boys: The Official Book.* Delacorte, 2000. QP 2001.

The yearbook-like layout of photos and comments from the band members is sanctioned by Howie, AJ, Kevin, Brian, and Nick.

Daldry, Jeremy. *The Teenage Guy's Survival Guide: The Real Deal on Girls, Growing Up, and Other Guy Stuff.* Little, Brown, 1999. QP 2000; PPYA 2000 (Self-Help).

Readers or browsers will discovers lots of frank, commonsense advice on adolescent problems like dating, body changes, and drugs.

Davis, James. *Skateboarding Is Not a Crime: 50 Years of Street Culture.* With photographs by Skin Phillips. Firefly, 2004. QP 2006; PPYA 2007 (I'm Not Making This Up).

Evolved from surfing, the sport of skateboarding is documented through photos and text that introduce its stars, culture, and movies as well as necessary gear and techniques.

Dee, Catherine, and Ali Douglas, eds. *The Girl's Book of Wisdom: Empowering,*

Inspirational Quotes from 400 Fabulous Females. Little, Brown, 1999. QP 2000; PPYA 2000 (Self-Help).

Organized into 44 categories, including friends, leadership, beauty, adventure, and success, are these humorous or motivational quotes from women of all races, ages, and careers.

Deem, James M. *Bodies from the Bog.* Houghton Mifflin, 1998. QP 1999.

Striking photographs reveal the well-preserved bodies and relics found in peat bogs that aid scientists in learning about life thousands of years ago.

DeFalco, Tom. *Hulk: The Incredible Guide.* DK, 2003. QP 2004.

Details now explain what happens when Dr. Bruce Banner, a superhero for more than 40 years, becomes angry and transforms into the 700-pound Hulk.

Defede, Jim. *The Day the World Came to Town: 9/11 in Gander, Newfoundland.* HarperTrade, 2003. PPYA 2004 (If It Weren't for Them).

When the United States closed its airspace after the September 11 attack, 38 jetliners and 6,595 passengers were diverted to Gander for six days, where townspeople cared for them.

DeVito, Basil V., Jr., with Joe Layden. *WWF Wrestlemania: The Official Insider's Story.* HarperCollins, 2001. QP 2002.

Behind the scenes of wrestlemania, the in-the-ring excitement is captured through color action photos, interviews with wrestlers and celebrities, and a DVD.

Diagram Group. *How to Hold a Crocodile.* Firefly, 2003. QP 2004.

All the info needed for those activities no one teaches you can be found here, from tying a bow tie to drilling for oil, playing castanets, and catching a cockroach.

Diary of a Junior Year. Real Teens series, vol. 1. Scholastic, 1999. QP 2000.
Diary entries from eight juniors paint a realistic view of high school life.

DiClaudio, Dennis. *The Hypochondriac's Pocket Guide to Horrible Diseases You Probably Already Have.* Bloomsbury, 2005. PPYA 2007 (I'm Not Making This Up).
If you need a quick disease, here's a list of the 50 worst, including symptoms, treatment, prognosis, and, just in case, a little prevention.

Dingle, Adrian. *The Periodic Table: Elements with Style.* Illustrated by Simon Basher. Houghton Mifflin, 2007. QP 2008.
The elements receive a 21st-century update—each with its own "home page," complete with photo, as might be found on a website.

Donkin, Andrew. *The Truly Tasteless Scratch and Sniff Book.* DK, 2000. QP 2001.
This 24-page board book will offend everyone with its reprehensible rhymes and scents of smelly feet, rotten fish, sour milk, and skunk odors.

Dougall, Alastair. *James Bond: The Secret World of 007.* Illustrated by Roger Stewart. DK, 2000. QP 2001.
Everything Bond-related can be found here, including his love life, cases, intricate workings of his cars and gadgets, and master plans of the villains he has encountered.

Drill, Esther, Heather McDonald, and Rebecca Odes. *Deal with It! A Whole New Approach to Your Body, Brain and Life as a gURL.* Pocket, 1999. QP 2001; PPYA 2000 (Self-Help).
Using a blend of humor and frankness, the creators of gURL.com advise girls on concerns such as rape, masturbation, zits, depression, drugs, and family life.

Duffy, Carol Ann, ed. *I Wouldn't Thank You for a Valentine: Poems for Young Feminists.* Holt, 1997. PPYA 2001 (Poetry).
This wide-ranging compilation of poetry goes beyond poems for the feminist movement alone and includes ones that involve women and their emotions in many different ways.

Duncan, Lois. *Who Killed My Daughter?* Dell, 1994. PPYA 2004 (Guess Again).
Noted YA author Duncan relates her own mystery after her daughter Kaitlyn is shot and killed; the police think it's a random shooting, but Kaitlyn's live-in boyfriend has gang ties.

Edelman, Bernard. *Dear America: Letters Home from Vietnam.* Simon & Schuster, 1991. PPYA 2002 (War).
More than 100 letters and poems let Americans view the war through the eyes of the soldiers who served, with the "death letters" being especially poignant.

Edgar, Jim. *Bad Cat: 244 Not-So-Pretty Kitties and Cats Gone Bad.* Workman, 2004. QP 2006.
Felines shaved to resemble strange topiaries or garbed in costumes are among the cats with attitude pictured here.

Edut, Tali, and Ophira Edut. *Astrostyle: Star-Studded Advice for Love, Life, and Looking Good.* Simon & Schuster, 2003. QP 2004.
Official astrologers for *Teen People,* twins Tali and Ophira help teens use their astrological signs to succeed in choosing clothing, romance, and friendships.

Edwards, Gavin, and Chris Kalb. *'Scuse Me While I Kiss This Guy, and Other Misheard Lyrics.* Fireside, 1995. PPYA 1999 (Teen Culture).
If you've been singing the wrong lyrics, you're not alone, as proved by these 275 commonly misheard song lyrics, taken from 1960s–1990s pop songs.

Eleveld, Mark, ed. *The Spoken Word Revolution: Slam, Hip Hop and the Poetry of a New Generation.* Sourcebooks, 2003. QP 2004.
The works of 50 poets, with performances on CD by 20 of them, are showcased in this overview of contemporary poetry.

Elffers, Joost. *Play with Your Food.* Stewart, Tabori, & Chang, 1997. QP 1999.
Cleverly cutting up and arranging yellow peppers, yams, lemons, cucumbers, or turnips can create a wide variety of birds, pigs, cats, and other critters.

Emert, Phyllis Raybin. *Mysteries of People and Places.* Strange Unsolved Mysteries series, book 3. Tor, 2000. PPYA 2004 (Guess Again).
Unsolved puzzles from the past still haunt us, including the identity of Jack the Ripper, secrets of the pyramids, and the phenomena inside the Bermuda Triangle.

Eminem. *Angry Blonde.* HarperCollins, 2000—QP 2002; HarperCollins, 2002—PPYA 2004 (On That Note).
Uncensored lyrics fill the pages of this authorized biography of a rap superstar who understands the power of words.

Erlbach, Arlene. *Worth the Risk: True Stories about Risk Takers plus How You Can Be One, Too.* Free Spirit, 1999. PPYA 2000 (Self-Help).
Taking a chance can be positive or negative, and the case studies of teens who took risks help illustrate the difference; suggestions for making good decisions are included.

Escher, M. C., and J. L. Locher. *The Magic of M. C. Escher.* Abrams, 2000. QP 2001.
Though many teens are familiar with Escher's work, this volume contains his graphic illustrations, woodcuts, and lithographs, with accompanying foldouts and commentary.

Everhart, Mike. *Sea Monsters: Prehistoric Monsters of the Deep.* National Geographic, 2007. QP 2008.
This companion to the movie of the same name features computer-generated and 3-D images of huge underwater predators that swam the seas 80 million years ago.

Farley, Christopher John. *Aaliyah: More Than a Woman.* Pocket, 2002. PPYA 2004 (On That Note).
Aaliyah Dana Haughton was a beautiful hip-hop soul artist who became an actress and then died in a plane crash at the age of 22.

Feiffer, Jules. *The Great Comic Book Heroes.* Fantagraphics, 2003. PPYA 2004 (If It Weren't for Them).
An essayist and artist himself, Feiffer records the history of the comics business, from 1937 to the early 1950s, in a classic work that analyzes appeal and artistic techniques.

Fishbein, Amy. *The Truth about Girlfriends.* Seventeen series. HarperCollins, 2001. QP 2002.
Seventeen magazine's collection of quizzes and activities enables teens to learn what a friend could and should be.

Flaherty, Mike. *American Chopper: At Full Throttle.* Meredith, 2004. QP 2006.
A behind-the-scenes look at the popular

Discovery channel program allows readers to see construction of the incredible customized, theme-oriented motorcycles.

Fleischman, John. *Phineas Gage: A Gruesome but True Story about Brain Science.* Houghton Mifflin, 2004. PPYA 2007 (I'm Not Making This Up).
In the realm of medical legend is railroad worker Phineas Gage, who survived 11 years after a 13-pound tamping rod pierced his left cheek and emerged from the top of his head.

Fletcher, Ralph J. *Relatively Speaking: Poems about Family.* Illustrated by Walter L. Krudop. Orchard, 1999. QP 2000.
This series of poems by a youngest child describes the interactions of one family, from an accident to a new baby, a funeral, and a family reunion.

———. *Room Enough for Love: The Complete Poems of "I Am Wings" and "Buried Alive."* Aladdin, 1997. PPYA 2001 (Poetry).
This one volume contains all the romance poems found in two of Fletcher's earlier titles and allows teens to explore the highs and lows of being in love.

Fong-Torres, Ben. *The Rice Room: Growing Up Chinese-American; From Number Two Son to Rock 'n' Roll.* Plume, 1995. PPYA 2002 (Tales of the Cities).
Entertainment journalist for *Rolling Stone* magazine, the author struggles growing up Chinese in America and shocks his parents with his musical interests.

Fontaine, Smokey D. *E.A.R.L.: The Autobiography of DMX.* HarperCollins, 2002. QP 2003.
From a childhood of abuse and neglect when no one ever listened to him,

Earl Simmons is now rapper DMX and expresses the thoughts of thousands of kids living like he did.

Forman, Ruth. *We Are the Young Magicians.* Beacon, 1993. PPYA 2001 (Poetry).
Recipient of the Barnard New Women Poets Prize, this young African American incorporates her memories of growing up urban and black into her poetry.

Fornay, Alfred. *Born Beautiful: The African American Teenager's Complete Beauty Guide.* Wiley, 2002. QP 2003.
Information about skin care, the correct makeup, hairstyles, and the best colors to wear and scents to use are provided so African American teens look and feel great.

Foxworthy, Jeff. *Jeff Foxworthy's Redneck Dictionary: Words You Thought You Knew the Meaning Of.* Illustrated by Layron DeJarnette. Villard, 2005. QP 2006.
As Foxworthy points out, learning to speak his unique southern dialect is easier than learning any other foreign language.

Franco, Betsy, ed. *Things I Have to Tell You: Poems and Writings by Teenage Girls.* With photographs by Nina Nickles. Candlewick, 2001. QP 2002.
Thirty traditional and free-form poems explore the unique world of teen girls, from the women's movement to loneliness to bad hair days.

———. *You Hear Me? Poems and Writing by Teenage Boys.* Candlewick, 2000. QP 2001.
A diverse group of teens write straight from the heart in free verse or rhyme about their lives, including love, anger, sex, drugs, and conformity.

Frank, Anne. *Anne Frank: The Diary of a Young Girl.* Bantam, 1993. PPYA 2003 (Lock It, Lick It, Click It).
Just before Anne and her family go into hiding in Amsterdam, she receives a diary for her 13th birthday but never learns how important her writings of Nazi occupation will become.

Freedman, Russell. *Cowboys of the Wild West.* Clarion, 1990. PPYA 2001 (Western).
Fifty historic photos depict the difficult life on cattle drives for these independent, usually teenage, men—not the cowboys seen in movies.

Fricke, Jim. *Yes Yes Y'all: The Experience Music Project Oral History of Hip-Hop's First Decade.* Da Capo, 2002. QP 2004.
Interviews with early hip-hoppers and disc jockeys provide a rich history of this musical movement that originated in the streets of the Bronx.

Friedman, Linda, and Dana White, eds. *Teen People: Real Life Diaries; Inspiring True Stories from Celebrities and Real Teens.* HarperCollins, 2001. QP 2002.
Six celebrities, including Carson Daly and Moby, along with six teens share personal stories of challenges each has had to face and overcome.

Fulghum, Hunter S. *Don't Try This at Home: How to Win a Sumo Match, Catch a Great White Shark, and Start an Independent Nation and Other Extraordinary Feats (for Ordinary People).* Broadway, 2002. QP 2004.
If you want to ride over Niagara Falls in a barrel or sink a submarine, detailed instructions on carrying out such really stupid and dangerous activities can be found here.

Gaiman, Neil, et al. *9-11: The World's Finest Comic Book Writers and Artists Tell Stories to Remember,* vol. 2. DC Comics, 2002. QP 2003.
Award-winning cartoonists such as Will Eisner, Neil Gaiman, Michael Moorcock, and Stan Lee portray personal thoughts and drawings about this horrific day in America.

Gaines, Thom. *Digital Photo Madness! 50 Weird and Wacky Things to Do with Your Digital Camera.* Lark, 2006. PPYA 2007 (Get Creative).
After covering the basics in easy-to-understand terminology, manipulating images to swap heads or zebra-stripe bodies are just two of the many creative activities you can take on.

Galvez, Jose, and Luis Alberto Urrea. *Vatos.* Cinco Puntos, 2000. QP 2002.
The combination of Urrea's poetry and Galvez's photos offer up a tribute to all Chicano, Latino, and Hispanic men who are often overlooked in today's society.

Gantos, Jack. *Hole in My Life.* Farrar, Straus, & Giroux, 2004. PPYA 2006 (Criminal Elements).
Trying to get rich in a drug scam, at the age of 20 this noted author ends up in prison, where he uses the time to hone his writing skills.

Ganz, Nicholas. *Graffiti World: Street Art from Five Continents.* Abrams, 2004. QP 2006.
Collected from Brooklyn to Brazil, more than 2,000 illustrations highlight the political and social commentary of street art.

Garza, Mario. *Stuff on My Cat: The Book.* Chronicle, 2006. QP 2007.
The popular website www.stuffonmycat .com is the source of these hilarious photos

of cats draped with gummi bears, action figures, wigs, and even cheeseburgers.

Gee, Joshua. *Encyclopedia Horrifica: The Terrifying TRUTH! about Vampires, Ghosts, Monsters and More.* Scholastic, 2007. QP 2008.
Photos and text describing psychic phenomena, ghosts, vampires, aliens, sea monsters, and werewolves attempt to separate fact from fiction and history from legend and lore.

Genat, Robert. *Funny Cars.* Motorbooks International, 2000. QP 2002.
The archives of the National Hot Rod Association yield photographs of 1960s factory experimental cars that eventually morphed into funny cars.

————. *Lowriders.* Motorbooks International, 2001. QP 2002; PPYA 2007 (I'm Not Making This Up).
Bilingual and filled with color photos, this book for all car enthusiasts includes the major types of lowriders, including bombs, Euros, trucks, new age, and even bicycles.

George-Warren, Holly, ed. *Rolling Stone: The Complete Covers, 1967–1997.* Abrams, 1998. QP 1999.
Thirty years of memorable *Rolling Stone* magazine covers include the work of such famous photographers as Annie Leibovitz and Richard Avedon.

Gerard, Jim. *Celebrity Skin: Tattoos, Brands, and Body Adornments of the Stars.* Thunder's Mouth, 2001. QP 2003.
Take a look at the tattoos on such celebrities as the Dixie Chicks, Angelina Jolie, Dennis Rodman, and the Backstreet Boys.

Gilroy, Tom, et al. *The Haiku Year.* Soft Skull, 1998. PPYA 2001 (Poetry).
Seven friends decide to write one haiku poem a day for a year. At the end of that time, they discover that their poems reflect the beauty in their everyday lives.

Ginsberg, Allen. *Howl and Other Poems.* City Lights, 1991. PPYA 2001 (Poetry).
First published in 1965 and disruptive for the social taboos it broke, "Howl" eradicated many barriers for poets and is today considered a classic.

Golden, Christopher, and Nancy Holder. *The Watcher's Guide.* Buffy the Vampire Slayer series, vol. 1. Pocket, 1998. PPYA 1999 (Teen Culture).
Summaries of episodes, scenes from original scripts, "Quote of the Week," fun facts, cast interviews, and Buffy's weapons and spells fill this guide to the popular TV show.

Golus, Carrie. *Tupac Shakur.* Just the Facts Biographies series. Lerner, 2007. QP 2008.
Readable text and abundant photos chronicle the life of this famous rapper, who was murdered in 1996 but whose music and fame live on.

Gootman, Marilyn E. *When a Friend Dies: A Book for Teens about Grieving and Healing.* Free Spirit, 1994. PPYA 2000 (Self-Help).
Compassionate advice—some from teens who have lost friends or family members—aids parents, counselors, and teens in the grieving process.

Gottesman, Jane. *Game Face: What Does a Female Athlete Look Like?* Edited by Geoffrey Biddle. Random House, 2001. QP 2002.
A time line of women's athletics, photos of famous and unknown female athletes representing many sports, and a complete index make this an excellent reference source.

Gottlieb, Andrew. *In the Paint: Tattoos of the NBA and the Stories behind Them.* Hyperion, 2003. QP 2005.
With 70 percent of the NBA players sporting tattoos, many of which are hidden, the photos and stories about their tats reveal a lot about the person wearing them.

Gottlieb, Lori. *Stick Figure: A Diary of My Former Self.* Simon & Schuster, 2000— QP 2001; Berkley, 2000—PPYA 2006 (What Ails You?).
This memoir, rife with humor, reveals Lori's decision at the age of 11 to control one thing in her life, dieting, and her desire to be the thinnest girl "on the planet."

Grahame-Smith, Seth. *How to Survive a Horror Movie: All the Skills to Dodge the Kills.* Chronicle, 2007. QP 2008.
Learn how to survive every possible horror movie situation, from scary nights babysitting to murderous dolls, exorcism, and corrupt local sheriffs.

Grandberry, Omari. *O.* MTV, 2005. QP 2006.
A member the Los Angeles–based R&B group B2K, Omari describes the group's breakup and his continued attempt to make it in the entertainment industry.

Grandits, John. *Blue Lipstick: Concrete Poems.* Clarion, 2007. QP 2008.
Imaginative poetry describes Jessie's high school life, from her dislike of cheerleaders to crowded school hallways, cranky days, and volleyball practice.

———. *Technically, It's Not My Fault: Concrete Poems.* Clarion, 2004. QP 2005.
Combining physical form, typeface, and verse, this collection of concrete poems illustrates a middle schooler's concerns, including pizzas, homework, and older sisters.

Gravelle, Karen. *5 Ways to Know about You.* Walker, 2001. QP 2002.
Though these five ways of predicting personality sound new age, astrology, palm reading, numerology, Chinese horoscopes, and handwriting analysis are centuries old.

Grealy, Lucy. *Autobiography of a Face.* HarperPerennial, 1995. PPYA 1999 (Different Drummers).
Nine-year-old Lucy's pain from jaw surgery and subsequent treatments for cancer are matched by her classmate's taunts about her face in this heartbreaking memoir.

Greatest Stars of the NBA series. Vol. 1, *Shaquille O'Neal;* vol. 2, *Tim Duncan;* vol. 3, *Jason Kidd;* vol. 4, *Kevin Garnett.* Tokyopop, 2004–2005. QP 2006.
This debut series of NBA sports manga uses action digital images and the manga technique of word balloons to highlight the careers of these four players.

Greenberg, Gary. *Pop-Up Book of Phobias.* Illustrated by Balvis Rubess. Morrow, 1999. QP 2001.
The pop-ups give a three-dimensional edge to the fear of peering down from a skyscraper, confronting a spider, or sitting in an airplane as all the oxygen masks drop down.

Greenberg, Jan, and Sandra Jordan. *Vincent Van Gogh: Portrait of an Artist.* Yearling, 2003. PPYA 2007 (Get Creative).
Correspondence between artist and brother reveals the man behind the myth as an exceptional artist who was passionate about and dedicated to his art.

Greenfield, Lauren. *Thin.* Chronicle, 2006. QP 2008.
Photographs and interviews of 20 female residents of an eating disorder clinic disclose varied reasons for anorexia, bulimia, and a false image of the perfect body.

Gregory, Julia. *Sickened: The Memoir of a Munchausen by Proxy Childhood.* Bantam, 2004. PPYA 2006 (What Ails You?).
A victim of her mother's desire for attention, the author was half starved, overmedicated, and a regular at doctors' offices until college.

Gregory, Leland. *Hey Idiot! Chronicles of Human Stupidity.* Andrews McMeel, 2003. QP 2004.
More than 200 examples of stupidity, from burning down your firehouse to exploding your oxygen tent by lighting a cigarette, are found in this work by a *Saturday Night Live* writer.

———. *Stupid Crook Book.* Andrews McMeel, 2002. QP 2004.
Siphoning gas from an RV only to receive gallons of sewage and locking keys inside a getaway car prove that criminals really are stupid.

Grody, Steve, and James Prigoff. *Graffiti L.A.: Street and Art.* Abrams, 2007. QP 2008.
Interviews with artists of the often short-lived graffiti art and Grody's photographs keep alive a unique culture that dates from the 1930s, when it began as gang territory marks.

Groening, Matt. *The Simpsons: A Complete Guide to Our Favorite Family.* HarperPaperbacks, 1997. PPYA 1999 (Teen Culture).
A decade's worth of episodes, couch gags, theme song lyrics, and "Top Homerisms" are found in this seasonal arrangement of the popular TV show *The Simpsons*.

———. *Simpsons Comics Royale.* HarperCollins, 2001. QP 2002.
Ten stories, some televised, are featured along with comments from Groening about Bart's spiky hair, his previous career, and an essay about secrets of the Simpsons.

Guzzetti, Paula. *Jim Carrey.* Dillon, 1998. QP 1999.
Jim Carrey is today a funny Hollywood comedian who has wanted to make people laugh ever since he was a child and now is living that dream.

Haab, Sherri. *The Hip Handbag Book: 25 Easy-to-Make Totes, Purses and Bags.* Illustrated by Nina Edwards. Watson-Guptill, 2004. QP 2006.
Simple, well-illustrated instructions enable readers to make clutch and shoulder bags, coin purses, and cell phone carriers out of blue jeans, socks, and duct tape.

———. *Nail Art.* Klutz, 1997. PPYA 1999 (Teen Culture).
Tips and techniques help teens paint hundreds of different designs on their nails, both fingers and toes.

Halls, Kelly Milner, Rick Spears, and Roxyanne Young. *Tales of the Cryptids: Mysterious Creatures That May or May Not Exist.* Darby Creek, 2006. QP 2007.
Legendary animals and monsters from around the world are the subject of this engaging work featuring tales, drawings, and photographs of Nessie, Bigfoot, and their friends.

Hamilton, Bethany, with Sheryl Berk and Rick Bundschuh. *Soul Surfer: A True Story of Faith, Family, and Fighting to Get Back on the Board.* MTV, 2006. PPYA 2008 (Anyone Can Play).

Though losing her arm to a shark while surfing, Bethany credits God for enabling her to return to her board within a month after surgery.

Hamilton, Jake. *Special Effects: In Film and Television.* DK, 1998. QP 1999.
Want to know about specific effects? Check out this book to learn how pouring rain, computer-animated dragons, and latex alien heads are created.

Handy, Roger, and Karen Elsener, eds. *Found Photos: Rear Ends.* Abrams, 2007. QP 2008.
Strange as it may sound, this is a fun, charming collection of bottoms, photographed on beaches or in parks, garbed or not, reclining or playing, and belonging to all ages.

Hareas, John. *NBA's Greatest.* DK, 2003. QP 2005.
More than 300 photos highlight the careers of some of basketball's greatest players and coaches as well as memorable moments in outstanding games.

Harrington, Jane. *Extreme Pets Handbook.* Scholastic, 2007. QP 2008.
Looking for a pet that's not a cute puppy or kitten? Suggestions here include detachable-fur rodents and eyeball-licking lizards, plus tips for persuading parents.

Hart, Christopher. *Anime Mania: How to Draw Characters for Japanese Animation.* Watson-Guptill, 2002. QP 2003.
Writing for aspiring cartoonists, Hart illustrates necessary shapes and angles for animating as well as techniques for storyboarding and sketching.

————. *Manga Mania Chibi and Furry Characters: How to Draw the Adorable Mini-Characters and Cool Cat Girls of Japanese Comics.* Watson-Guptill, 2006. QP 2007.
Instructions for drawing doe-eyed little people called chibi, as well as chibi monsters and human-cat hybrids, go beyond basic manga illustration.

————. *Manga Mania Fantasy Worlds: How to Draw the Amazing Worlds of Japanese Comics.* Watson-Guptill, 2003. QP 2004.
Noted illustrator Hart provides step-by-step instructions to create the ogres, knights, warriors, and gothic beasts that populate the magical worlds of manga mania.

————. *Manga Mania: How to Draw Japanese Comics.* Watson-Guptill, 2001. QP 2002; PPYA 2007 (Get Creative).
Wildly popular among the Japanese, this primer on manga illustration also includes background on manga genres and an interview with a large U.S. manga publisher.

————. *Manga Mania Villains: How to Draw the Dastardly Characters of Japanese Comics.* Watson-Guptill, 2003. QP 2004.
In this continuing series, it's time to learn to draw the bad guys, beginning with their head, body, and poses and moving on to expressions, costumes, and weaponry.

————. *Manhwa Mania: How to Draw Korean Comics.* Watson-Guptill, 2004. QP 2006.
Novice illustrators receive instruction in the techniques of drawing manhwa, the Korean form of the popular Japanese comic style manga.

————. *Mecha Mania: How to Draw the Battling Robots, Cool Spaceships, and Military Vehicles of Japanese Comics.* Watson-Guptill, 2002. QP 2003.

This noted cartoonist encourages young artists with a sampling of techniques for drawing robots, cyborgs, spaceships, and space battles.

Hart, Tony. *Microterrors: The Complete Guide to Bacterial, Viral and Fungal Infections.* Firefly, 2004. PPYA 2006 (What Ails You?).
Pathogenic characteristics of these microscopic agents of such diseases as AIDS and SARS are described and illustrated.

Hass, Robert, ed. *The Essential Haiku: Versions of Bashō, Buson and Issa.* Essential Poets series. HarperCollins, 1995. PPYA 2001 (Poetry).
The best works of Bashō, Buson, and Issa, masters of the 17-syllable poems that are uniquely Japanese, can be found in these selections.

Hautzig, Esther Rudomin. *The Endless Steppe: Growing Up in Siberia.* HarperTrophy, 1995. PPYA 2003 (This Small World).
Transported by cattle car from their home in Poland to Siberia, Esther, her mother, and her grandmother survive five years of exile in bitterly cold Siberia during World War II.

Hawk, Tony. *Between Boardslides and Burnout: My Notes from the Road.* HarperCollins, 2002. QP 2003.
This professional skateboarder's tour diary, complete with color photos and graphics, takes the reader on the road to competitions, demos, autograph sessions, and movie sets.

Hawk, Tony, with Sean Mortimer. *Hawk: Occupation, Skateboarder.* HarperCollins, 2000. QP 2001.
Tony Hawk was considered an old-timer when he retired at 32. His memoir covers his scrawny childhood and rise to prominence as a champion in the skateboarding world.

Hayhurst, Chris. *Bicycle Stunt Riding! Catch Air.* Extreme Sports Collection. Rosen, 2000. QP 2001.
Jumps, spins, and other exciting moves, along with information about the special freestyle bikes needed for stunt riding, can be found in this easy-to-read work.

———. *Mountain Biking: Get on the Trail.* Extreme Sports Collection. Rosen, 2000. QP 2001.
Photos add to the technique tips, necessary equipment, and training for mountain biking in a sport that requires skill and daring.

Hear Me Out: True Stories of Teens Educating and Confronting Homophobia. Second Story, 2004. PPYA 2006 (GLBTQ).
An assortment of young people from the Toronto area, involved in the T.E.A.C.H. project, write personal accounts of discovering their sexual identity.

Heimberg, Jason, and Justin Heimberg. *The Official Movie Plot Generator: 27,000 Hilarious Movie Plot Combinations.* Brothers Heimberg, 2004. QP 2005.
By flipping this book's tabs, the reader combines plot elements to create unusual movies, like the single-mother crime fighter who coaches sports and is aided by robots or monsters.

Hess, Jared, and Jerusha Hess. *Napoleon Dynamite: The Complete Quote Book.* Simon & Schuster, 2005. QP 2006.
All the best one-liners from Napoleon, Pedro, and the gang are included in this hilarious book of quotes extracted from the hit film of the same name.

Hess, Nina. *A Practical Guide to Monsters.* Mirrorstone, 2007. QP 2008.
Line drawings, paintings, and maps bring to life fantastic, mythic monsters that are also found inhabiting the world of *Dungeons and Dragons.*

Hillstrom, Kevin, Laurie Hillstrom, and Roger Matuz. *The Handy Sports Answer Book.* Visible Ink, 1998. PPYA 1999 (Good Sports).
Organized by type of sport and blind-tested in pubs, 1,000 snippets of sports facts, figures, and trivia are available in a question-and-answer format.

Hinojosa, Maria. *Crews: Gang Members Talk to Maria Hinojosa.* With photographs by German Perez. Harcourt, 1995. PPYA 2002 (Tales of the Cities).
NPR reporter Hinojosa interviews Latino gang members in New York City who regard their gang as an extended family, allowing escape from a multitude of problems.

Hip Hop Divas. Three Rivers, 2001. QP 2002.
This work profiles women in the hip-hop field, long dominated by guys, beginning with the ones who opened up the field to those who, like Lauryn Hill, are now hot stars.

Hoffman, Mat, with Mark Lewman. *The Ride of My Life.* HarperCollins, 2002. QP 2003.
Though he is now retired, photos and his memories testify that Hoffman was a fantastic BMX stunt rider who relished the surge of adrenalin needed for competing in the X Games.

Hogya, Bernie, and Sal Taibi. *Milk Mustache Mania.* Scholastic, 2002. QP 2003.
Kermit the Frog, Batman, Mike Myers, and Britney Spears are a few of the 65 celebrities who helped popularize the "Got Milk" ad campaign.

Holdsclaw, Chamique, with Jennifer Frey. *Chamique Holdsclaw: My Story.* Aladdin, 2001. PPYA 2004 (If It Weren't for Them).
Raised by her grandmother who made her believe in herself, Holdsclaw relates her college and professional basketball success and failures.

Holliday, Laurel. *Why Do They Hate Me? Young Lives Caught in War and Conflict.* Simon Pulse, 1999. PPYA 2002 (War).
Holliday includes interviews, diaries, notes, and essays from teens who have lived in war zones, enduring events over which they have no control.

Holt, David, and Bill Mooney. *Spiders in the Hairdo: Modern Urban Legends.* August House, 1999. QP 2000; PPYA 2000 (Short Takes).
Fifty brief stories of modern folklore will intrigue and terrify teens as they hear of the vanishing hitchhiker or those alligators living in the sewers of New York City.

Hoye, Jacob, ed. *MTV Uncensored.* Pocket, 2001. QP 2002.
The hit shows, fashion, music, and controversy of MTV's first 20 years are accompanied by quotes, color photos, and short interviews with the stars.

Hoye, Jacob, and Karolyn Ali, eds. *Tupac: Resurrection, 1971–1976.* Atria, 2003— QP 2004; Atria, 2006—PPYA 2007 (I'm Not Making This Up).
Companion to the documentary film of the same name, this scrapbook of Tupac's words and photos captures his life and thoughts in a moving biography.

Huebner, Mark, and Brad Wilson. *Sports Bloopers: All-Star Flubs and Fumbles.* Firefly, 2003. QP 2004.
Even talented athletes make mistakes, as shown by photos that reveal their missteps, blunders, and oopsies.

Huegel, Kelly. *GLBTQ: The Survival Guide for Queer and Questioning Teens.* Free Spirit, 2004. PPYA 2006 (GLBTQ).
Teens questioning their sexuality, or interested in learning more about GLBTQ, find answers through nonjudgmental advice, teen quotes, and resources.

Hughes, Dave, and Eric Fogel. *The Celebrity Deathmatch Companion.* Universe, 2000. QP 2001.
Fan mail and fighter stats accompany MTV's epic celebrity battles between clay animated figures, such as Pacino vs. DeNiro and Tyson vs. Stallone.

Hughes, Langston. *The Dream Keeper and Other Poems.* Illustrated by Brian Pinkney. Knopf, 1996. PPYA 2001 (Poetry).
With poetry as representative today of the lives of young people as when it was written in 1932, this is a collection to be shared with all teen readers.

In the Line of Duty: A Tribute to New York's Finest and Bravest. Forewords by Bernard B. Kerik, Police Commissioner, and Thomas Von Essen, Fire Commissioner. HarperCollins, 2001. PPYA 2004 (If It Weren't for Them).
Setting the scene, the police and fire commissioners dedicate this photo-essay to the courageous policemen and firefighters who assisted after September 11.

Inside Cheerleading, ed. *Cheerleading: From Tryouts to Championships.* Rizzoli, 2007. QP 2008.
Following a historical overview of competitive cheerleading are tips for developing a team with the right attitude, fitness, performance, and athletic ability.

Irons, Diane. *Teen Beauty Secrets: Fresh, Simple and Sassy Tips for Your Perfect Look.* Sourcebooks, 2002. QP 2003.
Former fashion model Irons provides practical beauty tips, including makeup, skin care, and fashion hints designed for a natural look.

Irwin, Cait. *Conquering the Beast Within: How I Fought Depression and Won . . . and How You Can, Too.* Times Books, 1999. QP 2001; PPYA 2000 (Self-Help).
Calling her depression a "hungry beast" for devouring her good feelings, Irwin describes how friends, family, and good medicines aided her recovery.

Issa, Kobayashi. *Inch by Inch: 45 Haiku by Issa.* Translated by Nanao Sakaki. La Alameda Press, 1999. PPYA 2001 (Poetry).
Works of the famous 19th-century Japanese poet Issa are translated by the equally famous contemporary poet Sakaki, who handwrites the haiku in English and Kanji.

Jackman, Ian. *TRL: The Ultimate Fan Guide.* Pocket, 2000. QP 2002.
Live TV is both fun and stressful, as this behind-the-scenes look at *Total Request Live* reveals, including comments from Carson Daly, Dave Holmes, and Amanda Lewis.

Jacobs, Thomas. *They Broke the Law, You Be the Judge: True Cases of Teen Crime.* Free Spirit, 2003. QP 2005; PPYA 2006 (Criminal Elements).
Presented with 21 actual cases, the reader decides if the sentence is correct based on available options and the rationale for the judge's decision.

————. *What Are My Rights? 95 Questions and Answers about Teens and the Law.* Free Spirit, 1997. QP 1999; PPYA 2000 (Self-Help).
If you have ever wondered about your rights, such as staying in school, the legitimacy of property searches, or the privacy of your grades, check here for answers.

Jamal, Joseph. *Tupac Shakur Legacy.* Simon & Schuster, 2006. QP 2008.
More than a biography, this scrapbook is filled with family photos, reproductions of the rap icon's handwritten song lyrics and poetry, and special stories of Tupac's short life.

Japanese Comickers: Draw Anime and Manga like Japan's Hottest Artists. HarperCollins, 2003. QP 2004.
Short biographies of 14 anime and comic artists are accompanied by samples of their best work, instructions on drawing, and a list of their favorite supplies.

Jenkins, Martin. *Vampires.* Informania series. Candlewick, 1998. QP 1999.
A graphic novelization of Stoker's famous vampire novel *Dracula* leads into photos and descriptions of all kinds of suckers, from vampire bats to leeches.

Jenkins, Steve. *The Top of the World: Climbing Mount Everest.* Houghton Mifflin, 1999. QP 2000.
A picture book with crushed- and cut-paper collages documents early mountaineers, necessary equipment, and the challenging climb up Mount Everest.

Jennings, Peter, Todd Brewster, and Jennifer Armstrong. *The Century for Young People.* Doubleday, 1999. QP 2000.
An adaptation of Jennings's adult work, this book relates history through interviews with people who lived it and archival images in 12 chronologically arranged chapters.

Jeter, Derek. *Game Day: My Life on and off the Field.* Edited by Kristen Kiser. Three Rivers, 2001. QP 2002.
One of the stalwarts of the Yankees, this popular Yankee shortstop takes readers on a tour of his private and personal life with candid photos of his family, home, and stadium life.

Jewel. *A Night without Armor: Poems.* HarperCollins, 1998. QP 1999.
A celebrity who was brought up on an Alaska farm, Jewel writes what she knows: birthing cows, saunas and snow, howling wolves, biker bars, lovers, and singing.

Jiang, Ji-Li. *Red Scarf Girl: A Memoir of the Cultural Revolution.* HarperTeen, 1998. PPYA 2003 (This Small World).
Ji-Li's autobiography paints a picture of her family's suffering because her grandfather was once a landlord, even though choosing to be a follower of Chairman Mao.

Jillette, Penn, and Teller. *Penn and Teller's How to Play with Your Food.* Villard, 1993. PPYA 1999 (Teen Culture).
The comic team of Penn and Teller shares a variety of food tricks, from writing fake fortune cookie messages to tying a cherry stem and surreptitiously stealing appetizers.

Johns, Michael-Anne. *Cool in School: What the Stars Were Like When They Went to School.* Scholastic, 1999. QP 2001.
Students will be happy to learn that celebrities also worried about acne and their grades, didn't always get the lead in a play, and were often left out of the "in" group.

Johnson, Dave, ed. *Movin': Teen Poets Take Voice.* Illustrated by Chris Raschka. Orchard, 2000. PPYA 2001 (Poetry).
Written by teens affiliated with a poetry project of the New York Public Library and Poets House, these works should inspire other teens to share their lives in poetic form.

Johnson, Stephen T. *Alphabet City.* Puffin, 1999. PPYA 2002 (Tales of the Cities).
This wordless picture book captures the energy of city life through the author's drawings of the alphabet, from the A of a sawhorse to the Z of a fire ladder.

Johnstone, Mike. *NASCAR: The Need for Speed.* Lerner, 2002. QP 2003.
The facts and figures, photos of stock cars and monster trucks, and information about racing organizations will appeal to racing fans and nonfans alike.

Jones, Diana Wynne. *The Tough Guide to Fantasyland.* Puffin, 2006. PPYA 2007 (What's So Funny?).
Arranged alphabetically, this tongue-in-cheek guide to fantasyland provides explanations of every fairy, dwarf, and boggart, along with jokes, maps, and plotlines.

Jordan, Michael. *For the Love of the Game: My Story.* Edited by Mark Vancil. Crown, 1998. QP 2000.
Though he is known for his basketball career, this autobiography also highlights Jordan's baseball play, membership on the 1992 Olympic basketball team, and time with his family.

Jukes, Mavis. *The Guy Book: An Owner's Manual; Maintenance, Safety and Operating Instructions for Boys.* Crown, 2001. QP 2003.
Information on sexuality, dating, going to the prom, and learning how to tie a tie will enable teen boys to survive their adolescent years.

Kahl, Jonathan. *First Field Guide: Weather.* National Audubon Society First Field Guides series. Scholastic, 1998. QP 1999.
Clouds, fronts, dust devils, and green flashes are a few of the meteorological phenomena explained in this weather guide.

Kalergis, Mary Motley, ed. *Seen and Heard: Teenagers Talk about Their Lives.* Stewart, Tabori, & Chang, 1998. QP 2000.
Fifty-one teens share stories of their adolescent years, which should help other young people realize they're not alone in feeling lonely, worried, or angry.

Kennedy. *Hey Ladies! Tales and Tips for Curious Girls.* Doubleday, 1999. PPYA 2000 (Self-Help).
Former MTV VJ offers humorous but sensible advice to help young teen girls handle potentially catastrophic situations, from their first kiss to getting along with Mom.

Kenner, Rob, and George Pitts. *VX: 10 Years of Vibe Photography.* Abrams, 2003. QP 2005.
The fastest-growing music magazine celebrates its first decade with a compilation of articles and photographs chronicling hip-hop's urban culture.

Kerven, Rosalind. *King Arthur.* Eyewitness Classic series. Illustrated by Tudor Humphries. DK, 1998. QP 1999.
This retelling of the famed classic of Arthur is enriched by callouts, sidebars, and full-color illustrations, bringing that historical period to life.

Keys, Alicia. *Tears for Water: Songbook of Poems and Lyrics.* Penguin Putnam, 2004. QP 2006.
Classically trained, Grammy award–winning Keys shares her prose, poetry, and lyrics.

Kilpatrick, Nancy. *Goth Bible: A Compendium for the Darkly Inclined.* St. Martin's, 2004. QP 2006.
All things historically Goth, including the Germanic tribe that battled the Huns, Victorian romanticism, and the contemporary dark image are described in this sourcebook.

Kimmel, Elizabeth Cody. *Ice Story: Shackleton's Lost Expedition.* Clarion, 1999. QP 2000.
This attempt to be first to cross the inhospitable Antarctic continent is brought to life by original expedition photos and Shackleton's memoir.

Kirberger, Kimberly. *Teen Love: On Relationships; A Book for Teenagers.* Health Communications, 1999. QP 2001.
Letters from teens, along with poetry, stories, and comics, help explain the new and mysterious experience for teens called love.

Klancher, Lee. *Monster Garage: How to Customize Damn Near Anything.* Motorbooks International, 2003. QP 2005; PPYA 2007 (Get Creative).
From *Monster Garage,* popularized on the Discovery Channel, come the how-tos for customizing any vehicle, from planning the project to bodywork and paint.

Kleh, Cindy. *Snowboarding Skills: The Back-to-Basics Essentials for All Levels.* Firefly, 2002. QP 2004.
Learning the lingo, board purchase, slopes etiquette, and professional tips are necessary for every snowboarder.

Knapp, Jennifer. *Cheap Frills: Fabulous Facelifts for Your Clothes.* Chronicle, 2001. QP 2003.
Tired of your boring clothes? Here are 40 projects using ribbons, beads, sequins, and other trimmings to achieve a fashionable, wearable wardrobe.

Knowles, Beyonce, Kelly Rowland, and Michelle Williams. *Soul Survivors: The Official Autobiography of Destiny's Child.* HarperCollins, 2002. QP 2003.
Learn more about the likes and dislikes of this popular singing group, their personal style, slights from peers, and reaction to the rumors that swirl around them.

Knowles, Tina. *Destiny's Style: Bootylicious Fashion, Beauty, and Lifestyle Secrets from Destiny's Child.* HarperCollins, 2002. QP 2003.
Beyonce's mother shares style secrets about the shopping, sewing, favorite recipes, home decorating, and entertaining of Destiny's Child.

Kool Moe Dee. *There's a God on the Mic: The True 50 Greatest MCs.* With photographs by Ernie Paniccioli. Thunder's Mouth, 2003. QP 2005; PPYA 2007 (I'm Not Making This Up).
Based on 17 categories, from lyricism to social impact, rapper Kool reports on 50 talents, including photos and discography of emcees and rap artists.

Koon, Jeff, and Andy Powell. *Wearing of This Garment Does Not Enable You to Fly: 101 Real Dumb Warning Labels.* Free Press, 2003. QP 2004.
The authors have selected the "best" of all the dumb warning labels sent to their website; among the 100 cautions is the warning that a beach ball is "NOT a lifesaving device."

Kramer, Nika. *We B*Girlz.* With photographs by Martha Cooper. powerHouse, 2005. QP 2007.
The underground subculture of break dancing is documented through photographs and interviews as the women of hip-hop dance enjoy their moment of fame.

Krulik, Nancy. *Lisa Lopes: The Life of a Supernova.* Simon & Schuster, 2002. QP 2003.
A creative, energetic R&B singer and rapper, Lisa recorded as part of TLC and as a solo artist before dying in an automobile accident when she was only 30 years old.

Kubert, Joe. *Fax from Sarajevo: A Story of Survival.* Dark Horse, 1998. PPYA 2002 (War).
Graphics, photos of the family, and copies of faxes sent from the Rustemagic family reveal their wartime struggles and eventual escape after the Serbian invasion.

Kurland, Michael. *Complete Idiot's Guide to Unsolved Mysteries.* Macmillan, 2000. PPYA 2001 (Paranormal).
The Shroud of Turin, Bermuda Triangle, UFOs at Roswell, and assassinations of Lincoln and Kennedy continue to puzzle us.

Lane, Billy. *Billy Lane Chop Fiction: It's Not a Motorcycle, Baby, It's a Chopper!* With photographs by Michael Lichter. Motorbooks International, 2004. QP 2006.
In Lane's autobiography, after he graduates from college his reputation as a creative chopper builder leads to television roles on *Monster Garage.*

Lanier, Troy, and Clay Nichols. *Filmmaking for Teens: Pulling Off Your Shorts.* Michael Wiese, 2005. PPYA 2007 (Get Creative).
Instructions for shooting a five-minute short subject film, to be shot over a weekend, include scriptwriting, production, topic selection, shooting, and editing.

Laurer, Joanie, with Michael Angeli. *Chyna: If They Only Knew.* HarperCollins, 2001. QP 2002.
WWE star Chyna, born Joanie Laurer, graphically describes her childhood, early belly dancing career, and ultimate success doing what she loves—professional wrestling.

Lee, John. *Street Scene: How to Draw Graffiti-Style.* F&W, 2007. QP 2008.
Everything you need to draw graffiti, including adding characters such as skaters or hip-hop artists to street art, becomes easier with this book.

Leiker, Ken, and Mark Vancil, eds. *Unscripted.* Pocket, 2003. QP 2005.
Though fans relish the sight of wrestling superstars in the ring, they will also enjoy a behind-the-scenes look at the homes, lives, travel, and daily routines of the wrestlers.

Leonetti, Mike, and John Iaboni. *Football Now.* Firefly, 2006. QP 2007.
Short bios of 70 current National Football League players, including personal stats, career highlights, and photographs, will please all football enthusiasts.

Leslie, Jeremy, and David Roberts. *Pick Me Up.* DK, 2006. QP 2007.
Combining the best of almanacs, trivia books, and the Internet results in this fascinating compendium of randomly arranged, well-illustrated, fun facts.

Levy, Joel. *Really Useful: The Origins of Everyday Things.* Firefly, 2002. QP 2004.
Everyday objects such as razor blades,

buttons, bar codes, neon lights, Post-it notes, tea bags, and corkscrews become intriguing and colorful in Levy's work.

Lewry, Fraser, and Tom Ryan. *Kittenwar: May the Cutest Kitten Win!* Chronicle, 2007. QP 2008.
The popular website kittenwar.com, where voters choose the cuter of two kittens, is now in book format with more kittenwars, history of wartime kittens, and kitten naming.

Locker, Sari. *Sari Says: The Real Dirt on Everything from Sex to School.* HarperCollins, 2001. QP 2002.
The advice columnist for *Teen People Online* responds to questions from teens about tattoos, interracial dating, kissing, braces, and ways to turn down a date.

Loheed, M. J. *The Finger: A Comprehensive Guide to Flipping Off.* With photographs by Stephanie Hernstadt. Acid Test Productions, 1998. PPYA 1999 (Teen Culture).
Color photos and satirical essays explore the history, uses, and worldwide versions of this universal sign of contempt and disdain.

Lord, Trevor. *Big Book of Cars.* DK, 1999. QP 2000.
James Bond–type vehicles, the Batmobile, and even a "slug car" are a few of the amazing cars highlighted by color photos and poster-like spreads.

Loukes, Keith. *Ask Dr. Keith: Candid Answers to Queer Questions.* Whitecap, 2004. PPYA 2006 (GLBTQ).
Questions about HIV/AIDS, coming out, sexuality, and relationships are answered in this easy-to-understand resource for GLBTQ teens.

Macdonald, Andy. *Dropping In with Andy Mac: The Life of a Pro Skateboarder.* Simon Pulse, 2003. QP 2004.
Riding his Big Wheels into traffic when he was a child set the stage for Macdonald's future as a professional skateboarder; an inspiring autobiography complete with photos.

Macy, Sue. *A Whole New Ball Game: The Story of the All-American Girls Professional Baseball League.* Puffin, 1995. PPYA 1999 (Good Sports).
Both the sport and the postwar social history of American women are described in this history of a unique league that began in 1943 when the men were away at war.

———. *Winning Ways: A Photohistory of American Women in Sport.* Scholastic, 1998. PPYA 1999 (Good Sports).
Black-and-white photographs and text chronicle 150 years of sports for women, from initial restrictions to growing popularity and interest.

Macy, Sue, and Jane Gottesman. *Play like a Girl: A Celebration of Women in Sports.* Holt, 1999. QP 2000.
Professional, college, amateur, and Olympic athletes are captured in spectacular photographs playing the sport they love.

Mad about the '90s. DC Comics, 2005. QP 2006.
Combing through its issues from the 1990s, *Mad* magazine collects previously published articles on such topics as Bill Clinton, the Internet, and the Gulf War.

Mah, Adeline Yen. *Chinese Cinderella: The True Story of an Unwanted Daughter.* Random House, 2001. PPYA 2002 (Relationships).

Blamed because her mother died giving birth to her, Adeline is ignored by her father until she wins an award for writing; only then does he agree to send her to college.

Malone, Bonz. *Hip-Hop Immortals: The Remix.* Thunder's Mouth, 2003. QP 2004.
Nearly 200 black-and-white and color photographs, along with text, reflect the unique style of such hip-hop artists as Eminem, Kool Herc, Ice T, and Flava Flav.

Mannarino, Melanie. *The Boyfriend Clinic: The Final Word on Flirting, Dating, Guys and Love.* HarperCollins, 2000. QP 2001.
Seventeen magazine advises girls about finding the right boyfriend, saying yes or no to a date, and surviving breakup.

Manoy, Lauren. *Where to Park Your Broomstick: A Teen's Guide to Witchcraft.* Fireside, 2002. QP 2003.
Beginning with the history of paganism and witchcraft, this evenhanded explanation covers Wiccan rituals, holidays, celebrations, and positive spells.

Marron, Maggie. *Stylin': Great Looks for Teens.* Friedman, 2001. QP 2003.
Want to look like your favorite star? Insider info reveals the latest in celebrity tattoos, shoes, haircuts, cosmetics, and clothes.

Masessa, Ed. *The Wandmaker's Guidebook.* Illustrated by Daniel Jankowski. Scholastic, 2006. QP 2007.
Burgeoning wizards and witches need this book, which is filled with paper foldouts, inset artifacts, illustrations, and a wand, complete with the seven rules of wandmaking.

Masoff, Joy. *Fire!* Illustrated by Barry D. Smith and Jack Resnick. Scholastic, 1998. QP 1999.
Color photos of firefighters, their equipment, and actual fires capture the drama and excitement of this dangerous profession that can include rescues and hazmat spills.

———. *Oh, Yuck! The Encyclopedia of Everything Nasty.* Illustrated by Terry Sirrell. Workman, 2000. QP 2002.
Photos and cartoons add the perfect touch to this A/acne to Z/zits account of all things disgusting—body lint, farts, maggots, rats, lice, toilets, and dandruff.

———. *Snowboard! Your Guide to Freeriding, Pipe and Park, Jibbing, Backcountry, Alpine, Boardercross, and More.* Extreme Sports series. National Geographic 2002. QP 2003.
Photos and text combine to explain both the insider lingo and the many moves used by snowboarders as they compete in the X Games.

Masyga, Mark, and Martin Ohlin. *Peeps: A Candy-Coated Tale.* Abrams, 2006. QP 2007.
When the yellow marshmallow Peeps family is missing, the media cover the story, along with craft ideas for making use of the Peeps if they're not found by their sell-by date.

Maynard, Christopher. *Sharks.* Informania series. Candlewick, 1997. QP 1999.
Tabbed chapters allow the reader to search for neon-colored photos and illustrations of shark attacks, species information, and captivating facts.

McCune, Bunny, and Deb Traunstein. *Girls to Women, Women to Girls.* Ten Speed, 1998. PPYA 2000 (Self-Help).

Girls and women share their personal history of transitioning from their teens into adulthood.

McFarlane, Evelyn, and James Saywell. *If . . . : Questions for Teens.* Random House, 2001. QP 2002.
Instead of answering questions, these authors ask them, forcing teens to consider how they feel about friends, a fashion trend, or a favorite book, movie, or CD.

McGrath, Jeremy, with Chris Palmer. *Wide Open: A Life in Supercross.* HarperCollins, 2004. QP 2005.
Supercross bad boy McGrath's autobiography is filled with photos of his races, endorsement deals, and tips for motorcycle maintenance.

McManners, Hugh. *Ultimate Special Forces.* DK, 2003. QP 2005.
Elite military units of Europe, Russia, Israel, and the United States, including the Royal Marines, Green Berets, and French Foreign Legion, are profiled in this photo-rich work.

Meglin, Nick, and John Ficarra, eds. *"Mad" about Super Heroes.* DC Comics, 2002. QP 2003.
Mad magazine's collection of commentaries, written by its "usual gang of super-idiots," spoofs all spandex-garbed superheroes, from Superman to the X-Men.

———. *The "Mad" Gross Book.* DC Comics, 2001. QP 2002.
Truly tasteless, inappropriate material from *Mad* magazine is collected in this tribute to vomit jokes, dismemberment, morgues, and cannibal hilarity.

Menzel, Peter, and Faith D'Aluisio. *Man Eating Bugs: The Art and Science of Eating Insects.* Ten Speed, 1998. QP 2000.
Recipes and photos highlight this team's sampling of insect delicacies in 13 countries, including stir-fried dragonflies, live termites and scorpions, and roasted grubs.

Meserole, Mike. *Ultimate Sports Lists.* DK, 1999. QP 2000.
The stats and trivia from all sports events, including most pass completions and top-grossing sports movies, can be found in this browser's delight.

Metallica, with Steffan Chirazi. *So What? The Good, the Mad and the Ugly: The Official Metallica Illustrated Chronicles.* Broadway, 2004. QP 2005.
This scrapbook of Metallica concert memories, interviews with band members, and collages of candid and concert photos will delight their metalhead fans.

Milan, Garth. *Freestyle Motorcross 2 Air Sickness: More Jump Tricks from the Pros.* Motorbooks International, 2002. QP 2003.
Photos document the step-by-step sequence for each jump trick while freestyle riders describe how each of the 25 tricks is performed.

Milano, Selene. *Unforgettable Color: Makeup with Confidence.* Carlton, 2003. QP 2004.
Organized by color, each of seven chapters contains information on makeup style and applications, eyebrow shaping, pedicures, manicures, and skin care.

Milholland, Charlotte. *The Girl Pages: A Handbook of the Best Resources for Strong, Confident, Creative Girls.* Hyperion, 1998. PPYA 2000 (Self-Help).
A founder of the girls movement, Milholland enriches girls' lives with this useful set of resources, including camps, websites, associations, books, and movies.

Miller, Jean-Chris. *The Body Art Book: A Complete Illustrated Guide to Tattoos, Piercings, and Other Body Modifications.* Berkley, 1997. PPYA 1999 (Teen Culture).
Want a tattoo but unsure what to do? Check this source for design, style and placement suggestions, artist names, and safety information.

Miller, Steve, and Bryan Baugh. *Scared! How to Draw Fantastic Horror Comic Characters.* Watson-Guptill, 2004. QP 2006.
Following a brief history of horror comics are step-by-step instructions for drawing vampires, werewolves, mummies, and piranhas.

Miller, Timothy, and Steve Milton. *NASCAR Now!* Firefly, 2004—QP 2005; Firefly, 2006—PPYA 2008 (Anyone Can Play).
This feature on NASCAR racing, second in popularity only to NFL football, includes driver profiles, histories of the racing teams, and a racing primer.

Milner-Halls, Kelly. *Albino Animals.* Darby Creek, 2004. QP 2005.
Photos explain the consequences of albinism, a genetic deviation based on recessive genes, which leaves a creature without any coloration and often at the mercy of predators.

Mintzer, Rich. *The Everything Money Book.* Adams, 1999. PPYA 2000 (Self-Help).
As this book explains, it's not enough to work hard and earn a good salary; one also needs financial goals and investments.

Mirra, Dave, with Mark Losey. *Mirra Images: The Story of My Life.* HarperCollins, 2003. QP 2004.
Six months after being hit by a drunk driver and told he would never ride again, this daring BMX rider returns to competition and wins X Games medals; color photos.

Mitton, Jacqueline. *Aliens.* Informania series. Candlewick, 1999. QP 2000.
Part of a series that also covers ghosts and sharks, this tabbed work includes UFOs, extraterrestrial communication, and a portfolio of movie aliens.

Moench, Doug. *The Big Book of the Unexplained.* DC Comics, 1997. PPYA 2001 (Paranormal).
This companion work to *The Big Book of Conspiracies* examines strange phenomena, such as alternate dimensions and alien abductions, with illustrations by noted cartoonists.

Montano, Mark. *Super Suite: The Ultimate Bedroom Makeover Guide for Girls.* Universe, 2002. QP 2004.
Before and after shots of 15 bedrooms, instructions for redoing them, and interviews with their occupants provide teens creative ways to make over their own rooms.

Morgan, David Lee, Jr. *LeBron James: The Rise of a Star.* Gray, 2003. QP 2005.
An up close, personal look at this phenomenal basketball star, enriched by interviews with LeBron's friends and two inserts of photos.

Morgenstern, Mindy. *The Real Rules for Girls.* Girl Press, 1999. QP 2001.
Practical, often irreverent advice shows girls the real world and how to deal with it, from putting jocks into perspective to accepting your family as normal.

Morrison, Bill, ed. *The Homer Book.* The Simpsons Library of Wisdom series. HarperCollins, 2004. QP 2005.

The deep, introspective thoughts of a lovable guy who likes his beer, his friends, and his refrigerator in this continuing series of "wisdom."

Morrison, Jim. *Wilderness.* The Lost Writings of Jim Morrison series, vol. 1. Vintage, 1989. PPYA 1999 (Teen Culture).
This compilation of unpublished poems, drawings, photos, and even a probing self-interview are drawn from the literary estate of the former Doors lead singer.

Morse, Jenifer Corr. *Scholastic Book of World Records 2004.* Scholastic, 2003. QP 2004.
Part of a continuing series, the 2004 edition sports a redesign of its format with new graphs, photos, and records.

MTV Photobooth. MTV Overground series. Universe, 2002. QP 2003.
Four-panel strips of goofy-acting celebrities, such as Kid Rock, Janet Reno, Queen Latifah, and Snoop Dog, are pulled from MTV's files.

Muharrar, Aisha. *More Than a Label: Why What You Wear and Who You're with Doesn't Define Who You Are.* Free Spirit, 2002. PPYA 2005 (Own Your Freak).
In a label-driven world, teens receive suggestions for resisting clique peer pressure and being independent thinkers, based on results from the teen author's survey.

Murillo, Kathy Cano. *Crafty Chica's Art de la Soul: Glittery Ideas to Liven Up Your Life.* HarperCollins, 2006. PPYA 2007 (Get Creative).
Photographs, instructions, and a resource guide are provided for 30 crafts, including jewelry, Mexican coffee coasters, and stylish candles, all from craftychica.com.

Myers, Walter Dean. *Bad Boy: A Memoir.* Amistad, 2002. PPYA 2008 (What Makes a Family?).
Growing up with foster parents in 1940s Harlem was difficult for noted YA author Myers as he struggled to fit in with peers who lacked his writing talent and intelligence.

————. *The Greatest: Muhammad Ali.* Scholastic, 2001. QP 2002.
Now battling Parkinson's disease, Ali was born Cassius Clay and became a great boxer during the time of the American civil rights movement and the Vietnam War.

Nagatomo, Haruno. *Draw Your Own Manga: All the Basics.* Kodansha, 2003. QP 2005.
Used as a textbook at a Japanese school for artists, these easy-to-follow instructions enable anyone to begin drawing in the manga style.

Nathan, M. M. *Cribs: A Guided Tour inside the Homes of Your Favorite Stars.* Pocket, 2002. QP 2003.
From the MTV show *Cribs* comes this compilation of home tours of the bungalows, lofts, and mansions inhabited by singers, actors, and other stars.

Naylor, Caroline. *Beauty Trix for Cool Chix: Easy-to-Make Lotions, Potions, and Spells to Bring Out a Beautiful You.* Watson-Guptill, 2003. QP 2005.
At the next slumber party, select from these 20 recipes and tips to make lip gloss, paint fingernails, or apply hair glitter.

Nelson, Peter. *Left for Dead: A Young Man's Search for Justice for the USS Indianapolis.* Random House, 2003. PPYA 2007 (I'm Not Making This Up).
In 1945, after the worst ship disaster in U.S. naval history, the ship's captain was

made a scapegoat, until 11-year-old Hunter Scott's history fair project cleared his name.

Newson, Lesley. *Devastation: The World's Worst Natural Disasters.* DK, 1998. QP 1999.
Maps, more than 400 full-color photographs, and text cover all kinds of disasters, from asteroids to mad cow disease, ice ages, droughts, floods, tsunamis, and fires.

Nicolay, Megan. *Generation T: 108 Ways to Transform a T-Shirt.* Workman, 2006. PPYA 2007 (Get Creative).
Illustrated instructions for revamping T-shirts, some requiring no sewing, are accompanied by historical tidbits about this popular garment.

Norman, Michael, and Beth Scott. *Haunted America.* Haunted America series. Tor, 1995. PPYA 1999 (Teen Culture).
From each state and Canadian province come documented tales of wraiths, ghosts, and other spirits who appear in all types of locales, from battlefields to the White House.

————. *Historic Haunted America.* Haunted America series. Tor, 1999. PPYA 2001 (Paranormal).
This final volume in the series relates new tales of ghosts emanating from old forts in Tucson, haunted plantations, railroad cars, and battlefields in Indiana.

Northcutt, Wendy. *The Darwin Awards: Evolution in Action.* Plume, 2002. PPYA 2007 (I'm Not Making This Up).
Anecdotes from the DarwinAwards .com site humorously illustrate how the ineptness of some humans proves Darwin's theory that only the fit survive.

Novas, Himilce, and Rosemary Silva. *Remembering Selena: A Tribute in Pictures and Words.* St. Martin's, 1995. PPYA 2004 (On That Note).
Black-and-white and color photos complement this bilingual account of Selena's early years, her rise to fame, and the tragic stabbing by her fan club president.

Odes, Rebecca, Esther Drill, and Heather McDonald. *The Looks Book: A Whole New Approach to Beauty, Body Image, and Style.* Penguin Putnam, 2002. QP 2003.
The history, psychology, body anatomy, and culture of beauty are presented for teens interested in their looks, though the main message is to be happy with who you are.

O'Donnell, Kerri. *Inhalants and Your Nasal Passages: The Incredibly Disgusting Story.* Incredibly Disgusting Drugs series. Rosen, 2001. QP 2002.
Making use of photos of body parts diseased from drugs, alcohol, or inhalants, this book describes the dangers of "huffing" graphically.

Oh, Minya. *Bling Bling: Hip Hop's Crown Jewels.* Wenner, 2005. QP 2006.
A wealth of photos illustrates the connection between hip-hop superstardom and a penchant for splashy, expensive jewelry.

O'Hearn, Claudine Chiawei, ed. *Half and Half: Writers on Growing Up Biracial and Bicultural.* Pantheon, 1998. PPYA 2000 (Short Takes).
Currently living and writing in America, these writers represent a combination of every ethnic group possible, yet each writes of their difficult search for a place to call home.

Okey, Shannon. *Knitgrrl: Learn to Knit with 15 Fun and Funky Projects.* Watson-Guptill, 2005. PPYA 2007 (Get Creative).
Want to knit a fake fur stole, mittens that can be used while texting, or leg warmers? Maybe throw a knitting party? Details for all these projects are available in this guide.

Okutoro, Lydia Omolola, ed. *Quiet Storm: Voices of Young Black Poets.* Jump at the Sun, 1999. QP 2000.
Sixty-one poems, submitted by young writers with a common heritage rooted in Africa, explore the African diaspora and the resulting passion it arouses in these poets.

Oldershaw, Cally. *Rocks and Minerals.* 3-D Eyewitness series. DK, 1999. QP 2000.
Experiments and activities designed for young people make it easier to understand information about the geological and geophysical characteristics of rocks and minerals.

Olmstead, Kathleen. *Girls' Guide to Tarot.* Illustrated by Sandie Turchyn. Sterling, 2002. QP 2003.
This guide to the centuries-old card game of tarot enables novices to understand the cards, decipher some sample spreads, and learn what the cards can and cannot do.

O'Neil, Dennis. *The DC Comics Guide to Writing Comics.* Watson-Guptill, 2001. PPYA 2007 (Get Creative).
Though there are many books about illustrating comics, this is one of the few that also explains how to write a story to match the graphics.

Opdyke, Irene Gut. *In My Hands: Memories of a Holocaust Rescuer.* Random House, 1999. PPYA 2002 (War).
A Polish Catholic who suffered many atrocities during World War II, Opdyke always helped Jews, even hiding 12 of them in the home of a German major for whom she worked.

Osborne, Jennifer. *Monsters: A Celebration of the Classics from Universal Studios.* Del Rey, 2006. QP 2007.
Photos and essays celebrate the directors, writers, actors, and makeup artists who brought to life such famous movie monsters as Frankenstein and Dracula.

Oser, Bodhi. *Fuck This Book.* Chronicle, 2005. QP 2000.
Photos illustrate this author's mischievousness in using stickers with the ubiquitous four-letter "F" word to change signs so that "No Parking" now reads "No F***ing."

Owen, David. *Hidden Evidence: Forty True Crime Stories and How Forensic Science Helped to Solve Them.* Firefly, 2000. QP 2001; PPYA 2007 (I'm Not Making This Up).
Beginning with early forms of forensics used in ancient China, case studies show the progression of technological enhancements that aid in crime solving.

————. *Hidden Secrets: The Complete History of Espionage and the Technology Used to Support It.* Firefly, 2002. PPYA 2003 (I've Got a Secret).
Organized by information sources, from agents to coded transmissions and overhead surveillance, a brief history of intelligence gathering is followed by spy case studies.

Packer, Alex J. *Highs! Over 150 Ways to Feel Really, Really Good . . . without Alcohol or Other Drugs.* Illustrated by Jeff Tolbert. Free Spirit, 2000. QP 2001.
Activities to reduce stress, learn to breathe properly, and meditate, as well as the fun of optical illusions and the joy of mental stimulation, provide diversions for teens.

————. *How Rude! The Teenager's Guide to Good Manners, Proper Behavior, and Not Grossing People Out.* Free Spirit, 1997. QP 1999; PPYA 2000 (Self-Help).
Traditional etiquette tips coexist with contemporary suggestions for sharing bathrooms, traveling in cyberspace, and hearing rude noises, all handled in a light, humorous tone.

Paint Me like I Am: Teen Poems. HarperTempest, 2003. QP 2004.
Poems by at-risk teens are organized into seven chapters under such categories as artists, friendship, and furious.

Palmer, Chris. *Streetball: All the Ballers, Moves, Slams and Shine.* HarperCollins, 2004. QP 2006; PPYA 2007 (I'm Not Making This Up).
This guide to street basketball includes profiles of top players, the history of the sport, and the nation's top street courts.

Pardes, Bronwen. *Doing It Right: Making Smart, Safe and Satisfying Choices about Sex.* Simon & Schuster, 2007—QP 2008; Simon Pulse, 2007—PPYA 2008 (Sex Is . . .).
A nonjudgmental discussion of sexuality answers teen questions and stresses the importance of being informed.

Parker, Julia, and Derek Parker. *The Complete Book of Dreams.* DK, 1998. PPYA 1999 (Teen Culture).
Learn to interpret dreams as they relate to personal life or the future as a way to better understand yourself.

Partridge, Elizabeth. *Restless Spirit: The Life and Work of Dorothea Lange.* Puffin, 2001. PPYA 2007 (Get Creative).
As 60 of Lange's famous photographs illustrate in this biography, she captured the personal side of the Great Depression and the Japanese internment camps of World War II.

Patnaik, Gayatri, and Michelle T. Shinseki. *The Secret Life of Teens: Young People Speak Out about Their Lives.* HarperCollins, 2000. QP 2001.
Organized by topics such as divorce, love, and substance abuse are writings teens submitted to bolt.com about their lives, thoughts, and dreams.

Patterson, Lindsay, ed. *A Rock against the Wind: African American Poems and Letters of Love and Passion.* Perigee, 1996. PPYA 2001 (Poetry).
Revised from the 1973 edition, more than 100 poems about pride, romance, lessons learned, and memories are organized thematically.

Paulsen, Gary. *My Life in Dog Years.* Illustrated by Ruth Wright Paulsen. Delacorte, 1998. QP 1999.
Paulsen tells about eight of his dogs, from Snowball, his first, to the sled dog Cookie, as he coincidentally reveals much about his own life.

Pavanel, Jane. *The Sex Book: An Alphabet of Smarter Love.* Millennium Generation series. Illustrated by Grant Cunningham. Lobster, 2001. QP 2003.
This frank and informative alphabetical arrangement of sexual terms informs curious teens about everything from tampons to blue balls, AIDS, homosexuality, and abstinence.

Payment, Simone. *Navy SEALs: Special Operations for the U.S. Navy.* Inside Special Operations series. Rosen, 2003. QP 2004.
Color photographs and short sidebars, plus many first-person stories, make this an exciting, easy-to-read account of the work of the U.S. Navy's elite sailors.

Pearce, Fred. *Earth Then and Now: Amazing Images of Our Changing World.* Firefly, 2007. QP 2008.

More than 300 photographs show before and after landscapes over the past 100 years, revealing such changes as melting glaciers, development, and the effect of wars.

Pearson, Felicia "Snoop," and David Ritz. *Grace after Midnight: A Memoir.* Grand Central, 2007. QP 2008.
Born a crack-addicted, three-pound baby, Felicia discloses her feisty ways, prison sentence for a self-defense killing, and luck in becoming an actress on *The Wire.*

Pelzer, Dave. *A Child Called "It": One Child's Courage to Survive.* Health Communications, 1995. PPYA 2002 (Relationships).
Dave is abused, tormented, starved, burned, and practically killed by an alcoholic mother who calls him "It" until a teacher reports the abuse and he is rescued by foster care.

Perdomo, Willie. *Where a Nickel Costs a Dime.* Norton, 1996. PPYA 2001 (Poetry).
Influenced by rap and the streets, Perdomo's poetry reflects life for a Puerto Rican living in New York City.

Perel, David, and the editors of the Weekly World News. *Bat Boy Lives! "The Weekly World News" Guide to Politics, Culture, Celebrities, Alien Abductions, and the Mutant Freaks That Shape Our World.* Sterling, 2005. QP 2006; PPYA 2007 (What's So Funny?).
From the kind of pizza served at Jesus' Last Supper to the escapades of Bat Boy to sightings of Elvis Presley, the "best" stories from tabloid news fill these pages.

Pfetzer, Mark, and Jack Galvin. *Within Reach: My Everest Story.* Dutton, 1998— QP 1999; Puffin, 2000—PPYA 2003 (Lock It, Lick It, Click It).

Caught by the mountain-climbing bug, Pfetzer shares his experiences as he twice tries to reach Everest's summit, including a 1996 attempt when many climbers died.

Pierson, Stephanie. *Vegetables Rock! A Complete Guide for Teenage Vegetarians.* Bantam, 1999. QP 2000.
Recipes, lists of cookbooks, restaurants, organizations, websites, and nutritional information aid teens who are considering becoming vegetarians.

Pilobolus Dance Theater. *Twisted Yoga.* With photographs by John Kane. Chronicle, 2002. QP 2003.
With photos taken from all angles, a dance company poses in visual puns of basic yoga moves as two or more dancers bend, twist, and contort their bodies.

Pinsky, Drew, and Adam Carolla. *Dr. Drew and Adam Book: A Survival Guide to Life and Love.* Dell, 1998. QP 2000.
Part of MTV's show *Loveline,* Pinsky and Carolla offer their sarcastic, humorous advice on sexuality and other embarrassing topics.

Piven, Joshua, and David Borgenicht. *The Worst-Case Scenario Survival Handbook.* Chronicle, 1999. QP 2001.
After consulting with listed experts, the authors describe how to survive an unopened parachute, escape from a sinking car, land a plane, and other emergencies.

————. *The Worst-Case Scenario Survival Handbook: Travel.* Chronicle, 2001. QP 2002.
Wherever travel takes you, this book will help you if you need to bribe an official, remove leeches, escape a riptide, ride a camel, or catch a fish with your hands.

Platt, Larry. *Only the Strong Survive: The Odyssey of Allen Iverson.* HarperCollins, 2002. QP 2004.

A pithy biography that brings into the open race and culture as they affect this always controversial NBA point guard.

Platt, Richard. *Crime Scene: The Ultimate Guide to Forensic Science.* DK, 2003. QP 2004.
Photos of crime scenes, disasters, crime labs, and forensic tools enhance this step-by-step explanation of criminal investigations.

Pletka, Bob, ed. *My So-Called Digital Life: 2,000 Teenagers, 300 Cameras, and 30 Days to Document Their World.* Santa Monica Press, 2005. QP 2007.
Teens across California document their daily lives in words and photos to answer the proverbial question "What did you do today?" Organized by a school administrator.

Polhemus, Ted. *Hot Bodies, Cool Styles: New Techniques in Self-Adornment.* With photographs by the team of UZi PART B. Thames and Hudson, 2004. QP 2006.
Returning to earlier roots of body adorn-ment, text and photographs highlight designs for tattoos and body piercings as well as techniques for hair extensions and body painting.

Pollack, Pamela. *Ski! Your Guide to Jumping, Racing, Skiboarding, Nordic, Backcountry, Aerobatics, and More.* Extreme Sports series. National Geographic, 2002. QP 2003.
This series highlights the spine-tingling aspects of skiing as athletes push beyond normal limits to compete in the X Games.

Pollet, Alison. *The Real World—New Orleans: Unmasked.* Pocket, 2000. QP 2001.
What happened in the television reality show is revealed through interviews with roommates, cast members, friends, and family of the participants.

Powell, Kevin, ed. *Who Shot Ya? Three Decades of Hiphop Photography.* With photographs by Ernie Paniccioli. HarperCollins, 2002. QP 2003.
Thirty years of Paniccioli's photographs illustrate the history of hip-hop culture, with a fascinating look at such stars as Lauryn Hill and Will Smith in their youth.

Powell, Michael. *Superhero Handbook.* Sterling, 2005. QP 2006.
This tongue-in-cheek guide explains all it takes to become an amazing superhero, preferably from a far-off, dying solar system.

Pratt, Jane. *Beyond Beauty: Girls Speak Out on Looks, Style and Stereotypes.* Clarkson Potter, 1997. QP 1999; PPYA 1999 (Teen Culture).
Twenty-five short profiles of teenage girls, only some of whom are famous, reveal their thoughts about beauty, clothing, and the jobs they hold.

Preston, Richard. *The Hot Zone.* Random House, 1995. PPYA 2006 (What Ails You?).
Ebola is a devastating filovirus usually found only in the rain forest, so when it appears in a northern Virginia lab full of monkeys, the entire lab is contaminated.

Raab, Evelyn. *Clueless in the Kitchen: A Cookbook for Teens and Other Beginners.* Illustrated by George A. Walker. Firefly, 1998. PPYA 2000 (Self-Help).
A selection of traditional and contemporary recipes, along with preparation tips, grocery buying, and nutritional information, help the rookie cook.

Rachel, T. Cole, and Rita Costello, eds. *Bend, Don't Shatter: Poets on the Beginning of Desire.* Soft Skull, 2004. PPYA 2006 (GLBTQ).
Having reached adulthood, these poets reflect their initial realization and response to their sexuality in poems meant to be read by everyone.

Rain, Gwinevere. *Spellcraft for Teens: A Magical Guide to Writing and Casting Spells.* Llewellyn, 2002. QP 2003.
An overview of Wicca as a religion is followed by a guide to spells and magic potions, written by a teen witch who advises Wiccan followers to get out of "the broom closet."

Rannels, Melissa, Melissa Alvarado, and others. *Sew Subversive: Down and Dirty DIY for the Fabulous Fashionista.* Taunton, 2006. QP 2007.
The hipster founders of the Stitch Lounge, a drop-in sewing center in San Francisco, present 22 projects to embellish and customize clothing for that personal uniqueness.

Ravenwolf, Silver. *Teen Witch: Wicca for a New Generation.* Llewellyn, 1998. PPYA 2007 (Religion).
Disputing the myths of wearing black and lighting candles, this guide to Wicca explains what it's like to be a witch today.

Read magazine, ed. *Read for Your Life: Tales of Survival.* Millbrook, 1998. QP 1999.
Selected from the past 50 years of the *Weekly Reader* literary magazine are stories of survival from grizzly bear attacks, cobra strikes, and even killer ants.

Reid, Lori. *The Art of Hand Reading.* DK, 1999. PPYA 2001 (Paranormal).
Chiromancy, or determining the meaning of lines, nail size, shapes, mounts, and tracings of the hand, is a "pseudoscience" that can be learned to tell the future.

Reisfeld, Randi, and Marie Morreale. *Got Issues Much? Celebrities Share Their Traumas and Triumphs.* Scholastic, 1999. QP 2000.
Famous personalities such as Will Smith and Leonardo DiCaprio reveal some of their teen concerns, which may comfort or help many teens.

Reynolds, David West. *"Star Wars," Episode I: Incredible Cross-Sections.* DK, 1999. QP 2000.
Cutaways, accompanied by text, illustrate the armaments, propulsion systems, and other technical features of the equipment used in this episode of *Star Wars*.

———. *"Star Wars," Episode I: The Visual Dictionary.* DK, 1999. QP 2000.
Excellent annotated photographs reveal cross-sectional details of characters, costumes, and equipment that appear in the *Star Wars* prequel.

Riley, Andy. *The Book of Bunny Suicides.* Plume, 2003. QP 2005; PPYA 2007 (What's So Funny?).
Whether standing under stalactites or meeting the lethal end of Darth Vader's light saber, bunnies choose bizarre means to do themselves in.

———. *Return of the Bunny Suicides.* Plume, 2004. QP 2006.
The bunnies are back and as bent upon self-destruction as ever, whether it be from hiding under an elephant's footstool or swimming with rabbit-hungry fishes.

Ripley's Believe It or Not. Ripley Entertainment, 2004. QP 2005.
A trivia-filled book, complementing Ripley's cartoons and museums of the same name, shares such oddities as bog

snorkeling, public autopsies, and vampire bats.

Roach, Mary. *Stiff: The Curious Lives of Human Cadavers.* Norton, 2004. PPYA 2007 (I'm Not Making This Up).
With respect and humor, the "life" of a human cadaver is described, from mummification to anatomical studies, organ donation, and aid in solving medical mysteries.

Roberts, Jeremy. *Rock and Ice Climbing! Top the Tower.* Extreme Sports series. Rosen, 2000. QP 2001.
Though extolling the excitement and challenge of climbing, the book also lists necessary gear, tips for safety, and profiles of the top rock and ice climbers.

The Rock and Joe Layden. *The Rock Says . . . : The Most Electrifying Man in Sports-Entertainment.* HarperCollins, 2000. QP 2001.
Third-generation wrestler Dwayne Johnson, better known to WWF fans as "The Rock," relates the history of the sport along with tidbits from his career.

Rodriguez, Luis J. *Always Running: La Vida Loca; Gang Days in L.A.* Marion Boyars, 1996. PPYA 2002 (Tales of the Cities).
Poet and publisher Rodriguez describes his days as a Latino gang member, including arrests and jail time, in an effort to discourage his son from following in his footsteps.

Roeper, Richard. *Ten Sure Signs a Movie Character Is Doomed and Other Surprising Movie Lists.* Hyperion, 2003. QP 2004.
Movie critic Roeper assembles humorous lists of movies, from those featuring "The Worst Irish Accents" to "Films in Which Ben Affleck Cries like a Big Fat Baby."

Rogge, Hannah. *Hardware: Jewelry from a Toolbox.* With photographs by Marianne Rafter. Stewart, Tabori, & Chang, 2006. QP 2007.
Industrial designer Rogge provides DIY instructions to make necklaces, bracelets, and earrings using such hardware items as nuts, metal washers, rubber tubing, and O-rings.

———. *Save This Shirt: Cut It, Stitch It, Wear It Now!* With photographs by Adrian Buckmaster. Stewart, Tabori, & Chang, 2007. QP 2008.
What to do with all those T-shirts? Cut them up and make a tank top, a miniskirt, belt, or tote bag in less than an hour with these illustrated directions from a creative author.

Rohrer, Russ. *Ten Days in the Dirt: The Spectacle of Off-Road Motorcycling.* Motorbooks International, 2004. QP 2005.
Ten popular events in off-road motorcycling are chronicled in this photographic tribute to event locations, motorcycles, and riders.

Rolling Stone magazine, eds. *Cobain.* Little, Brown, 1997. PPYA 1999 (Teen Culture).
Written after his death using information from *Rolling Stone* interviews, this book discloses the life and times of rock-and-roll musician Kurt Cobain and his band Nirvana.

Rothbart, Davy. *Found: The Best Lost, Tossed and Forgotten Items from around the World.* Fireside, 2004. QP 2005; PPYA 2007 (I'm Not Making This Up).
Pulled from *Found* magazine, this compilation of found messages, notes, fliers, and even a kitten records the

poignant, humorous, and puzzling items discarded and then found.

Runyon, Brent. *The Burn Journals.* Vintage, 2005. PPYA 2007 (I'm Not Making This Up).
Attempting to commit suicide, Runyon sets himself on fire in an action he immediately regrets, then endures eights months of skin grafts, therapy, and rehabilitation.

Ryder, Bob, and Dave Scherer. *WCW: The Ultimate Guide.* DK, 2000. QP 2001.
Full-color photos from World Championship Wrestling archives reveal the wrestlers' training and show preparation.

Rylant, Cynthia. *God Went to Beauty School.* HarperCollins, 2003—QP 2004; HarperTempest, 2006—PPYA 2007 (Religion).
A series of whimsical poems describe what might happen if God came to Earth and took part in all that he had created, from watching cable television to making spaghetti.

RZA with Chris Norris. *The Wu-Tang Manual.* Riverhead, 2005. QP 2006.
This rap group incorporates martial arts, Eastern spiritualism, and chess into their music, as revealed in their lyrics encyclopedia and photographic history.

Sacco, Joe. *Safe Area Gorazde: The War in Eastern Bosnia 1992–1995.* Fantagraphics, 2002. PPYA 2002 (War).
Using the medium of cartooning, the author relates the human side of war as he experienced it living for four weeks in a Muslim section besieged by Serbs.

Salant, James. *Leaving Dirty Jersey: A Crystal Meth Memoir.* Simon & Schuster, 2007. QP 2008.
Raised in an upper-middle-class family, Salant affects the bad boy pose, with "Dirty Jersey" tattooed on his arm, in this memoir of rehab after addiction to crystal meth.

Salinger, Adrienne. *In My Room: Teenagers in Their Bedrooms.* Chronicle, 1995. PPYA 1999 (Teen Culture).
Admitted into the bedrooms of 43 teens over a two-year period, Salinger interviewed them and photographed their favorite objects, revealing many hopes and dreams.

Saltz, Ina. *Body Type: Intimate Messages Etched in Flesh.* Abrams, 2006. QP 2007.
Some tattoos are created from typography rather than images. This collection of photographs reveals messages, song lyrics, mottoes, and romantic ideas written on the body.

Salzman, Mark. *True Notebooks: A Writer's Year at Juvenile Hall.* Vintage, 2004. PPYA 2007 (Get Creative).
Teaching creative writing to incarcerated young men helps them cope with and look beyond the crimes they committed.

Sanchez, Reymundo. *My Bloody Life: The Making of a Latin King.* Chicago Review, 2001. PPYA 2006 (Criminal Elements).
Searching for structure and family, Sanchez (a pseudonym) finds them when he joins the Latin King gang, known for its violence, ritualistic beatings, and killings.

Santiago, Esmeralda. *Almost a Woman.* Vintage, 1999. PPYA 2002 (Tales of the Cities).
Continuing the memoir begun in *When I Was Puerto Rican,* Santiago tells of her large family, trips to the welfare office, and attempts to assimilate into 1960s America.

Satrapi, Marjane. *The Story of a Childhood.* Persepolis series, vol. 1. Pantheon, 2004. PPYA 2007 (I'm Not Making This Up).
Comic book images fill this memoir of the author's childhood during the Islamic revolution, when the Iranian shah was overthrown and torture became routine.

Savage, Candace. *Cowgirls.* Ten Speed, 1996. PPYA 2001 (Western).
Photos, quotes, posters, and historical data help round out the often overlooked role of women who were ranchers, performers in Wild West shows, and even cowpunchers.

Savas, Georgia Routsis. *Total Astrology: What the Stars Say about Life and Love.* HarperCollins, 2000. QP 2001.
Discover the real you with knowledge garnered from the meaning of sun signs, quizzes, and charts of the zodiac.

Scalora, Suza. *Fairies: Photographic Evidence of the Existence of Another World.* HarperCollins, 1999. QP 2000.
Glorious photographs make the reader consider, even if only for a few seconds, the reality of fairies.

Schatz, Howard. *Athlete.* HarperCollins, 2002. QP 2003.
Striking photos demonstrate the relation between form and function of athletes, from muscled bodybuilders to wiry sprinters, compact gymnasts, and others.

Schiff, Nancy Rica. *Odd Jobs: Portraits of Unusual Occupations.* Ten Speed, 2002. QP 2004.
Photo essayist Schiff profiles 65 professionals and the odd jobs they hold, from duck walker to coin polisher, Kentucky Derby bugle blower to Smithsonian duster.

Schreibman, Tamar. *Kissing: The Complete Guide.* Simon & Schuster, 2000. QP 2001.
From learning how to kiss to cultural customs and a history of the act during Roman times, this upbeat guide prepares teens for the ritualistic step of a first kiss.

Schulberg, Jay. *The Milk Mustache Book.* Ballantine, 1998. PPYA 1999 (Teen Culture).
The director of the team that created the milk mustache ads explains how the shots were taken, reveals unseen celebrity photos, and includes spoofs and copycat ads.

Schutz, Samantha. *I Don't Want to Be Crazy: A Memoir of Anxiety Disorder.* Scholastic, 2006. QP 2007.
Written in verse, this autobiography describes Schutz's college days as she relies on counseling and medication to subdue the debilitating anxiety attacks that rule her life.

Schwager, Tina, and Michele Schuerger. *Gutsy Girls: Young Women Who Dare.* Free Spirit, 1999. QP 2000.
Profiles of 25 "gutsy girls," websites about their activities and organizations, and suggestions for ways to become like them will motivate young women.

Scott, Damion, and Kris Ex. *How to Draw Hip Hop.* Watson-Guptill, 2006. QP 2007.
Graffiti art, video game graphics, and traditional manga combine in this exploration of illustration, which captures the unique energy and movement of hip-hop.

Scott, Jerry, and Jim Borgman. *Are We an "Us"?* Zits Sketchbook series, vol. 4. Andrews McMeel, 2001. QP 2002.
Perpetually 15, Jeremy personifies

the trials and tribulations of being an adolescent as he listens to his dad's lame jokes or plans a road trip with Hector in the comic strip "Zits."

———. *Growth Spurt.* Zits Sketchbook series, vol. 2. Andrews McMeel, 1999. QP 2000.
Jeremy's continuing saga captures the trauma of every 15-year-old boy as he reaches puberty and tries to survive high school.

Seate, Mike. *Choppers: Heavy Metal Art.* Motorbooks International, 2004. QP 2005.
Photographs and interviews detail the development of increasingly popular custom motorcycles, characterized by their long forks and chopped frames.

———. *Jesse James: The Man and His Machines.* Motorbooks International, 2003. QP 2004.
Distantly related to the infamous bandit of the same name, this James puts his outlaw skills to work building custom bikes on the Discovery Channel's *Monster Garage.*

———. *Streetbike Extreme.* Motorbooks International, 2002. QP 2003.
After a strong disclaimer, Seate's history of street bike stunts is followed by color photos of insane motorcycle stunts performed by Evel Knievel and the stunt team Starboyz.

Sebold, Alice. *Lucky.* Back Bay, 2002. PPYA 2007 (I'm Not Making This Up).
Overcoming the stigma of rape, Sebold discloses her attempt to normalize her life when she returns to college, sees her attacker, and presses for prosecution.

Seckel, Al. *The Art of Optical Illusions.* Carlton, 2000. QP 2001.
The author guides the reader through four galleries of full-color or black-and-white optical illusions, with explanations that can be read or ignored.

———. *Great Book of Optical Illusions.* Firefly, 2002. QP 2003.
Teens will look at their world differently after seeing this collection of classic and contemporary visual puzzles; answers and explanations provided in a notes section.

———. *Optical Illusions: The Science of Visual Perception.* Firefly, 2006. QP 2007.
Can you believe what you see? Hundreds of Escher-type, ambiguous figures and pictorial puzzles confuse the brain and the eyes in this fantastic collection of visual illusions.

Seventeen magazine, ed. *Seventeen Presents . . . Traumarama! Real Girls Share Their Most Embarrassing Moments Ever.* Sterling, 2005. QP 2006.
Gleaned from *Seventeen*'s popular "Traumarama" column, this compilation features the most traumatic, embarrassing, or ridiculous moments in teens' lives.

———. *Seventeen Real Girls, Real-Life Stories: True Crime.* Sterling, 2007. QP 2008.
Taken from the pages of *Seventeen* magazine, these short stories reveal horrifying crimes done to teens, often by other teens, and include the punishment given for each offense.

Shakur, Sanyika. *Monster: The Autobiography of an L.A. Gang Member.* Grove, 2004. PPYA 2006 (Criminal Elements).
Writing from his prison cell, "Monster" tells of joining the Crips when he was only 11 and earning a reputation for viciousness. Now he is a black nationalist who's renounced gangs.

Shakur, Tupac. *The Rose That Grew from Concrete.* Pocket, 1999. QP 2001.
Compelling poems of passion and anger, written before Tupac became famous, are reproduced in their original format, complete with spelling errors and corrections.

Shandler, Sara. *Ophelia Speaks: Adolescent Girls Write about Their Search for Self.* HarperPerennial, 1999. PPYA 2000 (Self-Help).
Collecting the writings of hundreds of teen girls from around the country, Shandler organizes their concerns by chapters, ranging from academic pressure to eating disorders.

Shaw, Maria. *Maria Shaw's Star Gazer: Your Soul Searching, Dream Seeking, Make Something Happen Guide to the Future.* Llewellyn, 2003. QP 2005; PPYA 2007 (I'm Not Making This Up).
Explanations of astrological signs, along with numerology, tarot reading, palmistry, auras, gemstones, crystals, and dreams, help develop the psychic ability in any teen.

Shaw, Tucker. *Dreams: Explore the You That You Can't Control.* Alloy, 2000. QP 2001.
Explanations of the biology of the mind while it's asleep, interpretations of a variety of nightly images, and beginning a journal can help teens understand their dreams.

———. *"What's That Smell?" (Oh, It's Me): 50 Mortifying Situations and How to Deal.* Illustrated by Mike Reddy. Alloy, 2003. QP 2004.
Suggestions are given for handling all types of embarrassing situations, from unstopping a toilet to knowing how to act if you wreck your dad's car or if you're arrested.

———. *Who Do You Think You Are: 12 Methods for Analyzing the True You.* Illustrated by Mike Reddy. Alloy, 2001. QP 2002.
Ways to determine the "true you" through astrology, numerology, palm reading, Chinese horoscopes, and chakras are described.

Shaw, Tucker, and Fiona Gibb. *Any Advice?* Alloy, 2000. QP 2001.
These two advice experts from Alloy.com offer divergent responses to the hundreds of daily e-mails asking about friends, crushes, sex life, and relationships.

Shields, Genie Bird, David Ellwand, and David Downton. *Fairie-ality: The Fashion Collection from the House of Ellwand.* Candlewick, 2002. QP 2004.
Color photos of the enchanting fairy fashions, constructed of petals, feathers, leaves, sticks, bark, and other natural materials, are sure to delight fashionistas.

Shivak, Nadia. *Inside Out: Portrait of an Eating Disorder.* Atheneum, 2007. QP 2008.
This author's 30-year battle with bulimia is revealed in her drawings on scraps of paper about the disorder she calls "Ed."

Sikes, Gini. *8 Ball Chicks: A Year in the Violent World of Girl Gangsters.* Anchor, 1998. PPYA 2006 (Criminal Elements).
Life for girl gangsters is as violent as it is for the guys, but with the additional worries of rape, pregnancy, abortion, and motherhood.

Silverstein, Ken. *The Radioactive Boy Scout: The Frightening True Story of a Whiz Kid and His Homemade Nuclear Reactor.* Villard, 2005. PPYA 2007 (I'm Not Making This Up).
A Detroit teen becomes a little carried away when studying for his merit badge in

atomic energy and builds a model nuclear reactor in his backyard.

Simonson, Louise. *DC Comics Covergirls.* Rizzoli, 2007. QP 2008.
Beginning with Wonder Woman from the 1940s, the covers featured in this assortment also include Supergirl, Batgirl, and Catwoman.

Simpson, Jessica. *Jessica Simpson I Do: Achieving Your Dream Wedding.* NVU Editions, 2003. QP 2004.
Photos of Jessica's sumptuous wedding to singer Nick Lachey, accompanied by tips and suggestions from professionals, assist anyone planning a wedding.

Skate and Destroy: The First 25 Years of "Thrasher" Magazine. Universe, 2006. QP 2007; PPYA 2008 (Anyone Can Play).
This combined history of a magazine and a popular extreme sport is enlivened by rejected covers, interviews with legendary skaters, and previously unpublished photographs.

Smedman, Lisa. *From Boneshakers to Choppers: The Rip-Roaring History of Motorcycles.* Annick, 2007. QP 2008.
Motorcycles have been used since the 1880s by the military, gangs, stunt riders, dirt bikers, and mainstream Americans, as shown in this well-illustrated historical overview.

Smith, Charles R., Jr. *Rimshots: Basketball Pix, Rolls, and Rhythms.* Dutton, 1999. QP 2000.
Photographs, poetry, anecdotes, and thoughts capture courtside conversations and basketball action on street courts.

———. *Short Takes: Fast-Break Basketball Poetry.* Dutton, 2001. QP 2002.
Part of a basketball trilogy, following

Rimshots and *Tall Tales,* Smith's poetry is accompanied by bright graphics and photos of the game.

Smith, Danny. *Lost Hero: Raoul Wallenberg's Dramatic Quest to Save the Jews of Hungary.* HarperCollins, 2001. PPYA 2004 (If It Weren't for Them).
Stationed in Budapest, the Swedish diplomat cajoled, threatened, and bribed officials to save thousands of Hungarian Jews, but he disappeared in 1945 after arrest by the Soviets.

Solomon, James. *"The Real World": The Ultimate Insiders Guide.* MTV, 1997. PPYA 1999 (Teen Culture).
Catch up on all the gossip and trivia of your favorite roommates from MTV's popular reality show *The Real World.*

Soto, Gary. *Neighborhood Odes.* Scholastic, 1994. PPYA 2001 (Poetry).
The sights, smells, and sounds of life in a Hispanic neighborhood are gathered in these 21 poems.

Sparks, Beatrice, ed. *It Happened to Nancy: By an Anonymous Teenager, a True Story from Her Diary.* Avon, 1994. PPYA 2006 (What Ails You?).
In this retro view of AIDS, Nancy is a happy-go-lucky teen involved with her first romance, until one horrible night when a not-so-gentle boyfriend ruins her life.

Squires, K. M. **NSYNC: The Official Book.* Bantam, 1998. QP 1999.
Stories of families, friends, music, and life offstage are related by Justin, Chris, Lance, Joey, and J.C., members of a hot teen band from the 1990s.

St. Stephen's Community House. *The Little Black Book for Girlz: A Book on Healthy Sexuality.* Annick, 2006. PPYA 2008.

Based on their own questions, teen girls at a Canadian social service agency write about sexuality; reviewed and edited by doctors and social workers.

Starwoman, Athena. *How to Turn Your Ex-Boyfriend into a Toad and Other Spells: For Love, Wealth, Beauty and Revenge.* HarperCollins, 1996. PPYA 2001 (Paranormal).
Ancient spells are brought into contemporary times with specific instructions for casting each spell, whether to find a soul mate or help determine the future.

Steer, Dugald. *Dr. Ernest Drake's Dragonology: The Complete Book of Dragons.* Candlewick, 2003. QP 2005.
This "scientific" sourcebook on dragons supplies diagrams, maps, chapters on spells, charms for dragon taming, booklets with riddles, and even dragonslayer profiles.

————. *Pirateology: The Sea Journal of Captain William Lubber, Pirate-Hunter General, Boston, Massachusetts.* Candlewick, 2006. QP 2007.
Written as a pirate hunter's log, Captain Lubber's entries describe knot typing, weaponry, navigation, battle tactics, and famous pirates, accompanied by maps and gold dust.

Steffans, Karrine. *Confessions of a Video Vixen.* HarperCollins, 2005. QP 2006.
Noted for her roles in hip-hop music videos, and praised for her dancing, Karrine portrays the true side of hip-hop, with its excessive drugs, sex, and jewelry.

Stewart, Mark. *Derek Jeter: Substance and Style.* Lerner, 1999. QP 2000.
Though he is from Kalamazoo, Michigan, Derek always said he'd be a shortstop for the New York Yankees, and photos and chronologies prove he's right.

Stine, Megan. *Trauma-Rama: Life's Most Embarrassing Moments . . . and How to Deal.* HarperCollins, 2001. QP 2002.
Living in a nutty family, wearing the same outfit as your archenemy, being caught talking about someone—these are mortifying moments, but this book tells how to handle each situation.

Sugiyama, Rika. *Comics Artists— Asia: Manga Manhwa Manhua.* HarperCollins, 2004. QP 2006.
Interviews and illustrations explain drawings and sources of ideas from the best young artists from Japan (manga), Korea (manhwa), and China (manhua).

Szpirglas, Jeff. *Gross Universe: Your Guide to All Disgusting Things under the Sun.* Maple Tree, 2006. PPYA 2007 (I'm Not Making This Up).
Every gross topic involving the body is covered in such chapters as "V is for Vomit" and "What a Gas!" with explanations of mucus, phlegm, scabs, ear wax, farts, and saliva.

Tanaka, Shelley. *Lost Temple of the Aztecs: What It Was Like When the Spanish Invaded Mexico.* I Was There series. Illustrated by Greg Ruhl. Hyperion, 1998. QP 1999.
Beginning with the excavation of the Great Temple of Tenochtitlan, the culture of the Aztecs is examined from the Spanish invasion to its eventual demise in 1521.

————. *Secrets of the Mummies: Uncovering the Bodies of Ancient Egyptians.* I Was There series. Illustrated by Greg Ruhl. Hyperion, 1999. QP 2000.
The process of mummifying the dead is described along with what scientists are able to learn about the deceased when a mummy is unwrapped and examined.

Tarbox, Katherine. *Katie.com: My Story.* Dutton, 2000. QP 2001.
Katie's memoir divulges what happened when she corresponded with "Mark" in an online chat room and agreed to meet him, not realizing that everything he told her was a lie.

Tattoo Nation: Portraits of Celebrity Body Art. Bulfinch, 2002. QP 2004.
Chosen from the pages of *Rolling Stone* magazine are illustrations and photographs of the body art of such celebrities as Mary J. Blige, Björk, Eminem, and Drew Barrymore.

Taylor, Clark. *The House That Crack Built.* Illustrated by Jan Thompson Dicks. Chronicle, 1992. PPYA 2001 (Poetry).
Using the beat of the traditional nursery rhyme "The House That Jack Built," this picture book explores the drug trade, from the coca farmers to the users, cops, and other victims.

Teen People magazine, ed. *"Teen People" Celebrity Beauty Guide: Star Secrets for Gorgeous Hair, Makeup, Skin and More!* Time, 2005. QP 2006.
The inside scoop on looking as glamorous as the stars is filled with tips and celebrity photos for achieving the best hair, makeup, or skin care to make you totally glam.

————. *Teen People: Sex Files.* Avon, 2001. QP 2002.
Answers to teen questions, a glossary, and eight stories of real situations help explain sexual identity, gender roles, virginity, and STDs.

Thalia, with Belen Atanda-Alvarado. *Thalia: Belleza! Lessons in Lipgloss and Happiness.* Chronicle, 2007. QP 2008.
Latina music star Thalia shares beauty tips on skin, hair, makeup, and internal beauty with other Latinas. Before and after shots highlight her suggested techniques.

Thatcher, Kevin, ed. *"Thrasher" Presents: How to Build Skateboard Ramps, Halfpipes, Boxes, Bowls and More.* Delacorte, 2001. QP 2003.
Detailed instructions for building skateboard ramps will help those with no carpentry skills, and experienced teens can construct the more complicated structures.

Thigpen, David E. *Jam Master Jay: The Heart of Hip-Hop.* Pocket, 2003. PPYA 2004 (On That Note).
Jam Master Jay, a member of the rap group Run-DMC, will be remembered for introducing hip-hop to the world in this biography of an exuberant rapper.

This Book Really Sucks: The Science behind Gravity Flight, Leeches, Black Holes, Tornadoes, Our Friend the Vacuum Cleaner, and Most Everything Else That Sucks. Planet Dexter, 1999. QP 2001.
Machines that suck up dust and dirt, dentist tools that remove drool, and leeches that suck out blood and infection are just a few of the "things that suck."

Thompson, Dave. *Never Fade Away: The Kurt Cobain Story.* St. Martin's, 1994. PPYA 2004 (On That Note).
When he was only 14, Kurt wrote, "I'm going to be a superstar musician, kill myself, and go out in a blaze of glory." Sadly, that's exactly what he did.

Thorley, Joe. *Avril Lavigne: The Unofficial Book.* Virgin, 2003. QP 2005.
Part of the current, hot rock scene, Canadian singer-songwriter Avril Lavigne began her career singing in the choir of her church.

"Thrasher": Insane Terrain. Universe, 2001. QP 2002.
Photos of skate parks and hangouts, profiles of the top skaters, along with skateboarding history, provide a portrait of the sport's ever-changing culture.

Todd, Mark, and Esther Pearl Watson. *Whatcha Mean, What's a Zine? The Art of Making Zines and Mini-Comics.* Graphia, 2006. PPYA 2007 (Get Creative).
Tired of blogging? Here's a complete set of how-tos for creating your own mini-magazine, better known as a zine, including zine writer interviews and zine examples.

Tom, Karen, and Kiki, eds. *Angst! Teen Verses from the Edge.* Illustrated by Matt Frost. Workman, 2001. QP 2002.
Collected from teen writings left at PlanetKiki.com, these 60 poems examine popularity, dating, fashion styles, alienation, and other angst-causing topics.

Tomlinson, Joe. *Extreme Sports: In Search of the Ultimate Thrill.* Firefly, 2004. PPYA 2008 (Anyone Can Play).
Color photos highlight air, land, and water extreme sports, including barefoot water-skiing, sky flying, street luge, bungee jumping, and free diving.

Trachtenberg, Robert, ed. *When I Knew.* Illustrated by Tom Bachtell. Regan, 2005. PPYA 2006 (GLBTQ).
Eighty gay contributors share that first moment when they knew, or accepted, their sexuality in well-illustrated anecdotes that range from the hilarious to the poignant.

Traig, Jennifer. *Accessories: Things to Make and Do.* Crafty Girl series. Chronicle, 2002. QP 2003.
Add glitz and sparkle to your wardrobe with these creative designs for bags, hats, kitten mittens, sunglasses, and backpacks that make use of sequins, fun fabrics, and stencils.

———. *Makeup: Things to Make and Do.* Crafty Girl series. Chronicle, 2003. QP 2004.
Not only are teens given instructions for making lip glosses and blushes and tweezing their eyebrows, but they also learn how to apply makeup for 20 different looks.

———. *Slumber Parties: Things to Make and Do.* Crafty Girl series. Chronicle, 2002. QP 2003.
Tired of boring parties? Select from more than a dozen themed parties, including Fright Night, Beadapalooza, and Gypsy Jubilee, with tips for food, games, movies, and crafts.

Trumbauer, Lisa Trutkoff. *A Practical Guide to Dragons.* Mirrorstone, 2006. QP 2007.
Illustrations and text describe the anatomy, behavior, lair, egg development, and combat skills of the dragons featured in *Dragonlance: The New Adventure.*

Tucker, Reed. *Osbournes Unf***ing-authorized: The Completely Unauthorized and Unofficial Guide to Everything Osbourne.* Bantam, 2002. QP 2003.
Biographies of family members, a guide to the first ten episodes of their television show, photos, and a discography round out this tale of the infamous Osbourne family.

Turner, Ann. *A Lion's Hunger: Poems of First Love.* Illustrated by Maria Jimenez. Marshall Cavendish, 1998. QP 1999.
Thirty-six free-verse poems recount a year of first love, from the initial crush to actual dating and then the sad-but-sweet memories of what might have been.

Ung, Loung. *First They Killed My Father: A Daughter of Cambodia Remembers.* HarperPerennial, 2001. PPYA 2003 (This Small World).
Loung was five when the Khmer Rouge stormed her city and her wealthy family

fled. They eventually scattered, but many other Cambodians were killed or sent to labor camps during a horrific time.

Vibe magazine, ed. *Tupac Shakur.* Three Rivers, 1998. PPYA 1999 (Teen Culture).
Explore the life and death of this young man considered a "lightning rod" in the world of hip-hop music and representative of other black men who are murdered too young.

Vitkus, Jessica. *AlternaCrafts: 20+ Hi-Style Lo-Budget Projects to Make.* With photographs by Brian Kennedy. Stewart, Tabori, & Chang, 2005. PPYA 2007 (Get Creative).
Recycle those old T-shirts, sweaters, or newspapers to create new clothing, housewares, and gifts using step-by-step instructions for these easy to challenging projects.

Vizzini, Ned. *Teen Angst? Naaah . . . : A Quasi-Autobiography.* Free Spirit, 2000. PPYA 2002 (Tales of the Cities).
Peppered with black-and-white cartoons, these magazine essays reveal the author's admittedly geeky, naïve teen years.

Von Ziegesar, Cecily, ed. *Slam.* Alloy, 2000. QP 2001; PPYA 2001 (Poetry).
The works of noted poets are interspersed with unknowns drawn from the Alloy.com Poetry Slam website.

Wakan, Naomi. *Haiku: One Breath Poetry.* Heian International, 1997. PPYA 2001 (Poetry).
Originating during the time of the samurai, haiku must be written like the sword is drawn—quickly. This work provides exercises and tips for writing haiku.

Wallace, Terry. *Bloods: An Oral History of the Vietnam War by Black Veterans.* Presidio, 1985. PPYA 2002 (War).
Twenty black veterans describe what it was like for them to serve in a war when they were fighting for a country that did not always treat blacks fairly.

Walls, Jeannette. *The Glass Castle: A Memoir.* Scribner, 2006. PPYA 2008 (What Makes a Family?).
Walls, raised with benign neglect by an alcoholic, jobless father and a self-centered artist mother, shares both her love for and anger toward her parents.

Wann, Marilyn. *Fat!So? Because You Don't Have to Apologize for Your Size.* Ten Speed, 1998. PPYA 2000 (Self-Help).
Wann's sensible advice, sprinkled with medical facts and diagrams, is to eat right, exercise, and stop worrying about pounds.

Warren, Frank. *A Lifetime of Secrets: A PostSecret Book.* Morrow, 2007. QP 2008.
From the ages of 8 to 80, people send the author their secrets on creatively decorated postcards, which he shares on his blog and in this book.

———. *PostSecret: Extraordinary Confessions from Ordinary Lives.* HarperCollins, 2005. QP 2007.
A website art project evolves when people send the author an anonymous secret on a postcard, resulting in a striking group art project referred to as "graphic haiku."

Watson, Esther Pearl, and Mark Todd, eds. *The Pain Tree, and Other Teenage Angst-Ridden Poetry.* Houghton Mifflin, 2000. QP 2001; PPYA 2001 (Poetry).
Twenty-five poems from a zine collection and from *READ* and *Seventeen* magazine reveal the honesty and worries of young teens.

Watterson, Bill. *The Calvin and Hobbes Tenth Anniversary Book.* Andrews

McMeel, 1995. PPYA 2007 (What's So Funny?).
The now-retired cartoonist explains the inspiration for his special strip about a six-year-old boy and his sometimes stuffed and sometimes human tiger.

Westbrook, Alonzo. *Hip Hoptionary: The Dictionary of Hip Hop Terminology.* Broadway, 2002. PPYA 2004 (On That Note).
This funny, brash guide defines more than 2,500 terms in slang-to-English and English-to-slang sections and adds a list of hip-hop artists.

Wick, Walter. *Walter Wick's Optical Tricks.* Scholastic, 1998. QP 1999.
Photographer Wick makes clever use of mirrors and other tricks to compose photographic illusions that will startle the reader. Luckily, he reveals his secrets.

Wiesel, Elie. *Night.* Hill & Wang, 2006. PPYA 2007 (Religion).
In his memoir, Wiesel discloses the guilt he feels at surviving the Holocaust and his questioning of a God who could let this happen.

Wilcox, Charlotte. *Mummies, Bones and Body Parts.* Lerner, 2000. QP 2001.
This photo-essay describes anthropologists, paleontologists, and other scientists as they work with the remains of the dead to determine the culture in which they lived.

Willet, Edward. *Jimi Hendrix: Kiss the Sky.* American Rebels series. Enslow, 2006. QP 2008.
Jimi's brilliant musical career is described, along with his nonexistent business sense, in this book about the life of a cultural icon who suffered an untimely death.

Williams, Stanley "Tookie," and Barbara Cottman Becnel. *Life in Prison.* Morrow, 1998—QP 1999; SeaStar, 2001—PPYA 2006 (Criminal Elements).
The cofounder of the Crips gang tells of his life in prison, which is so different from the glamorous, macho tales this ex-con heard as a young boy.

Williamson, Kate T. *Hello Kitty through the Seasons: Photographs and Haiku.* With photographs by Jennifer Butefish and Maria Fernanda Soares. Abrams, 2006. QP 2007.
Whether romping in the snow, sunbathing on the beach, or picnicking on a lovely spring day, Hello Kitty shares her haiku thoughts about the four seasons.

Wilson, Daniel H. *How to Survive a Robot Uprising: Tips on Defending Yourself against the Coming Rebellion.* Bloomsbury, 2005. QP 2006; PPYA 2007 (What's So Funny?).
Strategies to defend against mutinous robots, treat laser wounds, confuse speech recognition, or engage in hand-to-claw combat are covered in this humorous guide.

Winick, Judd. *Pedro and Me: Friendship, Loss, and What I Learned.* Holt, 2000. QP 2001; PPYA 2002 (Graphic Novels).
A professional cartoonist highlights his friendship with Pedro, an AIDS activist who tried to educate others about preventing AIDS, in a touching memoir.

Wong, Janet S. *Behind the Wheel: Poems about Driving.* Simon & Schuster, 1999. QP 2000.
Free-verse poems about driving that serve as metaphors for living, including not stealing someone else's parking spot and dealing with grandmothers, dead batteries, and tickets.

Wood, Nick. *360 Degrees New York.* Abrams, 2003. QP 2004.

With 360-degree digital photographs and a CD of QuickTime movies of cityscapes and favorite places, Wood enables a stay-at-homer to travel to New York City.

Worthington, Charles. *The Complete Book of Hairstyling.* Firefly, 2002. QP 2003.
The author, a famous hairdresser, shares instructions for fabulous hairstyles, tips for hair care, and secrets from his salon's stylists.

"YM": The Best of ("Say Anything"). Bantam, 2004. QP 2005.
Collected from the "Say Anything" column of *YM* are life's most embarrassing moments of their teen readers, including classics from the past 40 years.

Yoshinaga, Masayuki. *Gothic and Lolita.* Phaidon, 2007. QP 2008.
Cult photographer Yoshinaga captures the gothic fashion trend that Japanese teens emulate as they create or buy Victorian, rococo, and gothic fashions.

Youngblut, Shelly. *Way inside ESPN's X-Games.* Hyperion, 1998. PPYA 1999 (Teen Culture).
Heavily illustrated and complete with star athlete bios, equipment, and a glossary, this work covers summer extreme sports including skysurfing, street luge, and wakeboarding.

Zailckas, Koren. *Smashed: Story of a Drunken Girlhood.* Penguin, 2006. PPYA 2007 (I'm Not Making This Up).
This powerful memoir tells of Koren's first sip of liquor as a 14-year-old, an ER visit at 16, binge drinking in college, and finally abstinence when she's 23 and working.

Zimmerman, Keith, and Kent Zimmerman. *"Mythbusters": The Explosive Truth behind 30 of the Most Perplexing Urban Legends of All Time.* Simon Spotlight, 2005. PPYA 2007 (I'm Not Making This Up).
Learn the difference between truth and myth about exploding toilets and the danger of a penny falling from the sky in a work based on the popular Discovery Channel show.

CHAPTER 6

FICTION ANNOTATIONS
Quick Picks for Reluctant Readers and Popular Paperbacks for Young Adults, 1999–2008

Pam Spencer Holley

The original annotations, written with the teen reader in mind, are available on the YALSA booklists website (www.ala.org/yalsa/booklists/). The annotations below were rewritten to provide librarians with more descriptive information to aid them in collection development, readers' advisory service, and creation of displays, booklists, or pathfinders.

Abbott, Hailey. *The Bridesmaid.* Delacorte, 2005. PPYA 2006 (Books That Don't Make You Blush).
Abby and her sister Carol help their parents cater many weddings, so Abby is amazed when Carol turns into Bridezilla before her wedding.

————. *Summer Boys.* Summer Boys series, book 1. Scholastic, 2004. QP 2005.
Cousins Ella, Beth, and Jamie spend summer at their family's beach house and search for that perfect, but elusive, summer fling.

Abelove, Joan. *Go and Come Back.* Puffin, 2000. PPYA 2003 (This Small World).
Two anthropologists return home after studying a Peruvian tribe, but it's hard to determine if they or the tribespeople learned more about another culture.

Acito, Marc. *How I Paid for College: A Novel of Sex, Theft, Friendship, and Musical Theater.* Broadway, 2005. PPYA 2006 (GLBTQ).
Needing funds to attend Julliard, but unable to tap his father who has a new trophy wife, bisexual Edward and his friends concoct a scheme of fraud and forgery.

Adams, Douglas. *The Hitchhiker's Guide to the Galaxy.* Ballantine, 1995. PPYA 2001 (Humor).
Just as Earth is scheduled for demolition, Ford Prefect snatches Arthur from his home and the two embark on a memorable journey through space.

Adams, Leonora. *Baby Girl.* Simon Pulse, 2007. QP 2008.
Sheree reveals what her life was like being raised by a teen mother in letters she writes from a home for unwed teen mothers.

Adoff, Jaime. *Jimi and Me.* Jump at the Sun, 2005. QP 2006.
Moving to rural Ohio after the murder of his record producer father, biracial Keith takes refuge in the music of Jimi Hendrix.

Alexander, Caroline. *Mrs. Chippy's Last Expedition: The Remarkable Journey of Shackleton's Polar-Bound Cat.* HarperCollins, 1999. PPYA 2003 (Lock It, Lick It, Click It).
Mrs. Chippy, the carpenter's cat, has her own take on the voyage when explorer Shackleton's ship *Endurance* becomes trapped in Antarctic ice.

Allen, Will. *Swords for Hire.* Centerpunch, 2003. PPYA 2007 (What's So Funny?).
Sixteen-year-old farm boy Sam is sent to the Elite Guard, paired with the unbalanced mercenary Rigby Skeet, and departs on a hilarious quest to seek their rightful king.

Alphin, Elaine Marie. *Counterfeit Son.* Harcourt, 2000—QP 2001; Penguin, 2002—PPYA 2003 (I've Got a Secret).
Cameron, son of a serial killer who abducts young boys, passes himself off as one of his father's victims when his father dies in a shoot-out with police.

Alvarez, Julia. *Finding Miracles.* Laurel-Leaf, 2006. PPYA 2008 (What Makes a Family?).
Adopted from a third world country, Millie ignores her heritage until Pablo joins her class in Vermont, and she discovers they are probably from the same village.

Anderson, Laurie Halse. *Fever 1793.* Aladdin, 2002. PPYA 2006 (What Ails You?).
Yellow fever spreads across Philadelphia, and Matilda and her mother are separated when they leave town to stay with friends in the countryside.

———. *Speak.* Farrar, Straus, & Giroux, 1999—QP 2000; Puffin, 2001—PPYA 2003 (I've Got a Secret).
Melinda refuses to explain why she called the police during a preschool party, until the rapist comes after her again.

———. *Twisted.* Viking, 2007. QP 2008.
Returning his senior year as a "hottie" with a bad boy image, Tyler finds his relationships with girls so complicated that he wants to return to his former short, nerdy status.

Andora, Anthony. *Rhysmyth.* Illustrated by Lincy Chan. Tokyopop, 2007. PPYA 2008 (Anyone Can Play).
Banned from the gymnastics team for clumsiness, Elena tries one-on-one dance competitions performed on a glass grid in hopes of becoming a fast-dancing Rhysmyther.

Anonymous. *Go Ask Alice.* Avon, 1982. PPYA 2003 (Lock It, Lick It, Click It).
Reality or fiction? Whichever it is, this diary of a young girl's slide into drug use to forget parental pressure is chilling.

Anthony, Piers. *On a Pale Horse.* Incarnations of Immortality series, book 1. Del Rey, 1986. PPYA 2003 (Flights of Fantasy).
Living in a world where science and magic interact, Zane discovers that he's the new incarnation of Death and has the pale horse and power over life and death to prove it.

Appelt, Kathi. *Kissing Tennessee: And Other Stories from the Stardust.* Harcourt, 2000. QP 2001.
Eight stories disclose typical teen concerns about makeup, what to wear, and who doesn't have a date as they prepare to attend the graduation Stardust Dance.

Applegate, K. A. Everworld series. Book 1, *Search for Senna;* book 2, *Land of Loss;* book 3, *Enter the Enchanted;* book 4, *Realm of the Reaper.* Scholastic, 1999. QP 2000.
David, Senna, and three other friends first realize they are living in two parallel universes when Senna is dragged into Everworld and her friends must rescue her.

Arakawa, Hiromu. Fullmetal Alchemist series, vols. 1–4. VIZ, 2005. QP 2006.
Two brothers dabble in alchemy until one requires cybernetic replacement limbs and the other wraps his soul in armor; both are now government agents.

Araki, Hirohito. *Jojo's Bizarre Adventure.* Jojo's Bizarre Adventure series, vol. 1. Translated by Alex Kirsch. VIZ, 2005. QP 2007.
Finally available in English, this manga classic is the first of the adventures involving the Joestar family and the evil vampire Dio.

Armstrong, Jennifer, and Nancy Butcher. *The Kindling.* Fire-Us series, book 1. Eos, 2003. PPYA 2004 (Simply Science Fiction).
In 2007, a small band of teens struggle to survive in Florida, caught in a changed world after a mysterious virus eradicates most of the population.

Aronson, Sarah. *Head Case.* Roaring Brook, 2007. QP 2008.
Too many beers cause Frank to lose control of his car and kill two people; now he faces life as a quadriplegic and frets about being a "head case" in this first novel.

Asai, Carrie. Samurai Girl series. Book 1, *The Book of the Sword;* book 2, *The Book of the Shadow.* Simon Pulse, 2003. QP 2004.
A wealthy mobster adopts Heaven, the only survivor of a plane crash, but when the mobster murders her brother she flees to exact revenge as a samurai.

Asher, Jay. *Thirteen Reasons Why.* Razorbill, 2007. QP 2008.
After finding a package of audiocassettes on his front porch, Clay listens to Hannah's explanation of why each person named contributed to her decision to commit suicide.

Atkins, Catherine. *Alt Ed.* Puffin, 2004. PPYA 2005 (Own Your Freak).
A varied group of students, including a jock and a bully, eventually learn to get along after being in an after-school counseling group.

———. *When Jeff Comes Home.* Putnam, 1999. QP 2001.
After being abused and demeaned for over two years by his kidnapper, Jeff returns home but is haunted by images of his captor and isn't sure he can testify against him.

Atwater-Rhodes, Amelia. *Demon in My View.* Den of Shadows series. Delacorte, 2000. QP 2001.
Jessica writes a book about vampires that contains more truth than she realizes, then is caught between an angry, retaliatory vampire and a good witch who wants to save her.

———. *In the Forests of the Night.* Den of Shadows series. Delacorte, 1999—QP 2000; Laurel-Leaf, 2000—PPYA 2001 (Paranormal).

Vampire Risika lived in colonial America, where she transformed when she was 17. Now, 300 years later, she seeks revenge for the death of her human brother.

————. *Midnight Predator.* Den of Shadows series. Delacorte, 2002. QP 2003.
Vampire hunter Turquoise Draka goes undercover disguised as a human servant to eliminate a vampiress known for her cruelty.

————. *Shattered Mirror.* Den of Shadows series. Delacorte, 2001—QP 2002; Laurel-Leaf, 2003—PPYA 2005 (All Kinds of Creepy).
Vampire hunter Sarah meets Christopher, who she sadly discovers is the twin of a vampire her clan has hunted since the 1800s.

Austen, Jane. *Pride and Prejudice.* Bantam, 1981. PPYA 2000 (Romance).
In this well-loved novel of manners, poor Mrs. Bennett has the hard task of finding good, wealthy husbands for her five daughters.

Avi. *Devil's Race.* HarperTrophy, 1995. PPYA 2001 (Paranormal).
Hanged in the 1850s for being a demon, one of John Proud's many great-uncles selects John's body to inhabit.

————. *Midnight Magic.* Scholastic, 1999. QP 2000.
Magician Mangus and his servant are summoned to exorcise a ghost from Pergamentioto Castle, where they uncover a plot to overthrow the kingdom.

————. *Something Upstairs.* Avon, 1990. PPYA 1999 (Changing Dimensions).
Moving into an old home, Kenny meets the ghost of the murdered slave Caleb and together they time-travel to the 19th century to search for Caleb's killer.

————. *Wolf Rider: A Tale of Terror.* Bantam, 1993. PPYA 2004 (Guess Again).
"I just killed someone," claims the voice on the phone, but when Andy reports this strange call to the police no one believes him.

Azuma, Kiyohiko. Yotsuba&! series, vol. 1. A.D. Vision, 2005. PPYA 2007 (What's So Funny?).
In this manga tale a single father adopts energetic, green-haired, four-year-old Yotsuba, whose curiosity and misadventures leave the neighbors puzzling over her origins.

Bagdasarian, Adam. *Forgotten Fire.* Laurel-Leaf, 2002. PPYA 2003 (This Small World).
The author's grandfather survives the genocide of Turkish Armenians in the early 1900s but witnesses horrors no one should have to see.

Baldacci, David. *Absolute Power.* Warner, 1996. PPYA 2000 (Page Turners).
When a cat burglar picks up a letter opener that places the U.S. president at the scene of a murder, the executive staff mounts a manhunt to catch a thief.

Banks, Lynne Reid. *Melusine: A Mystery.* HarperTeen, 1997. PPYA 1999 (Changing Dimensions).
In France the Melusine of legend is part snake and part woman; the Melusine Roger meets shape-shifts to snake form when her father sexually abuses her.

Bardi, Abby. *The Book of Fred.* Washington Square, 2002. PPYA 2007 (Religion).
Raised in a fundamentalist sect ruled by traditions of the prophet Fred Brown, Mary Fred is sent to a foster home, where her obedience meshes with her new family's modern life.

Barker, Clive. *Abarat.* HarperCollins, 2004. PPYA 2005 (All Kinds of Creepy).
Disgruntled with her life, teenager Candy lets herself be swept into the mysterious sea of Izabella, unaware that the Lord of Midnight is out for her blood.

Barnes, Derrick. *The Making of Dr. Truelove.* Simon Pulse, 2006. QP 2007; PPYA 2008 (Sex Is . . .).
Dumped by his girlfriend for a jock, Diego Montgomery sets up an Internet site as Dr. Truelove, dispenses advice to the lovelorn, and hopes to win back his Roxy.

Barnes, Jennifer Lynn. *Tattoo.* Delacorte, 2007. QP 2008; PPYA 2008 (Magic in the Real World).
Temporary tattoos provide Bailey and her friends the powers they need to defeat an evil Fate who plans disaster at their school dance.

Barron, T. A. *The Lost Years of Merlin.* Lost Years of Merlin series, book 1. Ace, 1999. PPYA 2003 (Flights of Fantasy).
Young Emrys has no memory of his origins, but when he creates a fire that blinds him he explores his gift of "second sight" and is renamed Merlin.

Bauer, Cat. *Harley, like a Person.* Winslow, 2000—QP 2001; PPYA 2002 (Relationships); Knopf, 2007—PPYA 2008 (What Makes a Family?).
Convinced she was adopted and is not really part of her dysfunctional family, Harley searches for her biological father and discovers the proof she needs, along with some family secrets.

Bauer, Joan. *Backwater.* Putnam, 2000. PPYA 2006 (Books That Don't Make You Blush).
Eager to learn more about her family, whose roots trace back to the *Mayflower,* Ivy finds her aunt Jo living like a hermit in the Adirondack Mountains.

————. *Rules of the Road.* Putnam, 1998—QP 1999; Puffin, 2000—PPYA 2001 (Humor).
Learning from her elderly employer Mrs. Gladstone as she drives her to Texas to oversee her string of shoe stores, 17-year-old Jenna becomes a better shoe salesperson.

————. *Thwonk.* Laurel-Leaf, 1996—PPYA 1999 (Changing Dimensions); Penguin, 2005—PPYA 2007 (What's So Funny?).
A.J. gladly accepts romantic assistance from Cupid so Peter will fall for her, but after a few days of boring Peter she wishes she'd asked for homework help instead.

Beale, Fleur. *I Am Not Esther.* Hyperion, 2002—QP 2003; Hyperion, 2004—PPYA 2007 (Religion).
When her mother decides to work with refugees in Africa, Kirby is sent to live with fundamentalist relatives, who change her name to Esther and preach plain living.

Bechard, Margaret. *Hanging On to Max.* Roaring Brook, 2002—QP 2003; Simon Pulse, 2003—PPYA 2005 (Read 'Em and Weep).
Learning his girlfriend plans to give their child up for adoption, Sam adopts Max and spends his senior year of high school changing diapers instead of playing football.

Behrens, Andy. *All the Way.* Puffin, 2007. PPYA 2008 (Sex Is . . .).
Morose because his friends had great summer vacations while he worked, Ian takes a 1,000-mile road trip to meet a girl from a chat room, who is nothing like he expected.

Bell, Hilari. *A Matter of Profit.* HarperCollins, 2003. PPYA 2004 (Simply Science Fiction).

Ahrven has one year to find rebels who plot to assassinate his emperor, save his sister from marrying the emperor's son, and decide on a career other than being a warrior.

Bendis, Brian Michael. *Double Trouble.* Ultimate Spider-Man series, vol. 3. Illustrated by Mark Bagley. Marvel Comics, 2002. PPYA 2004 (If It Weren't for Them).
With villains to fight, a classmate who threatens to reveal his identity, and a new girl in school, Peter Parker is always busy.

———. *Learning Curve.* Ultimate Spider-Man series, vol. 2. Illustrated by Mark Bagley. Marvel Comics, 2001. QP 2004.
Peter Parker learns to better control his Spider-Man powers when he takes on the Enforcer in a quest to rid New York City of criminals.

———. *Power and Responsibility.* Ultimate Spider-Man series, vol. 1. Illustrated by Mark Bagley. Marvel Comics, 2000—QP 2002; Marvel Comics, 2001—PPYA 2002 (Graphic Novels).
The origin of Spider-Man's powers: high school student Peter Parker is bitten by an experimental spider, and the rest is history.

Bennett, Cherie. *The Haunted Heart.* Enchanted Hearts series, book 1. HarperTeen, 1999. QP 2000.
With two choices of boyfriend, Gina is not sure if she should select the aristocratic Jonathan or the moody Thomas, who also happens to be a ghost.

———. *Love Him Forever.* Enchanted Hearts series, book 6. Morrow, 1999. QP 2001.
Because she has a history of selecting the wrong guy, Colleen Belmont is torn between her yearlong love for Kevin and her fascination with newcomer Luke.

Benson, Ann. *The Plague Tales.* Dell, 1997. PPYA 2006 (What Ails You?).
Parallel stories tell of the bubonic plague, the first from a 14th-century Spaniard who describes treatment of the victims and the second from a 21st-century researcher.

Bernardo, Anilu. *Loves Me, Loves Me Not.* Pinata, 1998. PPYA 2000 (Romance).
Cuban American Margarita has a crush on popular Zach, but when she discovers his prejudice against Hispanics she turns her attention to new student Justin.

Berry, Liz. *The China Garden.* HarperTeen, 1999. PPYA 2001 (Paranormal).
Although abandoned and kept locked, the mysterious China garden at the country estate of Ravensmere exerts a tug from the past on two young people of today.

Billingsley, Franny. *Folk Keeper.* Simon & Schuster, 2001. PPYA 2003 (I've Got a Secret).
Corinna is happy keeping the savage, underground folk at bay in her role as folk keeper, so she is dismayed when she receives a summons to transfer to a wealthy estate.

Bird, Isobel. Circle of Three series. Vol. 1, *So Mote It Be;* vol. 2, *Merry Meet;* vol. 3, *Second Sight;* vol. 4, *What the Cards Said;* vol. 5, *In the Dreaming;* vol. 6, *Ring of Light;* vol. 7, *Blue Moon.* HarperCollins, 2001. QP 2002.
Three teens become interested in witchcraft, but when the love spell cast by one works too well they study Wicca and learn its healing spells.

Black, Holly. *Tithe: A Modern Faerie Tale.* Simon Pulse, 2004. PPYA 2005 (Gateway to Faerie).
In this deliciously dark urban fairy tale, Kaye returns to her childhood home, reacquaints herself with the fairies, and discovers that she is a pixie.

———. *Valiant: A Modern Tale of Faerie.* Simon & Schuster, 2005—QP 2006; Simon Pulse, 2006—PPYA 2008 (Magic in the Real World).

Betrayed by her mother, Val runs away to New York City where street kids introduce her to the world of Faerie, which lies hidden in the subway shadows.

Black, Jonah. The Black Book: Diary of a Teenage Stud series. Vol. 1, *Girls, Girls, Girls;* vol. 2, *Stop, Don't Stop.* HarperTeen, 2001. QP 2002; PPYA 2003 (Lock It, Lick It, Click It).

Expelled from prep school, Jonah returns home for public high school and keeps a "black book" of his feelings about two girls, often mixing fantasy with reality.

Blank, Jessica. *Almost Home.* Hyperion, 2007. QP 2008.

Seven teens loosely band together for Dumpster diving, prostitution, and drug use on the streets of Los Angeles.

Block, Francesca Lia. *Cherokee Bat and the Goat Guys.* HarperCollins, 1993. PPYA 2004 (On That Note).

Though Cherokee helps Witch Baby out of depression by letting her play drums in the Goat Guys band, magic and costumes don't guarantee success.

———. *Girl Goddess #9: Nine Stories.* HarperTrophy, 1998. PPYA 2000 (Short Takes).

Gay boyfriends, interracial dating, and leaving for college are a few of the offbeat topics in this group of short stories.

———. *I Was a Teenage Fairy.* HarperCollins, 1998. QP 1999.

Barbie meets a teeny-tiny fairy whose outspoken opinions give her the courage she needs to rein in her overbearing stage mother.

———. *Missing Angel Juan.* HarperTrophy, 1995. PPYA 2002 (Tales of the Cities).

Witch Baby heads to the Big Apple to find her boyfriend, aided by the ghost of Weetzie Bat's father.

———. *Violet and Claire.* HarperCollins, 1999. QP 2000.

Though opposite in personality, Violet and Claire are best friends who drift apart but after a crazy party head to the desert to restore their friendship.

———. *Witch Baby.* HarperTrophy, 1992. PPYA 1999 (Different Drummers).

Taken in by Weetzie Bat and her family, Witch Baby still feels excluded until meeting her real mother makes her realize how lucky she is to be loved by Weetzie.

Bloor, Edward. *Tangerine.* Scholastic Apple, 1998. PPYA 1999 (Good Sports).

Overshadowed by his football-playing brother and legally blind from an "accident," new student Paul is determined not to let his poor sight interfere with his soccer playing.

Blume, Judy. *Forever.* Simon Pulse, 2007. PPYA 2008 (Sex Is . . .).

Katherine knows her love for Michael will last forever, but when she goes away to college she discovers forever isn't quite as permanent as she once thought.

———. *Summer Sisters.* Dell, 1999. PPYA 2000 (Page Turners).

Spending six summers together on Martha's Vineyard bonds Caitlin and Vix as "summer sisters," yet their friendship may not be strong enough to withstand a betrayal.

Bo, Ben. *The Edge.* Lerner, 1999. QP 2001.

Surviving a warehouse fire started by fellow graffiti artists, Declan has six weeks of rehabilitation and channels his energy into death-defying snowboarding.

————. *Skullcrack.* Lerner, 2000. QP 2001. Escaping from a dreary life with his alcoholic father, Jonah surfs at Skullcrack off the coast of Ireland, where he sees strange figures in the Irish mist.

Bonner, Cindy. *Lily: A Love Story.* Onyx, 1994. PPYA 2000 (Romance).
Lily can't help but fall for Marion Beatty, youngest of the notorious Beatty brothers, though she doesn't realize she'll spend her honeymoon being chased by a posse.

Booth, Coe. *Tyrell.* Push, 2006. QP 2007.
Homeless 15-year-old Tyrell attempts to keep his Bronx family together, avoids the temptation of easy drug money, and deals with the heartbreak of first love.

Borchardt, Alice. *The Silver Wolf.* Legends of the Wolves series, book 1. Ballantine, 1999. PPYA 2000 (Page Turners).
Regeane's guardian hopes to wed her to a wealthy man in this tale of eighth-century Rome, but Regeane must keep secret her ability to shape-shift into a werewolf when the moon is full.

Bradbury, Ray. *Fahrenheit 451.* Ballantine, 1987. PPYA 2004 (Simply Science Fiction).
In a future society where firemen start fires to burn books, one fireman understands the joy brought by ideas found in books and joins a secret society of scholars.

Bradford, Richard. *Red Sky at Morning.* HarperPerennial, 1999. PPYA 2001 (Western).
Josh and his mother spend World War II in New Mexico, where Josh revels in their small town and its intriguing inhabitants while his mother enjoys bridge and sherry.

Bradley, Alex. *24 Girls in 7 Days.* Dutton, 2005. QP 2006.
Because Jack is dateless for the prom, his friends post an online ad for him in the school newspaper and 24 girls respond. Now he has just seven days to speed-date and make his choice.

Brand, Max. *Destry Rides Again.* Pocket, 1991. PPYA 2001 (Western).
When Destry is sent to jail for robbing the Express, he declares his innocence and vows to seek vengeance on the jury when his jail time is up.

Braun, Lillian Jackson. *The Cat Who Sniffed Glue.* The Cat Who series, book 8. Jove, 1989. PPYA 2004 (Guess Again).
Qwilleran, a retired newspaper reporter, and his Siamese cats Koko and Yum Yum sniff out the murderer of a rich banker and his wife.

Brennan, Michael. *Electric Girl.* Electric Girl series, vol. 1. AiT/Planet Lar, 2001. PPYA 2002 (Graphic Novels).
In this story of a seemingly normal girl and her dog, Virginia conducts electricity with her bare hands.

Brewer, Heather. *Eighth Grade Bites.* The Chronicles of Vladimir Tod series. Dutton, 2007. QP 2008.
Orphaned vampire Vlad contends with an English teacher who knows too much about him and vampires who are still angry that his father married a human.

Brian, Kate. *The Princess and the Pauper.* Simon & Schuster, 2004. QP 2004.
Princess Carina and look-alike Los Angeles teen Julia switch places so the princess can attend a rock concert sans bodyguards while Julia enjoys a date with handsome Markus.

————. *The Virginity Club.* Simon Pulse, 2005. PPYA 2008 (Sex Is . . .).
Thinking they need to remain pure in "soul and body" to win a college

scholarship, four girls organize a Virginity Club but meet with varying success.

Brin, David. *Startide Rising.* Uplift Saga, book 2. Bantam, 1983. PPYA 2004 (Simply Science Fiction).
While pursued by an alien armada, a spaceship crew of humans, dolphins, and a chimp discover the fate of the Progenitors, the race thought responsible for wisdom.

Brittain, Bill. *Wings.* HarperTrophy, 1995. PPYA 1999 (Changing Dimensions).
Enjoying the freedom of flying with his just-sprouted batlike wings, Ian quickly discovers how difficult it is to be different.

Brooks, Bruce. *Midnight Hour Encores.* HarperCollins, 2000. PPYA 2004 (On That Note).
When his cello prodigy daughter asks why she has no mother, a free-spirited father uses music to explain the culture of the 1960s.

———. *The Moves Make the Man.* HarperTrophy, 1995. PPYA 1999 (Good Sports).
Black Jerome and white Bix become friends through their shared love of basketball.

———. *What Hearts.* HarperTrophy, 1995. PPYA 2005 (Read 'Em and Weep).
Asa grows up fast as these four interrelated stories reveal how his depressed mother and series of four fathers always seem to let him down.

Brooks, Kevin. *Martyn Pig.* Scholastic, 2003. PPYA 2006 (Criminal Elements).
His good friend Alex helps Martyn cover up his father's accidental death so the authorities don't have to be notified, but then Alex calls the cops anyway.

Brooks, Martha. *Being with Henry.* Groundwood, 2002. PPYA 2002 (Relationships).
Kicked out of his home after a fight with his stepfather, homeless Laker is hired to do yard work by the crotchety widower Henry and the two become friends.

Brown, Tracy. *Criminal Minded.* St. Martin's, 2005. QP 2006.
Partners in crime, Lamin and Zio live the good life from their drug-dealing profits, but reality sets in after a shooting when it's obvious they don't know how to be legit.

Brownley, Margaret. *Buttons and Beaus.* Topaz, 1997. PPYA 2000 (Romance).
The sparks fly in 1880s New York City when Amanda Blackwell, owner of Blackwell's Cycling School, meets architect Damian Newcastle, who wants the land her school is on.

Bruchac, Joseph. *The Warriors.* Darby Creek, 2003. PPYA 2006 (Books That Don't Make You Blush).
Jake, who is proud of his Iroquois heritage, begins a term at boarding school, where he learns that his reverence for the Iroquois game of lacrosse is misunderstood.

Bujold, Lois McMaster. *Warrior's Apprentice.* Baen, 1997. PPYA 2004 (Simply Science Fiction).
Despite brittle bones and a dwarfish physique, Miles Vorkosigan uses his intelligence to create an unrivaled galactic mercenary force.

Bull, Emma. *Finder: A Novel of the Borderlands.* Illustrated by Elmer Damaso. Tor, 2003. PPYA 2006 (What Ails You?).
Magic and reality and humans and fairies all exist in Bordertown, where Orient is a finder of lost things, a necessary skill in Bordertown.

———. *War for the Oaks.* Orb, 2001. PPYA 2003 (Flights of Fantasy).
Rock singer Eddi is a mortal who doesn't know she's been selected to fight for the Seelies against the Unseelies in a war between the fairies.

Bunting, Eve. *Blackwater.* HarperCollins, 1999—QP 2000; HarperTrophy, 2000—PPYA 2003 (I've Got a Secret).
Though the town thinks he is a hero in his failed rescue attempt of two teens from the Blackwater River, Brodie struggles with whether or not to tell what really happened.

Burgess, Melvin. *Bloodtide.* Tor, 2002. PPYA 2004 (Simply Science Fiction).
In a futuristic, violent time, London is ruled by rival gangs and surrounded by creatures called halfmen, who are combinations of men and animals.

———. *Doing It.* Holt, 2006. PPYA 2008 (Sex Is . . .).
Three British lads talk and dream of sex as each enjoys a relationship, but they quickly discover that what seems so glamorous soon becomes confining and tawdry.

———. *Smack.* HarperTeen, 1999. PPYA 2002 (Tales of the Cities).
Running away from abusive, restrictive homes, Tad and Gemma become addicted to heroin, an addiction from which only Gemma is able to escape.

Burke, Morgan. The Party Room trilogy. *Get It Started; After Hours; Last Call.* Simon Pulse, 2005. QP 2006.
Kirsten hears that the murderer dubbed the "Prep School Killer" is dead, but her relief is short-lived when another student is found dead.

Burnard, Damon. *Burger!* Houghton Mifflin, 1998. PPYA 1999 (Changing Dimensions).
Vegetarian Clementine discovers Chef Jeff is an alien who plans to fatten up her classmate as the main course for his gourmand master in this early graphic novel.

Burnham, Niki. *Royally Jacked.* Simon Pulse, 2004. QP 2005.
When her mother announces she is divorcing and living with her girlfriend, Valerie decides to join her father, a chief of protocol for a European royal family.

Busiek, Kurt. *Kurt Busiek's Astro City: Life in the Big City.* Astro City series, vol. 1. Illustrated by Brent E. Anderson and Alex Ross. Homage Comics, 1996. PPYA 2002 (Graphic Novels).
Astro City is guarded by superheroes who patrol the skies, one of whom is the Samaritan, the featured superstar in this first volume.

———. *The Wizard's Tale.* Illustrated by David T. Wenzel. Wild Storm, 1999. PPYA 2003 (Flights of Fantasy).
Bafflerog Rumplewhisker is a kindhearted wizard charged with keeping the lineage of evil intact, but his attempts at spells usually backfire.

Butts, Nancy. *The Door in the Lake.* Front Street, 1997. QP 1999.
Unsure if he was captured by aliens and held for more than two years, Joey returns to the site of the camping trip where his memories ended.

Cabot, Meg (Meggin). *All-American Girl.* HarperCollins, 2002—QP 2003; HarperTrophy, 2003—PPYA 2006 (Books That Don't Make You Blush).
The artistic individualist in her family, Samantha experiences great changes when

she saves the president's life and ends up being the coolest kid in school.

———. *The Boy Next Door.* Avon, 2002. QP 2004.
This adult debut novel from popular YA author Meg Cabot uses e-mail to record gossip columnist Melissa Fuller's romance, which is aided by two cats and a Great Dane.

———. *The Princess Diaries.* Princess Diaries series, vol. 1. HarperCollins, 2000—QP 2001; HarperTeen, 2001—PPYA 2003 (Lock It, Lick It, Click It).
As noted in her diary, after learning she is a princess in Genovia and heir to the throne, Mia retains her sense of humor even when followed by the paparazzi.

———. *Princess in Love.* Princess Diaries series, vol. 3. HarperCollins, 2002. QP 2003.
Finally acknowledged as the Genovian heir to the throne, though an illegitimate one, Mia has a life in America just like any other teenage girl.

———. *Princess in the Spotlight.* Princess Diaries series, vol. 2. HarperCollins, 2001. QP 2002.
Mia's life becomes crazy when Grandmere turns Mia's mother's wedding plans into a state wedding.

———. *Ready or Not.* HarperTeen, 2007. PPYA 2008 (Sex Is . . .).
After meeting when Sam stops an assassination attempt on the president, she and the president's son David step up their dating but miscommunicate about sex.

Cadnum, Michael. *Rundown.* Viking, 1999. QP 2000.
A faked report of rape to garner some attention from her bride-to-be sister lands Jennifer in such a mess that she attempts

suicide before finally telling the detective the truth.

Cappo, Nan. *Cheating Lessons.* Simon Pulse, 2003. PPYA 2006 (Books That Don't Make You Blush).
Knowing it is impossible for her team to have the highest qualifying score for the State Classics Bowl, Bernadette is disappointed that her English teacher may have cheated.

Card, Orson Scott. *Enchantment.* Ballantine, 2000. PPYA 2005 (Gateway to Faerie).
Returning to Russia to see if the sleeping princess he found in the woods is still there, Ivan locates her, but kissing her brings more trouble than romance.

———. *Ender's Game.* Tor, 1992. PPYA 2000 (Page Turners).
Sent to Battle School, Ender Wiggins plays simulated war games to determine his potential as Earth's military commander in combat against insectoid aliens.

———. *Ender's Shadow.* Tor, 1998. PPYA 2004 (Simply Science Fiction).
Orphaned Bean is taken from the streets and sent to Battle School, where his intelligence proves he is capable of leadership. Questions about his origin keep him second to Ender.

———. *Magic Street.* Del Rey, 2006. PPYA 2008 (Magic in the Real World).
Found in a grocery bag and raised by a nurse and her neighbors, orphan Mack Street has the uncanny ability to slip into the dreams of others and learn their deepest wishes.

———. *Seventh Son.* Tales of Alvin Maker, book 1. Tor, 1993. PPYA 2003 (Flights of Fantasy).
This alternate-world fantasy about a seventh son of a seventh son who is born

with extraordinary psychic powers is set in a frontier America alive with magic.

Carey, Mike. *Re-gifters.* Illustrated by Sonny Liew and Marc Hempel. Minx, 2007. PPYA 2008 (Anyone Can Play).
A crush on a fellow hapkido student almost ruins Dixie's plans to compete successfully in a national tournament in this graphic novel.

Carlson, Lori M., ed. *American Eyes: New Asian-American Short Stories for Young Adults.* Fawcett, 1996. PPYA 2000 (Short Takes).
Growing up in a country where you are in the minority is the focus of these stories about Asian American teens.

Carlson, Melody. *Finding Alice.* Waterbrook, 2003. PPYA 2007 (Religion).
With touches of *Alice in Wonderland,* college student Alice suddenly hears voices in her head, slides into schizophrenia, and doesn't improve until the "Cat Lady" intervenes.

————. *It's My Life.* Diary of a Teenage Girl series, book 2. Multnomah, 2000. PPYA 2006 (Books That Don't Make You Blush).
Caitlin O'Conner records her attempts to help others as she puts her new Christian faith to work.

Carroll, Jenny. The Mediator series. Vol. 1, *Shadowland* (QP and PPYA); vol. 2, *Ninth Key* (QP). Simon Pulse, 2000. QP 2002; PPYA 2003 (I've Got a Secret).
Moving to California after her mother remarries, Suze helps ghosts resolve their issues so they can move on in this series by popular author Meg Cabot, writing as Jenny Carroll.

Cart, Michael, ed. *Love and Sex: Ten Stories of Truth.* Simon & Schuster, 2001. QP 2002.

Love and sex intertwine as teens consider if they are gay, ready to "do it," or experiencing infatuation or real love.

————. *Tomorrowland: Ten Stories about the Future.* Scholastic, 1999. QP 2000.
Characters from different centuries, including a caveman, a monk, and a girl born from donated sperm, contemplate their futures.

Carvell, Marlene. *Who Will Tell My Brother?* Hyperion, 2004. PPYA 2005 (Read 'Em and Weep).
Proud of his Mohawk heritage, Evan continues the unpopular crusade begun by his late brother to remove the Indian as their high school mascot.

Cary, Kate. *Bloodline.* Razorbill, 2005. QP 2006.
When wounded Lt. John Shaw is nursed at the hospital by Mary Seward, she learns through reading his diary about the mysterious "bloodline" linking his family to Dracula.

Cast, P. C., and Kristin Cast. The House of Night series. Book 1, *Marked;* book 2, *Betrayed.* St. Martin's, 2007. QP 2008.
Living in a world where vampires and humans coexist, Zoey enters the House of Night School to become a vampire but faces betrayal when human teens are killed.

Castellucci, Cecil. *Beige.* Candlewick, 2007. QP 2008.
In contrast to her outrageous, colorful father Rat, drummer for the legendary punk band Suck, conservative Katy lives up to her nickname, "Beige."

————. *Boy Proof.* Candlewick, 2005. QP 2006.
Science fiction and monster movie–loving teen Victoria is disdainful of boys until she meets Max.

Chambers, Veronica. *Marisol and Magdalena: The Sound of Our Sisterhood.* Hyperion, 2001. PPYA 2003 (This Small World).
Marisol spends the summer in Panama with her grandmother to learn some Spanish and a little more about her Panamanian heritage.

Chandler, Elizabeth. *The Deep End of Fear.* Dark Secrets series, book 4. Simon Pulse, 2003. QP 2004.
Returning to Westbrook Estate after a 12-year absence, Kate worries when her pupil Patrick tells her he talks to Ashley, his drowned sister.

———. *Don't Tell.* Dark Secrets series, book 2. Simon Pulse, 2001. QP 2002.
Returning to the riverfront home Wisteria, where her mother supposedly drowned seven years earlier, Lauren realizes that somebody wants her dead, too.

Charnas, Suzy McKee. *The Kingdom of Kevin Malone.* Magic Carpet, 1997. PPYA 1999 (Changing Dimensions).
While roller-skating in Central Park, Amy joins neighborhood bully Kevin in his fantasy kingdom of Fayre Farre, where he hides from his abusive father.

Chayamachi, Suguro. *Code One: Dante.* Devil May Cry series, vol. 1. Translated by Ray Yoshimoto. Tokyopop, 2005. QP 2007.
Twins Dante and Virgil, sons of the demon Sparda, who defended humans thousands of years ago, take two different paths in this classic tale of good versus evil.

Chbosky, Stephen. *The Perks of Being a Wallflower.* Pocket, 1999. QP 2000; PPYA 2002 (Relationships).
Charlie describes his first year of high school through a series of letters telling of new friends, his sister's pregnancy, the suicide of a best friend, and his bout with depression.

Chima, Cinda Williams. *The Warrior Heir.* Hyperion, 2007. PPYA 2008 (Magic in the Real World).
Unaware of his gifts, Jack is astounded when his superpowers are unleashed and he discovers a secret society of wizards, warriors, and enchanters called "the Weir."

Choyce, Lesley. *Thunderbowl.* Orca, 2004. QP 2005.
Jeremy comes alive when he plays guitar in his rock band Thunderbowl, but a weekly gig at a club interferes with school, making him long to drop out and focus on music.

Christie, Agatha. *Death on the Nile.* Berkley, 1997. PPYA 2004 (Guess Again).
When Linnett is killed on her honeymoon cruise, it's lucky Hercule Poirot is on board to track down the shipboard murderer.

Christopher, John. *The White Mountains.* The Tripods trilogy. Simon & Schuster, 1968. PPYA 2004 (Simply Science Fiction).
Will and some friends try to escape to the White Mountains to evade the mind control forced on humans by the invading aliens called tripods.

Cirrone, Dorian. *Dancing in Red Shoes Will Kill You.* HarperTrophy, 2006. PPYA 2007 (Get Creative).
Though Kayla is an outstanding ballerina, her Dolly Parton–sized breasts limit her dreams of a solo in *Cinderella;* instead she lands the role of the ugly stepsister.

Clark, Catherine. *Truth or Dairy.* Avon, 2000. PPYA 2001 (Humor).
Dumped by her boyfriend as he leaves for

college, angry Courtney fills her journal with stories of ignoring men, making great smoothies, and taking up school politics.

————. *Wurst Case Scenario.* HarperTeen, 2001. PPYA 2003 (Lock It, Lick It, Click It).
As Courtney describes in her diary, she worries about being a vegan in the middle of a rural Wisconsin campus where all meals are meat and potatoes.

Clarke, Arthur C. *Childhood's End.* Ballantine, 2001. PPYA 2004 (Simply Science Fiction).
Over the past 50 years the Overlords have eradicated poverty and disease from Earth—now they're ready to eradicate the humans.

Clarke, Miranda. *Night of a Thousand Boyfriends.* Quirk, 2003. QP 2004.
A choose-your-own adventure allows the reader to decide whether a young woman's search for love in the big city will be sexy, chaste, or the perfect match.

Clowes, Daniel. *Ghost World.* Fantagraphics, 2001. PPYA 2002 (Graphic Novels).
Urban friends Becky and Enid face the possibility of being apart when high school ends, as Enid thinks of college and Becky wants to keep everything the same.

Clugston-Major, Chynna. *Queen Bee.* Scholastic, 2005. QP 2006.
Two psychokinetic girls, nice Haley and not-so-nice Alexa, meet in this graphic novel in which each wants to be "Queen Bee" of seventh grade.

Cohn, Rachel. *Gingerbread.* Simon & Schuster, 2002. QP 2003; PPYA 2005 (Own Your Freak).
Sent to New York City to spend the summer with her biological father, Cyd

Charisse makes the most of a trip involving relatives who don't know what to do with her.

————. *The Steps.* Aladdin, 2004. PPYA 2008 (What Makes a Family?).
Her parents split, her mother dates a dweeby classmate's father, and Annabel visits her newlywed father in Australia, where she is startled to hear her stepsiblings call him Dad.

Cohn, Rachel, and David Levithan. *Nick and Norah's Infinite Playlist.* Knopf, 2006—QP 2007; Knopf, 2007—PPYA 2008 (Sex Is . . .).
Nick and Norah, two city teens, meet at a punk rock club and fall in love to an indie-rock sound track.

Colfer, Eoin. *Artemis Fowl.* Artemis Fowl series, book 1. Miramax, 2002. PPYA 2002 (Flights of Fantasy).
Determined to carry on the family tradition of thievery, Artemis kidnaps a fairy and demands a ransom of gold but instead is stuck with a feisty fairy and no ransom.

Conford, Ellen. *Crush.* HarperCollins, 1998—QP 1999; HarperTrophy, 1999—PPYA 2000 (Romance).
A collection of nine stories swirls around who's dating whom for the annual Valentine's Day dance, called the Sweetheart Stomp.

Connelly, Michael. *Blood Work.* Warner, 1998. PPYA 2000 (Page Turners).
How can retired FBI agent Terry McCaleb turn down Graciela Rivers's request to help solve her sister Grace's murder, when it is Grace's heart beating in his chest?

Cook, Karin. *What Girls Learn: A Novel.* Random House, 1998. PPYA 2006 (What Ails You?).
Moving when the mood hits their mother,

Tilden and Elizabeth are surprised when she packs up again to marry Nick but grateful after she dies that Nick is their stepfather.

Cooney, Caroline B. *Both Sides of Time.* Laurel-Leaf, 1997. PPYA 1999 (Changing Dimensions).
Walking the grounds of the historic Stratton mansion, Annie time-travels to the 1890s and falls in love with Strat, heir to the home.

————. *Burning Up.* Delacorte, 1999. QP 2000.
Concerned about her town's racism, Macey digs deep into the town's history and uncovers secrets her family would rather she not know.

————. *Diamonds in the Shadow.* Delacorte, 2007. QP 2008.
The Finch family shelters a Sierra Leone refugee "family" for their church, not realizing they are in danger from the refugees' forced diamond smuggling.

————. *Driver's Ed.* Random House, 1996. PPYA 2003 (I've Got a Secret).
Remy has a crush on Morgan and so goes along with the dare to steal highway signs, not thinking who might be killed when they take a stop sign.

————. *Hush Little Baby.* Scholastic, 1999. QP 2000.
When her ex-stepmother shoves a bundle containing a baby into Kit's arms, she becomes part of a complicated criminal plan.

————. *Wanted!* Scholastic, 1997. PPYA 2004 (Guess Again).
Pursued by the police, as well as her father's killer, Alice struggles to elude everyone as she tries to figure out why she's a suspect and what's on her father's computer file.

Cooper, Ilene. *Sam I Am.* Scholastic, 2006. PPYA 2007 (Religion).
When the family dog knocks over their Christmas tree/Hanukkah bush, 12-year-old Sam wonders about religion and its place in his interfaith household.

Cooper, Susan. *The Boggart.* Aladdin, 1995. PPYA 1999 (Changing Dimensions).
Hitching a ride on an inherited piece of furniture, an impish boggart leaves Scotland to follow an American family home, where he creates mischief for everyone.

Cormier, Robert. *Fade.* Random House, 1991. PPYA 2003 (I've Got a Secret).
Inheriting the family ability to fade, Paul tries it once or twice but vows never to intentionally fade, until he hears of an abused nephew who fades for evil purposes.

————. *Heroes.* Delacorte, 1998—QP 1999; Laurel-Leaf, 2000—PPYA 2004 (If It Weren't for Them).
Unable to stop the rape of his girlfriend by a World War II hero, Francis enlists, accidentally saves his company from a grenade, and returns home to face that local hero.

————. *Rag and Bone Shop.* Laurel-Leaf, 2003. PPYA 2006 (Criminal Elements).
Jason is the last person to have seen Alicia before she is murdered and, after hours of police interrogation, begins to wonder if perhaps he did kill her.

————. *Tenderness.* Delacorte, 2004— PPYA 2005 (All Kinds of Creepy); Laurel-Leaf, 1998—PPYA 1999 (Different Drummers).
In a touching tale, a serial killer is caught when the girl he genuinely cares for accidentally drowns. Eric knows he'll be blamed for Lori's death.

Covington, Dennis. *Lizard.* Laurel-Leaf, 1993. PPYA 1999 (Different Drummers).
Sent to a state school for the retarded only because of unfocused eyes and a flattened nose, "Lizard" escapes with a traveling actor and plays Caliban in Shakespeare's *Tempest.*

Coy, John. *Crackback.* Scholastic, 2005. QP 2006.
A new coach who reduces his playing time makes high school star Miles consider whether football should continue to be the center of his life.

Cray, Jordan. *Gemini7.* Danger.com series. Aladdin, 1997. QP 1999.
Trying to distance himself from his girlfriend, Jonah meets a "cyber girlfriend," but Nicole proves dangerous to his family and his former girlfriend.

Creech, Sharon. *Absolutely Normal Chaos.* HarperCollins, 1997. PPYA 2001 (Humor).
Mary Lou fills a summer journal for an English assignment with stories about her wacky family, her cousin's mysterious inheritance, and her first romance.

———. *The Wanderer.* HarperCollins, 2002. PPYA 2003 (I've Got a Secret).
Sophie talks her way into a trans-atlantic voyage on *Wanderer* to visit her grandfather Bompie, but she doesn't mention in her journal that she was adopted and has never met Bompie.

Crichton, Michael. *Sphere.* Ballantine, 1988. PPYA 2000 (Page Turners).
Sent to inspect a large spaceship lying on the ocean floor, scientists discover a mysterious sphere inside.

Cross, Gillian. *Tightrope.* HarperTrophy, 2001. PPYA 2002 (Tales of the Cities).
Ashley lives with an invalid mother, and tagging in hard-to-reach spaces is her only rebellious thrill, but it draws the attention of someone who leaves her threatening notes.

Cross, Shauna. *Derby Girl.* Holt, 2007. QP 2008.
Tired of her beauty pageant–obsessed mother, Bliss becomes enamored with derby skating and eventually earns a spot on the local team and the nickname "Ruthless Babe."

Crutcher, Chris. *Athletic Shorts: Six Short Stories.* Laurel-Leaf, 1992. PPYA 2000 (Short Takes).
These short stories provide an introduction to some of Crutcher's memorable characters, including fat Angus Bethune and the very offbeat Telephone Man.

———. *Deadline.* HarperCollins, 2007. QP 2008.
Learning he has only one year to live, Ben tells no one and forgoes any treatment so that he can live his year to the fullest without puke or pity.

———. *Ironman.* Laurel-Leaf, 1996. PPYA 1999 (Good Sports).
Anger at his domineering father's attempts to "make a man" of him fuels 17-year-old Bo's quest for victory in the triathlon.

———. *Staying Fat for Sarah Byrnes.* Laurel-Leaf, 1995. PPYA 1999 (Good Sports).
Fat Eric and badly scarred Sarah swim together, continuing even after he loses his "Moby Dick" weight and she stops talking.

———. *Whale Talk.* Laurel-Leaf, 2002. PPYA 2005 (Own Your Freak).
T.J. stands out in his white community not only for his independent streak but also because he is an adopted, biracial teen.

Curtis, Christopher Paul. *The Watsons Go to Birmingham—1963.* Bantam, 1997. PPYA 2001 (Humor).
When brother Byron gets in trouble, his family takes him south for a taste of his grandmother's discipline, but the Watsons ride right into a church bombing.

Danziger, Paula. *This Place Has No Atmosphere.* Bantam, 1989. PPYA 2001 (Humor).
Aurora can't believe her parents are making her leave their home in the mall and accompany them to the moon colony, a place that "has no atmosphere."

Danziger, Paula, and Ann M. Martin. *P.S. Longer Letter Later.* Scholastic, 1998—QP 1999; Scholastic, 1999—PPYA 2003 (Lock It, Lick It, Click It).
Though opposites, Elizabeth and Tara*Starr are best friends, so when Tara*Starr moves away their friendship continues through letters.

———. *Snail Mail No More.* Scholastic, 2000. QP 2001.
Switching from snail mail to e-mail makes it easier for Elizabeth and Tara*Starr to write but harder to remain friends.

David, Peter. *The Deadly Gourmet Affair.* Spyboy series, vol. 1. Dark Horse, 2001. QP 2002.
Alex's latent abilities as a superspy emerge and suddenly everyone is trying to dispose of him.

Davidson, Dana. *Jason and Kyra.* Jump at the Sun, 2004. QP 2005.
Opposites attract when supercool, superjock Jason teams up with smart, nonconformist Kyra on a research project and the two discover a mutual attraction.

———. *Played.* Jump at the Sun, 2005—QP 2007; Hyperion, 2007—PPYA 2008 (Sex Is . . .).
To be accepted into his high school's select fraternity, Ian agrees to charm plain Kylie into sleeping with him, but his deception is unveiled before the entire school.

Davis, Amanda. *Wonder When You'll Miss Me.* HarperPerennial, 2004. PPYA 2005 (Own Your Freak).
After a brutal assault and a failed suicide attempt, Faith returns to school thinner but still unnoticeable. Joining the circus gives her a new self-confidence.

Davis, Donald. *Barking at a Fox-Fur Coat.* August House, 1991. PPYA 2001 (Humor).
Davis regales readers with "true" stories of his North Carolina family as he describes the misadventures of aunts, uncles, grandparents, cousins, and critters.

Davis, Mark, Mike Davis, and Brandon Schultz. *Genesis.* Blokhedz series, book 1. Pocket, 2007. QP 2008.
Gifted rapper Blak's songs become reality as he avoids the violence of gangs and the temptations of street life in the Monarch Projects of Empire City.

Dayton, Anne, and May Vanderbilt. *Emily Ever After.* Broadway, 2005. PPYA 2007 (Religion).
Trying to maintain her Christian ideals while finally working in New York City is harder than Emily thought it might be, and soon her old flame is much more appealing.

de la Cruz, Melissa. *The Au Pairs.* The Au Pairs series, book 1. Simon & Schuster, 2004. QP 2005.
For different reasons, Eliza, Mara, and Jacqui leap at the $10,000 au pair job for two summer months of caring for the four Perry children in the fabulous Hamptons.

———. *Blue Bloods.* Blue Bloods series, book 1. Hyperion, 2006. QP 2007.
Schuyler and Bliss exhibit the first signs of vampirism that afflict most of their contemporaries but don't realize that they're now targets for murderous teen vampires.

———. *Masquerade.* Blue Bloods series, book 2. Hyperion, 2007. QP 2008.
The death of young Blue Bloods, upcoming members of the wealthy vampire aristocracy, casts a pall over the annual coming-out Masquerade Ball.

de la Peña, Matt. *Ball Don't Lie.* Delacorte, 2005—QP 2006; Delacorte, 2007—PPYA 2008 (Anyone Can Play).
Sticky is a 17-year-old white boy who bounces between foster and group homes almost as fast as his basketball, which is the only constant in his life.

de Lint, Charles. *The Blue Girl.* Puffin, 2006. PPYA 2008 (Magic in the Real World).
Imogene must defend herself against soul-sucking creatures, aided by Maxine and Ghost, the remains of a deceased student who still haunts the school.

———. *Jack of Kinrowan: Jack the Giant-Killer and Drink Down the Moon.* Tor, 1999. PPYA 2003 (Flights of Fantasy).
Thrown into the world of Faerie by a gang of bikers on Ottawa's streets, Jackie discovers she is considered the Jack of Kinrowan and has been sent to save them from evil.

De Oliveira, Eddie. *Lucky.* Scholastic, 2004. PPYA 2006 (GLBTQ).
Attracted to a fellow soccer player, Sam meets members of London's gay community, which helps him realize that he's attracted to both boys and girls; in short—he's just Sam.

Dean, Carolee. *Comfort.* Graphia, 2004. PPYA 2005 (Read 'Em and Weep).
Kenny hopes his writing skills will help him escape his unbearable home life. A winning piece of poetry starts his "Dallas" fund.

Dean, Zoey. *The A-List.* The A-List series, book 1. Little, Brown, 2003. QP 2004.
Traveling to Los Angeles to live with her wealthy father, Anna sheds her perfect image and has fun in a social world vastly different from her East Coast lifestyle.

———. *Blonde Ambition.* A-List series, vol. 3. Little, Brown, 2004. QP 2006.
Anna Percy's high living continues as she interns on a popular TV show and meets "the boy of her dreams."

Deaver, Jeffrey. *The Bone Collector.* Lincoln Rhyme series, book 1. Signet, 1998. PPYA 2000 (Page Turners).
A quadriplegic who is also a brilliant forensic scientist teams with a patrol officer to track down a serial killer who leaves macabre clues pointing to his next victim.

Deaver, Julie Reece. *The Night I Disappeared.* Simon & Schuster, 2002. PPYA 2003 (I've Got a Secret).
Jamie is so wrapped up in her fantasies that when a bike accident sends her to the hospital her mother seeks psychiatric help for Jamie and her imaginary friend.

Deem, James M. *3 NBs of Julian Drew.* Avon, 1996. PPYA 1999 (Different Drummers).
Trapped in a nightmarish existence of indifference and abuse from his stepmother, 15-year-old Julian corresponds with his deceased mother.

Delaney, Joseph. *Revenge of the Witch.* The Last Apprentice series,

book 1. Illustrated by Patrick Arrasmith. Greenwillow, 2005. QP 2006.
Making use of his supernatural powers, Tom apprentices to Mr. Gregory, the local "Spook," who teaches him to keep ghosts, boggarts, and witches under control.

Dessen, Sarah. *Dreamland.* Puffin, 2002, PPYA 2003 (I've Got a Secret).
Upset that her older sister eloped rather than attend Yale, Caitlin drifts into a relationship with wealthy, abusive Rogerson Biscoe but then is unable to escape.

———. *Keeping the Moon.* Viking, 1999. QP 2000.
Though Colie has lost 45 pounds she hasn't lost her insecurity, until she spends a summer with her large, eccentric aunt and learns to disregard the gossip of others.

———. *Someone like You.* Viking, 1998. QP 1999.
Halley's relationship with her best friend Scarlett changes during their junior year after Scarlett's boyfriend dies and news of Scarlett's pregnancy leaks out.

Deuker, Carl. *High Heat.* HarperTeen, 2005. PPYA 2008 (Anyone Can Play).
After Shane's father commits suicide because of financial problems, his privileged life falls apart faster than his legendary pitching.

———. *Runner.* Houghton Mifflin, 2005. QP 2006.
Desperate for money to pay the moorage fees for the boat he and his dad call home, Chance agrees to pick up and deliver packages while he's out running.

Dickey, Eric Jerome. *Thieves' Paradise.* Dutton, 2002. QP 2003.
When Dante's dot-com job is eliminated, his prison record makes it hard to find another, and he turns to grifting on the streets of Los Angeles to make ends meet.

Dickinson, Peter. *Eva.* Laurel-Leaf, 1990. PPYA 1999 (Changing Dimensions).
Unable to save Eva after a traffic accident, doctors transfer her neuron memory into the body of a chimpanzee, which raises moral and ethical issues about transplants.

Dines, Carol. *Talk to Me: Stories and a Novella.* Laurel-Leaf, 1999. PPYA 2000 (Short Takes).
Whether it is deciding which family member to live with or standing up for a person being bullied, these stories feature teens learning to make choices.

Dixon, Chuck, and Jordan Gorfinkel. *Birds of Prey.* DC Comics, 1999. PPYA 2002 (Graphic Novels).
Formerly known as Batgirl and now wheelchair-bound after an attack by the Joker, Oracle leads other superheroines in the fight against crime.

Dokey, Cameron. *Beauty Sleep.* Simon Pulse, 2002. PPYA 2005 (Gateway to Faerie).
In this entertaining retelling of *Sleeping Beauty,* the cursed Aurore flees her kingdom when she is 16 and meets Prince Charming, who is looking for a sleeping princess to kiss.

———. *The Storyteller's Daughter.* Illustrated by Kinuko Craft. Simon Pulse, 2002. PPYA 2005 (Gateway to Faerie).
To prevent the grim king from killing one wife a month, blind Shahrazad tells stories that finally melt his heart in this retelling of an *Arabian Nights* tale.

Donoghue, Emma. *Kissing the Witch: Old Tales in New Skins.* HarperTeen, 1999. PPYA 2000 (Short Takes).

Think fairy tales are full of beautiful, weak women who need to be rescued by strong, handsome men? Think again.

Douglas, Lola. *True Confessions of a Hollywood Starlet.* Razorbill, 2006. PPYA 2007 (What's So Funny?).
Actress Morgan Carter hits rock bottom from drugs, is sent to rehab, and now lives with a family friend in Indiana as she tries to act like a regular high school student.

Doyle, Arthur Conan. *The Great Adventures of Sherlock Holmes.* Penguin, 1991. PPYA 2004 (Guess Again).
This compilation features short stories by the acclaimed creator of one of literature's greatest sleuths, Sherlock Holmes.

Draper, Sharon M. *Darkness before Dawn.* Atheneum, 2001. QP 2002.
As Keisha delivers the graduation address, she remembers her tumultuous senior year when she had to defend herself against rape by the school's track coach.

————. *Forged by Fire.* Simon Pulse, 1998. PPYA 2002 (Relationships).
Taken from his aunt, he is reclaimed by his mother, but now Gerald protects his half-sister Angel from her abusive father.

Duane, Diane. *So You Want to Be a Wizard.* So You Want to Be a Wizard series, book 1. Magic Carpet, 2001. PPYA 2003 (Flights of Fantasy).
Novice wizards Nita and Kit learn protective spells to stand up against their bullying classmates.

DuMaurier, Daphne. *Rebecca.* Avon, 1996. PPYA 2000 (Romance).
Though Rebecca died in a boating accident, the second Mrs. DeWinter discovers that her memory hasn't faded from the rooms and servants of Manderley on the Cornish coast.

Duncan, Lois. *I Know What You Did Last Summer.* Dell, 1999. PPYA 2005 (All Kinds of Creepy).
Four teens involved in a hit-and-run accident take a vow of silence but are later tracked down by someone bent on revenge.

————. *Locked in Time.* Laurel-Leaf, 1986, PPYA 1999 (Changing Dimensions).
Spending the summer with her father and his new stepfamily, Nore is not sure how to interpret the dream warnings she receives from her deceased mother.

————. *The Third Eye.* Laurel-Leaf, 1991. PPYA 2001 (Paranormal).
Though terrified when she is first asked to help, Karen uses her psychic powers to assist the police to locate missing children.

————, ed. *Trapped! Cages of Mind and Body.* Simon Pulse, 1999. PPYA 2000 (Short Takes).
Young adult authors contribute tales of teens who feel trapped, whether working in a restaurant, contemplating marriage, lying to a psychiatrist, or living in a shelter.

Dygard, Thomas. *Halfback Tough.* Beech Tree, 1998. PPYA 1999 (Good Sports).
Former "bad boy" Joe Atkins enjoys his notoriety as a football star at his new school but worries when previous cronies show up at his games.

Easton, Kelly. *Aftershock.* Margaret K. McElderry, 2006. QP 2007.
Walking away from the Idaho car crash that kills his parents, Adam remains in a mute daze as he alternately walks and hitchhikes back to his home in Rhode Island.

———. *The Life History of a Star.* Simon Pulse, 2002. PPYA 2003 (Lock It, Lick It, Click It).
Her older brother David dies after returning home from Vietnam, but Kristin is comforted by his comment that atoms of a star don't die but are transformed.

Eberhardt, Thom. *Rat Boys: A Dating Experiment.* Hyperion, 2001. QP 2002.
Attending Spring Fling with hottie dates transformed from pet rats, Marci and Summer remember that there is one other thing rats like to do besides eating and sleeping.

Eddings, David. *Pawn of Prophecy.* The Belgariad series, book 1. Del Rey, 1986. PPYA 2003 (Flights of Fantasy).
Garion, an orphaned farm boy raised by his aunt Pol, sets out on a dangerous quest to locate an object that will decide the fate of his universe.

Ehrenhaft, Daniel. *The Last Dog on Earth.* Yearling, 2003. PPYA 2006 (What Ails You?).
Having just named his new mutt Jack, Logan fears Jack will die when a mysterious disease turns dogs into predators.

———. *10 Things to Do before I Die.* Delacorte, 2004. QP 2005.
Certain that a crazed fry cook poisoned him, Ted grabs the to-do list written by his friends and prepares to live out his wildest fantasies over the next 24 hours.

Eisner, Will. *Last Day in Vietnam: A Memory.* Dark Horse, 2000. PPYA 2002 (War).
Pulling from his experiences in World War II and later assignments to Korea and Vietnam, Eisner reveals the many forms of combat encountered by a soldier in this graphic novel.

Ellis, Deborah. *The Breadwinner.* Groundwood, 2001. PPYA 2003 (This Small World).
After her father's arrest, Parvana dons her deceased brother's clothes and reads and writes letters for pay, but she fears the Taliban will see through her disguise.

Ellis, Warren. *Force of Nature.* StormWatch series, vol. 1. DC Comics, 1999. QP 2001.
Up until now StormWatch has been a reactive, crisis intervention team, but the controller of the superhero team changes them to a proactive, "take no prisoners" group.

Ellison, Suzanne Pierson. *The Last Warrior.* Rising Moon, 1997. PPYA 2001 (Western).
Captured by the U.S. Army and sent to the Carlisle School in Pennsylvania to be "civilized," Solito hates his life and runs away, returning to his Apache home in Arizona.

Engdahl, Sylvia Louise. *Enchantress from the Stars.* Penguin, 2003. PPYA 2004 (Simply Science Fiction).
A stowaway aboard her father's spaceship, Elana lands on a medieval planet where inhabitants still believe in magic and consider her the "Enchantress from the Stars."

Erskine, Kathryn. *Quaking.* Philomel, 2007. QP 2008.
Moving to yet another foster home, Matilda achieves a sense of peace living with her Quaker family, which enables her to stand up to her school's bullying pro-war students.

Ewing, Lynne. Daughter of the Moon series. Vol. 1, *Goddess of the Night;* vol. 2, *Into the Cold Fire.* Hyperion, 2000. QP 2001.

Vanessa's invisibility, Catty's ability to time-travel, and Serena's mind reading are special powers these goddesses of the Daughters of the Moon need to combat evil Atrox.

————. *Drive-By.* HarperCollins, 1998. PPYA 2006 (Criminal Elements).
After his older brother is killed for skimming off drug money, the gang comes after Tito looking for the money and demanding that he join them.

————. *Party Girl.* Knopf, 1998—QP 1999; Laurel-Leaf, 1999—PPYA 2002 (Relationships).
When her very best friend and fellow gang member is killed, Kata doesn't know whether to seek revenge or get out of gang life entirely.

Feinstein, John. *Last Shot: A Final Four Mystery.* Yearling, 2006. PPYA 2008 (Anyone Can Play).
Winning a writing contest, two teens cover the Final Four of March Madness, where they overhear a conversation about throwing one of the basketball games.

Ferris, Jean. *Bad.* Farrar, Straus, & Giroux, 1998—QP 1999; Farrar, Straus, & Giroux, 2001—PPYA 2006 (Criminal Elements).
Caught while helping her boyfriend rob a convenience store, Dallas is sent to a rehab center where she discovers a love of reading.

————. *Eight Seconds.* Penguin, 2002. PPYA 2003 (I've Got a Secret).
Attending rodeo camp introduces John to the adrenalin rush of eight seconds on a bull but also makes him wonder about the rush he feels for a fellow cowboy.

————. *Love among the Walnuts.* Harcourt, 1998. PPYA 2006 (Books That Don't Make You Blush).

Evil uncles try to kill Sandy's wealthy family by poisoning the birthday cake, but Sandy and his valet skip dessert and rescue his parents and their pet chicken Attila.

————. *Of Sound Mind.* Sunburst, 2004. PPYA 2008 (What Makes a Family?).
Serving as the ears for his deaf parents and sibling, responsible Theo bonds instantly with Ivy, who performs similar tasks for her deaf father.

————. *Once upon a Marigold.* Harcourt Brace, 2004. PPYA 2005 (Gateway to Faerie).
A lost prince, a kindly troll, a lonely princess, and a helpful pigeon—who else would you expect to be characters in a fairy tale?

Fields, Terri. *Holdup.* Roaring Brook, 2007. QP 2008.
Naïve Joe unwittingly agrees to help a stranger and becomes an accessory to another "Ski Mask Bandit" robbery, where he accidentally shoots one of the hostages.

Finder, Joseph. *High Crimes.* Avon, 1999. PPYA 2000 (Page Turners).
High-powered attorney Claire Chapman defends her husband after he is accused of committing crimes in Vietnam while serving in the military under another name.

FitzGerald, Dawn. *Soccer Chick Rules.* Square Fish, 2007. PPYA 2008 (Anyone Can Play).
To Tess, the only reason to attend school is to play sports, so when she learns that budget problems may eliminate sports, she signs up to help pass the necessary tax levy.

Flake, Sharon. *Bang!* Jump at the Sun, 2005. QP 2006.

A father goes to extreme lengths to teach his son Mann and his friend Kee-lee how to survive their neighborhood, where people are shot "for no real reason."

―――. *Begging for Change.* Jump at the Sun, 2003. QP 2004.
Having once been homeless, Raspberry is obsessed with money, but when she steals from her best friend she worries that she's like her thieving, drug-addicted father.

―――. *The Skin I'm In.* Little, Brown, 1998. QP 1999.
A teacher with a blotchy complexion caused by a rare skin condition serves as a mentor for dark-skinned Maleeka, who studies the way Miss Saunders stands up to teasing.

―――. *Who Am I without Him? A Short Story Collection about Girls and the Boys in Their Lives.* Hyperion, 2004. QP 2005.
Ten short stories explore the problems involved with both securing and then hanging on to a boyfriend.

Flanagan, John. *The Ruins of Gorlan.* Ranger's Apprentice series, book 1. Philomel, 2005. QP 2006.
Disappointed not to be chosen for Battle School, Will apprentices as a Ranger and becomes the eyes and ears for his kingdom in this first of a series.

Fleischman, Paul. *A Fate Totally Worse Than Death.* Candlewick, 1997. PPYA 2001 (Humor).
Last year Danielle and her buddies pushed a classmate off a cliff; now her ghost haunts them and they show signs of aging in this spoof of the horror genre.

―――. *Seedfolks.* Scholastic, 1999. PPYA 2002 (Tales of the Cities).
When a young girl plants a few lima bean seeds and sprouts emerge, so do multiethnic neighbors who transform an abandoned city lot into a garden.

Flinn, Alex. *Beastly.* HarperCollins, 2007. QP 2008.
Kyle's shallow cruelty earns him a curse from a goth girl he offended, and he is left as ugly on the outside as he is on the inside.

―――. *Breaking Point.* HarperCollins, 2002. QP 2003.
A new scholarship student at a ritzy private school, Paul is ignored until popular Charlie pays attention to him, but Paul doesn't realize that he is being set up for a prank leading to jail time.

―――. *Breathing Underwater.* HarperCollins, 2001―QP 2002; HarperTeen, 2002―PPYA 2003 (Lock It, Lick It, Click It).
Sentenced to anger management class for hitting his girlfriend, Nick slowly understands the reasons for his actions and even takes the class again.

―――. *Nothing to Lose.* HarperCollins, 2004. QP 2005; PPYA 2006 (Criminal Elements).
When he learns his mother is standing trial for the murder of her husband, runaway Michael returns from a year of working in a carnival to speak in her defense.

Foon, Dennis. *Skud.* Groundwood, 2004. PPYA 2006 (Criminal Elements).
Four seniors watch their future plans fall apart before graduation when one dies, one is jailed, and one loses a tryout spot for an ice hockey team.

Frank, E. R. *America.* Atheneum, 2002― QP 2003; Simon Pulse, 2003―PPYA 2005 (Read 'Em and Weep).
Abandoned by his crack-addicted mother

and shuttled between foster homes, biracial America attempts suicide, which leads to much-needed help.

———. *Life Is Funny.* DK, 2000. QP 2001.
Eleven students share their stories of drugs, abusive parents, foster homes, racism, violence, and divorce, which illustrate the varied meanings of "life is funny."

Frank, Hilary. *Better Than Running at Night.* Houghton Mifflin, 2002. PPYA 2007 (Get Creative).
Ellie learns by the start of second semester that there is more to her freshman year at art school than line, perspective, and Nate.

Frank, Lucy. *Oy, Joy!* Simon Pulse, 2001. PPYA 2002 (Tales of the Cities).
Too shy to call anyone on her Match Quiz, though she longs to be in love, Joy Cooper steps back as her uncle Max takes over in the matchmaking department.

Fraustino, Lisa Rowe, ed. *Dirty Laundry: Stories about Family Secrets.* Viking, 1998. QP 1999.
These 11 short stories reveal that every family has some "dirty laundry" they want to keep secret.

Freymann-Weyr, Garret. *My Heartbeat.* Puffin, 2003. PPYA 2006 (GLBTQ).
Upset that someone would ask if her brother Link and his friend James are a twosome, Ellen realizes she doesn't know her brother as well as she thought she did.

Friedman, Aimee. *South Beach.* Scholastic, 2005. QP 2006.
Former best friends Alexa and Holly escape from New Jersey and head to South Beach, Florida, for a spring break adventure.

Friedman, Hal. *Over the Edge.* HarperCollins, 1999. PPYA 2000 (Page Turners).

Hired to replace teacher Elaine Wilkins, who died after falling from a cliff on an eighth-grade field trip, Meg wonders if Elaine was really pushed over the edge.

Friend, Natasha. *Lush.* Scholastic, 2006. QP 2007.
Long letters to an unknown correspondent about her father's alcoholism help Samantha cope with her unhappy family life.

Friesner, Esther. *Tempting Fate.* Puffin, 2007. PPYA 2008 (Magic in the Real World).
Assigned as a temp secretary to the three sister owners of Tabby Fabricant Textiles, Ilana is surprised to type up "death receipts," until she learns she is working for the Fates.

Frost, Helen. *Keesha's House.* Farrar, Straus, & Giroux, 2007. PPYA 2008 (What Makes a Family?).
The intricate poetry of sestinas and sonnets tells of troubled teens who reach safety and become part of an extended family when they stay in "Keesha's House."

Fujishima, Kosuke. *1-555-Goddess.* Oh My Goddess series. Dark Horse, 1996. PPYA 2002 (Graphic Novels).
When college student Keiichi Morisato dials a wrong number and connects with the Goddess Technical Help Line, Belldandy visits him . . . and stays.

———. *Oh My Goddess! Wrong Number.* Oh My Goddess series. Dark Horse, 2002. QP 2003.
This remastered first volume of *1-555-Goddess* includes the original Belldandy story plus answers to many previously unexplained questions.

Fullerton, Alma. *Walking on Glass.* HarperCollins, 2007. QP 2008.

After saving his mother from her suicide attempt, the unnamed narrator is now conflicted about the life support she's on, knowing he'll have to decide about "pulling the plug."

Funke, Cornelia. *Inkheart.* Scholastic, 2005. PPYA 2008 (Magic in the Real World).

Meggie's father Mo is able to read a character out of a book into life, which leads to trouble when one character wants to remain free and Mo must ask the author to rewrite the book.

Gabaldon, Diana. *Outlander.* Dell, 1992. PPYA 2000 (Page Turners).

Accidentally traveling back in time to 18th-century Scotland, Claire stays long enough to fall in love but then returns to the 20th century and her husband.

Gaiman, Neil. *Coraline.* Illustrated by Dave McKean. HarperTrophy, 2004. PPYA 2005 (All Kinds of Creepy).

Entering a door that leads into the other half of her old house, Coraline discovers mirror images of her parents, but ones with curious button eyes and papery skin.

———. *Death: The High Cost of Living.* Vertigo, 1994. PPYA 2002 (Graphic Novels).

Once a century Death assumes human form and walks the Earth so that she doesn't forget just what she is taking away. Today is the day.

———. *Neverwhere.* Avon, 1998. PPYA 2008 (Magic in the Real World); PPYA 1999 (Changing Dimensions).

When he helps an injured woman, Richard discovers a subterranean London, known as London Below, which leaves him unseen by everyone except the London Belowers.

———. *Stardust.* HarperPerennial, 2001. PPYA 2003 (Flights of Fantasy).

Promising his love he will bring her a falling star they spotted, Tristan crosses into Faerie and hunts down his "star," but he discovers that others seek her special powers.

Gaiman, Neil, and Terry Pratchett. *Good Omens: The Nice and Accurate Prophecies of Agnes Nutter, Witch.* HarperTorch, 2006. PPYA 2007 (What's So Funny?).

When Agnes Nutter predicts the end of the world, she can't control the switching of babies, which leads to substituting an Antichrist for Christ in this wacky, pun-filled work.

Gallo, Donald R., ed. *Join In: Multiethnic Short Stories by Outstanding Writers for Young Adults.* Laurel-Leaf, 1995. PPYA 2000 (Short Takes).

Foreign-born writers and writers with close ties to a culture describe ways ethnic teens adapt to American life.

———. *No Easy Answers: Short Stories about Teenagers Making Tough Choices.* Laurel-Leaf, 1999. PPYA 2000 (Short Takes).

Teens face moral crises as they make choices in areas such as peer pressure, gang membership, and even blackmail.

———. *On the Fringe.* Puffin, 2003. PPYA 2005 (Own Your Freak).

Noted young adult authors write about the insiders and outsiders of high school life.

———. *Ultimate Sports: Short Stories by Outstanding Writers for Young Adults.* Laurel-Leaf, 1997. PPYA 1999 (Good Sports).

Sports, sports, and more sports, from racquetball to wrestling, are the focus of these 11 stories about winning, losing, and growing up.

Galloway, Priscilla. *Truly Grim Tales.* Laurel-Leaf, 1998. PPYA 2000 (Short Takes).
Familiar fairy tales appear here, but rewritten with a wicked, satirical touch to appeal to those who enjoy a grisly twist.

Garden, Nancy. *Dove and Sword: A Novel of Joan of Arc.* Scholastic, 1997. PPYA 2004 (If It Weren't for Them).
Gabrielle's neighbor Jeannette hears voices, yet Gabrielle accompanies her as she gathers an army to fight the English, until the fateful day Jeannette is burned at the stake.

Garwood, Julie. *For the Roses.* Pocket, 1996. PPYA 2000 (Romance).
Four orphaned boys retrieve a baby from a New York alley and move to Montana to raise her, but then are threatened by the Englishman sent to claim their "sister" Mary Rose.

Gerritsen, Tess. *Life Support.* Pocket, 1998. PPYA 2000 (Page Turners).
ER doctor Toby Harper often visits her Alzheimer's-afflicted mother, so when other elderly patients die at her mother's retirement home Dr. Harper is the first suspect.

Gerrold, David. *Jumping Off the Planet.* Tor, 2002. PPYA 2004 (Simply Science Fiction).
Chigger, Weird, and Stinky's vacation with their father turns ominous when they ride the elevator to the moon.

Giberga, Jane Sughrue. *Friends to Die For.* Puffin, 1999. PPYA 2004 (Guess Again).
Part of an A-list group, Crissy worries when someone is murdered at a party she attends, and she thinks her best friend's boyfriend may be involved.

Giffen, Keith. I Luv Halloween series, vols. 1–2. Illustrated by Benjamin Roman. Tokyopop, 2005–2006. QP 2007.
Every Halloween varies for a group of friends: one year they receive apples instead of candy; the next year their trick-or-treat space is invaded by zombies.

Gilbert, Barbara Snow. *Broken Chords.* Laurel-Leaf, 2001. PPYA 2004 (On That Note).
Clara is a gifted 17-year-old pianist who is pushed by her musically talented parents until a wrist injury prevents any practice for two weeks and she discovers other interests.

———. *Stone Water.* Front Street, 2003. PPYA 2005 (Read 'Em and Weep).
His terminally ill grandfather's last request to assist him to commit suicide leaves Grant battling his conscience over what is morally right in life and death.

Giles, Gail. *Dead Girls Don't Write Letters.* Roaring Brook, 2003. QP 2004.
Sunny's favored, older sister Jazz runs away to New York but dies in an apartment fire, so how can Sunny explain the letter she just received from her?

———. *Playing in Traffic.* Roaring Brook, 2004. QP 2005.
Quiet, unassuming Matt is the object of goth girl Skye's affections, but he doesn't understand her twisted mind.

———. *Shattering Glass.* Roaring Brook, 2002—QP 2003; Simon Pulse, 2003— PPYA 2005 (Own Your Freak).
Manipulative new student Rob decides to transform nerdy Simon Glass into Mr. Popular, but Simon catches on and exhibits some deviousness of his own in this first novel.

———. *What Happened to Cass McBride?* Little, Brown, 2006. QP 2007.
Kyle captures Cass and buries her alive, convinced her refusal to date his brother caused him to commit suicide.

Gilmore, Kate. *The Exchange Student.* Houghton Mifflin, 1999. QP 2000.
A seven-foot alien exchange student visits Earth and stays with the Wells family, but steals DNA to restock his planet's dwindling number of animals.

Gilstrap, John. *Nathan's Run.* Warner, 1997. PPYA 2000 (Page Turners).
Twelve-year-old orphan Nathan Bailey, accused of murdering a cop as he escaped from jail, is now chased by authorities as well as a hit man.

Glenn, Mel. *Foreign Exchange: A Mystery in Poems.* Morrow, 1999. QP 2000.
A group of city teens spend the weekend in a small town, but when a popular local teen is found strangled, authorities immediately pinpoint mixed-race Kwame as the killer.

———. *Split Image.* HarperTeen, 2002. PPYA 2003 (I've Got a Secret).
Poems from students and teachers at Tower High offer insight into Laura Li, who lives two lives: model student by day and dance club party girl at night.

———. *Who Killed Mr. Chippendale?* Puffin, 1999. PPYA 2001 (Poetry).
The saga of Mr. C's murder and feelings about violence are revealed in verse format by teachers, students, and community leaders whose lives he touched.

Glovach, Linda. *Beauty Queen.* HarperCollins, 1998. QP 1999.
Escaping an abusive home situation, Samantha turns to topless dancing to earn enough to live. When she becomes a heroin addict, it's not long before she's placed in a coffin.

Godfrey, Rebecca. *Torn Skirt.* HarperCollins, 2002. QP 2003.
Sara takes to the streets of British Columbia to hunt down Justine, a street girl in a torn skirt, and enters a world filled with drugs, prostitution, and violence.

Going, K. L. *Fat Kid Rules the World.* Puffin, 2004. PPYA 2005 (Own Your Freak).
After punk rock legend Curt convinces fat Troy to join his band, both their lives change.

Golden, Christopher. *Meets the Eye.* Body of Evidence series, book 4. Simon & Schuster, 2000. QP 2001.
Reading about the culprits responsible for a recent spate of robberies and murders, Jenna realizes she helped autopsy these crooks weeks earlier and they should all be buried.

Golden, Christopher, and Rick Hautala. *Throat Culture.* Body of Evidence series, book 8. Simon & Schuster, 2005. PPYA 2006 (What Ails You?).
Part-time coroner Jenna investigates the paralyzing disease that strikes her new stepmother and many of the wedding guests.

Goldman, William. *The Princess Bride.* Ballantine, 1990. PPYA 2001 (Humor).
In this timeless fairy tale Westley battles everything, including death, to be reunited with his true love Buttercup.

Goldschmidt, Judy. *The Secret Blog of Raisin Rodriguez.* Penguin, 2006. PPYA 2007 (What's So Funny?).
A newcomer to Philadelphia, Raisin blogs to all her California friends with stories of her unhappiness, until a classmate reads, prints, and shares her blog at school.

Gonzalez, Julie. *Ricochet.* Delacorte, 2007. QP 2008.
Four boys gather on a rooftop to play "idiot's roulette." When the gun is aimed at the next person, Connor's best friend is killed and he is left to mourn.

Goobie, Beth. *Something Girl.* Orca, 2005. QP 2006.
A hospital visit from a young girl she used to babysit finally convinces badly beaten Sophie to tell the truth about her "upstanding" father.

———. *Sticks and Stones.* Orca, 2002. QP 2003.
Called a slut at school as part of a campaign started by a boy she said "No" to on a date, Jujube fights back, helped by many of her female classmates.

Gould, Stephen. *Jumper.* Tor, 1993. PPYA 1999 (Changing Dimensions).
Discovering he can teleport, or "jump," Davy flees his abusive father in search of other jumpers and soon is teleporting across continents to fight terrorism.

———. *Wildside.* Tor, 1996. PPYA 2004 (Simply Science Fiction).
When Charlie inherits a ranch from his uncle, he discovers a concealed door leading to a parallel world filled with plants and animals but no sign of human life.

Grant, Cynthia D. *Mary Wolf.* Simon Pulse, 1997. PPYA 1999 (Different Drummers).
After losing his job, Mary's father takes the family around America in their RV. But the longer they're on the road, the more Mary wants to return to their own home.

———. *The White Horse.* Atheneum, 1998. QP 1999.
Her mother is a crack addict, her boyfriend is a druggie, and the only constant in Raina's life is school. When her boyfriend dies, she turns to her English teacher.

Grant, Vicki. *Dead-End Job.* Orca, 2005. QP 2006.
Saving money for art school, Frances works the graveyard shift at a local convenience store, where she meets mentally disturbed Devin, who tries to woo her.

———. *I.D.* Orca, 2007. QP 2008.
When Chris picks up a wallet on the street, he starts to return it but realizes he resembles the owner and thinks he will have a chance for a better life if he switches his identity.

———. *Pigboy.* Orca, 2006. QP 2007.
Class nerd Dan Hogg finally earns the respect of his classmates when he saves them from an escaped convict who poses as the pig farmer on their class field trip to a working farm.

Gratz, Alan. *Something Rotten.* Dial, 2007. QP 2008.
In a combination of Shakespeare and Raymond Chandler mysteries, Horatio helps his friend Hamilton Prince investigate his father's death and mother's recent remarriage.

Green, John. *Looking for Alaska.* Dutton, 2005. QP 2006.
Arriving at boarding school, outsider Miles rooms with popular, prank-loving Chip and falls in love with beautiful, troubled Alaska.

Greenberg, Martin, and Russell Davis, eds. *Faerie Tales.* DAW, 2004. PPYA 2005 (Gateway to Faerie).
A dozen magical tales from fantasy writers including de Lint, Huff, and Scarborough share the mystery and wonder of the world of faerie.

Griffin, Adele. *Amandine.* Hyperion, 2001. QP 2002.

When insecure Delia tires of Amandine's habitual downgrading of people and pulls away from her, she retaliates by spreading destructive, hateful lies about Delia's father.

Grimes, Nikki. *Bronx Masquerade.* Dial, 2002—QP 2003; Puffin, 2003—PPYA 2007 (Get Creative).

An assignment linked to an "Open Mike" night bonds a class of Bronx high school students through their shared poetry.

——. *Jazmin's Notebook.* Puffin, 2000. PPYA 2003 (Lock It, Lick It, Click It).

Reading Jazmin's journal, one learns how she stood firm, stayed in the academic track, and did not succumb to sexual overtures from a boy she liked.

Grisham, John. *The Client.* Dell, 1994. PPYA 2000 (Page Turners).

Sneaking a forbidden cigarette, 11-year-old Mark Sway is the recipient of a dying man's message telling the whereabouts of a U.S. senator's body. Now everyone is after Mark.

Groening, Matt. *Bart Simpson's Treehouse of Horror: Spine-Tingling Spooktacular.* HarperCollins, 2001. PPYA 2002 (Graphic Novels).

Year-round Halloween escapades fill the pages of this chilling yet hysterically funny book featuring giant cockroaches, teen acne, flying monkeys, and school dances.

——. *Simpsons Comics A-Go-Go.* HarperCollins, 2000. QP 2001.

More adventures from those baffling Simpsons as Marge contemplates running a day care center and worries that Lisa is becoming bohemian.

——. *Simpsons Comics Barn Burner.* HarperCollins, 2005. PPYA 2007 (What's So Funny?).

Whether Homer is running for mayor or Bart is squealing on the school bullies, laughter follows when reading this collection of Simpsons antics.

——. *Simpsons Comics Madness.* HarperCollins, 2003. QP 2004.

Cartoons graphically describe the wacky Simpsons family as Bart tries to be smart, Homer takes part in a dangerous game show, and Lisa and Martin are substitute teachers.

——. *Simpsons Comics Unchained.* HarperCollins, 2002. QP 2003.

Four comics continue the escapades of this unusual family as Grampa helps senior citizens, Homer fights for free speech, and Mr. Burns pays his workers in jelly donuts.

Gruner, Jessica, and Buzz Parker. *The Lost Issue.* Emily the Strange series. Dark Horse, 2005. QP 2007.

Join tweens, teens, and adults who love mysterious Emily and her world of talking black cats and the playful ghosts of famous quirky people.

Gutman, Dan. *Honus and Me: A Baseball Card Adventure.* HarperTrophy, 1998. PPYA 1999 (Good Sports).

Acquiring a Honus Wagner baseball card brings Joe thoughts of money but also a face-to-face meeting with the famed player in a time-travel journey.

Guy, Rosa. *The Disappearance.* Laurel-Leaf, 1979. PPYA 2004 (Guess Again).

After being acquitted of murder, Imamu is offered a place in a foster home with Mrs. Aimsley, but two days later the Aimsley daughter disappears.

Ha, Thu-Huong. *Hail Caesar.* Push, 2007. PPYA 2008 (Sex Is . . .).
Proud to have earned the nickname Caesar because of his ability to conquer women, John has a comeuppance when he meets Eva, who is oblivious to his charms.

Haddix, Margaret Peterson. *Among the Betrayed.* Shadow Children series, book 3. Simon & Schuster, 2002. QP 2003.
With families limited to only two children, "shadow child" Nina's identity has been discovered and she now faces execution.

————. *Among the Hidden.* Shadow Children series, book 1. Simon & Schuster, 1998—QP 2000; Simon & Schuster, 2002—PPYA 2003 (I've Got a Secret).
Born a third child just as the government issues the edict for families to have only two children, Luke has been hidden his entire life.

————. *Among the Imposters.* Shadow Children series, book 2. Simon & Schuster, 2001. QP 2002.
An illegal third child, Luke assumes the identity of an unreported, deceased child and finally attends boarding school, but he worries that a classmate will report him.

————. *Don't You Dare Read This, Mrs. Dunphrey.* Simon Pulse, 1997. PPYA 2003 (Lock It, Lick It, Click It).
Changes are made in Trish's dysfunctional family after she finally allows Mrs. Dunphrey to read her English journal, in which she has recorded her abuse and neglect.

————. *Just Ella.* Simon & Schuster, 1999—QP 2000; Aladdin, 2001—PPYA 2005 (Gateway to Faerie).
In this continuation of the Cinderella tale, Ella is living in Prince Charming's castle awaiting marriage but discovers that he is boring and she dislikes royal etiquette.

————. *Leaving Fishers.* Simon Pulse, 1999. PPYA 2007 (Religion).
Dorry accepts an invitation to join the religious group Fishers of Men, but the organization occupies all her time and she ignores her grades and family.

————. *Running Out of Time.* Aladdin, 1997. PPYA 2004 (Guess Again).
When Jessica is sent out of her frontier village to seek help for the diphtheria that strikes her town, she is stunned to learn that she really lives in the 1990s, not the 1840s.

Haddon, Mark. *The Curious Incident of the Dog in the Night-Time.* Vintage, 2004. PPYA 2006 (What Ails You?).
Autistic math genius Christopher Boone wants to solve the mystery of his neighbor's murdered poodle, a task that leads to questions about his own family.

Hahn, Mary Downing. *Gentleman Outlaw and Me—Eli: A Story of the Old West.* HarperTrophy, 1997. PPYA 2001 (Western).
Disguised as a boy and calling herself Elijah, Eliza is helped by the "Gentleman Outlaw" as she searches for her gold miner father.

————. *Look for Me by Moonlight.* HarperTeen, 1997. PPYA 2001 (Paranormal).
When Cynda falls for a pale, aristocratic guest at her parents' inn, she is unaware she has placed everyone in danger.

Halam, Ann. *Dr. Franklin's Island.* Dell, 2002. PPYA 2005 (All Kinds of Creepy).
Stranded on an island, three teens meet the weird Dr. Franklin, who uses them for transgenic treatments. Returning to their former selves is now more important than escape.

Halliday, John. *Shooting Monarchs.*
Margaret K. McElderry, 2003. QP 2004.
While photographing monarch butterflies,
physically handicapped Danny stops a
serial killer from kidnapping and attacking
his beautiful classmate Leah.

Halpern, Julie. *Get Well Soon.* Feiwel &
Friends, 2007. QP 2008.
Increased panic attacks send Anna to the
"loony bin," as she refers to it, where she
has fun, loses weight, meets some bizarre
people, and finally has a boyfriend.

Halvorson, Marilyn. *Bull Rider.* Orca,
2003. QP 2004.
Having lost his rodeo father to an angry,
trampling bull, Layne keeps his bull riding
a secret from his mother.

———. *Cowboys Don't Cry.* Fitzhenry &
Whiteside, 1994. PPYA 2001 (Western).
After his mother is killed in a car accident,
Shane and his rodeo star father start a new
life on a small ranch they inherit, but Shane
thinks he and his father are drifting apart.

Hamill, Pete. *Snow in August.* Warner,
1999. PPYA 2002 (Tales of the Cities).
Linked by their love of baseball, a rabbi
and a young boy stand firm against racial
prejudice.

Hamilton, Laurell K. *Guilty Pleasures.*
Ace, 1993. PPYA 2000 (Page Turners).
Though Anita Blake hunts vampires, she
has just been hired by a powerful vampire
to track down the serial killer who is
murdering his comrades.

Hamilton, Virginia. *The House of Dies
Drear.* Aladdin, 1984. PPYA 2004
(Guess Again).
When the Smalls move to Ohio, they
discover that the home they bought is
filled with passageways from its days as a
stop on the Underground Railroad.

Harazin, S. A. *Blood Brothers.* Delacorte,
2007. QP 2008.
Clay and Joey come from different
economic backgrounds but have been best
friends since grade school. Joey is now
lying in the ICU and Clay is devastated.

Harmon, Michael. *Skate.* Knopf, 2006. QP
2008.
When boarder Ian loses his temper and
decks a coach, he grabs his brother Sammy
and the two "skate" across Washington
State in search of the father who
abandoned them.

Harrar, George. *Not as Crazy as I Seem.*
Houghton Mifflin, 2003. PPYA 2006
(What Ails You?).
Being wrongfully accused of tagging
lockers upsets Devon but forces him to
learn techniques to manage his obsessive
mannerisms.

Harris, Thomas. *The Silence of the Lambs.*
St. Martin's, 1991. PPYA 2005 (All
Kinds of Creepy).
To stop a serial killer, FBI trainee Clarice
Starling interviews the imprisoned Dr.
Hannibal Lector, who provides snippets of
data in exchange for information.

Harrison, Lisi. *The Clique.* The Clique
series, book 1. Little, Brown, 2004. QP
2005.
New student Claire's choice of clothing
is ridiculed by a clique of four middle
school girls, but Claire enjoys the last
laugh.

Hartinger, Brent. *The Geography Club.*
HarperTempest, 2004. PPYA 2005 (Own
Your Freak).
Using the cover of a geography club, a
group of gay and lesbian high school
students meet weekly at school and
provide support for one another.

———. *Last Chance Texaco.* HarperCollins, 2004—QP 2005; HarperCollins, 2005—PPYA 2006 (Criminal Elements).
Troubled 15-year-old Lucy receives a "last chance" to put mistakes from her past behind her when she is sent to a progressive group home for teens.

———. *The Order of the Poison Oak.* HarperTeen, 2006. PPYA 2008 (Sex Is . . .).
At a summer camp with many burn victims, counselor and gay teen Russell organizes the Order of the Poison Oak, which is open to outcasts of all types.

Harvey, Sarah N. *Bull's Eye.* Orca, 2007. QP 2008.
Emily turns to vandalism when she learns that everything about her family is a lie, but she stops when she realizes that family can be more than just people related to you.

Hautman, Pete. *Godless.* Simon Pulse, 2005. PPYA 2007 (Religion).
Rebelling against his Catholic father, Jason and his good friend Shin create a new religion that worships the town water tower.

———. *Hole in the Sky.* Simon & Schuster, 2005. PPYA 2006 (What Ails You?).
After an influenza attack either kills or leaves its victims violent and delusional, Ceej and other survivors search the Grand Canyon for a mysterious Hopi portal to another world.

———. *Mr. Was.* Aladdin, 1998. PPYA 1999 (Changing Dimensions).
Escaping from his abusive father, Jack ventures through a closet door in his deceased grandfather's house, travels back in time, and has a chance to change family events.

———. *Stone Cold.* Simon & Schuster, 1998. QP 1999.
Denn begins a lawn care service when his father abandons the family, but he switches careers when he discovers that poker brings in more money.

———. *Sweetblood.* Simon Pulse, 2005. PPYA 2006 (What Ails You?).
Diabetic Lucy is convinced her disease is linked with vampirism, but her teachers only think she is weird and her parents restrict her to the house.

Hawes, Louise. *Rosey in the Present Tense.* Walker, 2001. PPYA 2002 (Relationships).
Romantic Franklin refuses to let go of the girl he loves, until deceased Rosey convinces him she has to move on to her next world.

Hawthorn, Rachel. *The Boyfriend League.* HarperTeen, 2007. PPYA 2008 (Anyone Can Play).
Dana and Bird can't believe their good luck when they read that the local college baseball team needs host families for the summer—what a great opportunity to find a boyfriend!

Hayes, Daniel. *Flyers.* Aladdin, 1998. PPYA 2001 (Humor).
When Gabe and other members of his Gifted and Talented class film a monster movie project at Blood Red Pond, their costumes create confusion among the townspeople.

Hayes, Stormcrow. *Afterlife,* vol. 1. Illustrated by Rob Steen. Tokyopop, 2006. QP 2007.
As the Afterlife decays, Thaddeus leaves his post as guardian to search for the meaning of life and his true love Anabelle.

Headley, Justina Chen. *Nothing but the Truth (and a Few White Lies).* Little, Brown, 2007. PPYA 2008 (What Makes a Family?).
Patty Ho is a "hapa," half Asian and half white, who struggles with her split heritage until she gains some insight into her controlling Taiwanese mother.

Hee-Joon, Son. *PhD: Phantasy Degree,* vols. 1–2. Tokyopop, 2005. QP 2006.
Sang, a young girl masquerading as an old wizard, infiltrates the Demon School Hades to learn how to stop Medosa Guild's killing of potentially threatening students.

Heinlein, Robert. *Starship Troopers.* Ace, 1987. PPYA 2004 (Simply Science Fiction).
Juan Rico endures a grueling boot camp in outer space in preparation for the battle against Earth's biggest enemy, the "bugs," in a science fiction classic.

Henderson, J. A. *Bunker 10.* Harcourt, 2007. QP 2008.
A desire to take a girlfriend on a real date off base leads to time travel, computer simulations, and a destructive explosion at the top-secret Pinewood Military Installation.

Heneghan, James. *Hit Squad.* Orca, 2003. QP 2005.
Popular, beautiful Birgit tires of her high school's acceptance of bullying and orga-nizes a group of like-minded students who help her retaliate.

Henry, April. *Shock Point.* Penguin, 2006. QP 2007.
Sent to a camp for troubled teens by her unscrupulous stepfather, Cassie Streng is determined to escape and expose his unethical medical practices.

Herrera, Juan Felipe. *CrashBoomLove: A Novel in Verse.* University of New Mexico Press, 1999. QP 2001.
Chicano Cesar Garcia is a new student who doesn't fit in and feels isolated until he falls into "crashboomlove."

Hesse, Karen. *Letters from Rifka.* Puffin, 1993. PPYA 2003 (Lock It, Lick It, Click It).
Rifka records her immigration experiences among the verses of a book of Pushkin's poetry, telling her Russian cousin how ringworm almost keeps her out of America.

Hesser, Terry Spencer. *Kissing Doorknobs.* Delacorte, 1998—QP 1999; Laurel-Leaf, 1998—PPYA 2006 (What Ails You?).
Tara's life is filled with strange compulsions, which leave her with no friends, an upset mother, and perplexed therapists until she meets another teen just like her.

Heuston, Kimberley. *The Shakeress.* Puffin, 2004. PPYA 2007 (Religion).
Orphan Naomi and her siblings leave the home of their austere aunt to join a Shaker community, though Naomi continues to search for the right religion for herself.

Hiaasen, Carl. *Flush.* Knopf, 2005. QP 2006.
Outraged by the unsound ecological practices of the floating casino *Coal Queen,* Noah's dad sinks the ship, serves jail time, and divides his family's loyalty.

Hilgartner, Beth. *A Murder for Her Majesty.* Houghton Mifflin, 1992. PPYA 2006 (Books That Don't Make You Blush).
Fleeing from her father's murderers, young Alice settles into the perfect hiding place by disguising herself and joining the Yorkshire Cathedral boys choir.

Hillerman, Tony. *Dance Hall of the Dead.*
Joe Leaphorn and Jim Chee series,
book 2. HarperTrade, 1990. PPYA 2001
(Western).
When two boys disappear, leaving
behind a trail of blood, Navajo policeman
Leaphorn investigates but the Zuni rituals
inhibit his search for the killer.

Hinton, S. E. *The Outsiders.* Puffin, 1997.
PPYA 2006 (Criminal Elements).
In this classic young adult novel, the
greasers fight the wealthy socs, but more
than a life is lost in the rumble that ensues.

Hirano, Kohta. Hellsing series, vols. 1–4.
Dark Horse, 2003–2004. QP 2005.
The secret English organization Hellsing
protects the queen and her countrymen
in this manga series featuring the vampire
Alucard as its most successful monster
hunter.

Ho, Minfong. *The Clay Marble.* Farrar,
Straus, & Giroux, 1993. PPYA 2003
(This Small World).
Forced to flee from their Cambodian
village, Dara and her family settle in a
refugee camp, but shelling separates her
from her family and she is left with only
her friend Jantu.

Hobbs, Valerie. *Letting Go of Bobby James,
or How I Found My Self of Steam.*
Farrar, Straus, & Giroux, 2004. QP 2005.
Abandoned by her abusive newlywed
husband at a gas station in Florida, teen
Jody uses her wits and the last of her cash
to start a new life far from their home in
Texas.

Hobbs, Will. *Jason's Gold.* Morrow, 1999.
QP 2000.
In this novel based on historical fact,
penniless Jason treks to Alaska to join his
brothers in the craze for Klondike gold.

———. *Kokopelli's Flute.* HarperTrophy,
1997. PPYA 1999 (Changing
Dimensions).
When he plays an ancient bone flute
found in some Anasazi ruins, Tep Jones
unleashes mystical powers beyond his
control.

———. *Leaving Protection.* HarperCollins,
2005. PPYA 2006 (Books That Don't
Make You Blush).
Excited to be working on a commercial
trawler fishing off the Alaskan coast,
Robbie puts himself in danger when he
suspects his captain is selling historical
Russian artifacts.

———. *The Maze.* HarperTrophy, 1999.
PPYA 2002 (Relationships).
Rick reports the corruption in his
detention center but then is forced to
flee, winding up in a rocky canyon of
Utah where he and a biologist bring some
criminals to justice.

Hoffman, Kerry Cohen. *Easy.* Simon &
Schuster, 2006. QP 2007.
When her parents divorce and the people
she cares about ignore her, Jessica follows
a dangerous path as she seeks love and
comfort in the arms of men and boys.

Hoffman, Nina Kiriki. *A Fistful of Sky.*
Ace, 2004. PPYA 2008 (Magic in the
Real World).
Gypsum LaZelle has just transitioned to
becoming a witch but is still learning to
control her powers. If she doesn't set a
curse, the power builds inside her and she
becomes ill.

Hoh, Diane. *Titanic: The Long Night.*
Scholastic, 1998. QP 1999.
Elizabeth in first class and Katie in third
both meet the "men of their dreams" on
the ill-fated voyage of the *Titanic*.

Holeman, Linda. *Search of the Moon King's Daughter.* Tundra, 2003. PPYA 2004 (If It Weren't for Them).
When her deaf brother is sold to a chimney sweep in 1830s industrialized England, Emmaline leaves home, works as a scullery maid in London, and searches for him.

Holman, Felice. *Slake's Limbo.* Aladdin, 1986. PPYA 1999 (Different Drummers).
On his own in New York City, Aremis Slake hides in a hole off the subway line with no plans to emerge, but then there is a subway accident.

Holmes, Barbara Ware. *Following Fake Man.* Yearling, 2001. PPYA 2004 (Guess Again).
Homer follows a disguised man who turns out to be a noted artist who knew Homer's father. For the first time, Homer hears about his father's death.

———. *Letters to Julia.* HarperTrophy, 1999. PPYA 2003 (Lock It, Lick It, Click It).
Sending chapters of a book she is writing to editor Julia Jones, Liz never imagines that Julia thinks these stories of her unhappy family are important.

Hoobler, Dorothy and Thomas. *The Ghost in the Tokaido Inn.* Puffin, 1999. PPYA 2004 (Guess Again).
Seikei can never be samurai since his father wasn't one, but it is possible for him to act like one when he discovers the kabuki member who stole a samurai's ruby.

Hooper, Mary. *At the Sign of the Sugared Plum.* Bloomsbury, 2005. PPYA 2006 (What Ails You?).
Candy, herbs, or dried flowers—can anything protect Hannah from the Black Death as it worms its way through the streets of London?

Hoover, H. M. *Winds of Mars.* Viking, 1999. PPYA 2004 (Simply Science Fiction).
Raised on Mars and daughter of its president, Annalyn discovers the tyranny of her father and has a hand in unseating him.

Hopkins, Cathy. Mates, Dates, and . . . series. *Mates, Dates, and Cosmic Kisses; Mates, Dates, and Designer Divas; Mates, Dates, and Inflatable Bras.* Simon Pulse, 2003. QP 2004.
Friends Izzie, Lucy, and Nesta deal with typical teen problems, from boyfriends to underarm waxing, in this humorous series.

———. Truth or Dare series. *The Princess of Pop; Teen Queens and Has-Beens; White Lies and Barefaced Truths.* Simon & Schuster, 2004. QP 2005.
Everything important to eighth-grade girlfriends, whether it is kissing a boy, entering a talent competition, or choosing lip gloss, is explored in these lighthearted titles.

Hopkins, Ellen. *Crank.* Simon Pulse, 2004. QP 2005; PPYA 2005 (Read 'Em and Weep).
On a court-ordered visit to her slimy father, perfect daughter Kristina is introduced to crystal meth, which transforms her into an out-of-control addict.

———. *Glass.* Margaret K. McElderry, 2007. QP 2008.
Certain she has her life together after becoming a mother and giving up meth, Kristina succumbs to the lure of speed when she tries to take off "baby weight."

———. *Impulse.* Margaret K. McElderry, 2007. QP 2008.
Three suicidal teens meet at the Aspen Springs treatment facility, become friends,

and support one another, even after one teen stops taking the prescribed medicine.

Horowitz, Anthony. *Eagle Strike.* An Alex Rider Adventure. Philomel, 2004. QP 2005.
When his girlfriend Sabina's journalist father is targeted by the assassin Yassen Gregorovich, Alex uses all his tricks to halt the madman.

————. *Point Blank.* An Alex Rider Adventure. Philomel, 2002. QP 2003.
Recruited by M16 to investigate some mysterious deaths, Alex is sent to a boarding school where a crazed scientist intends to replace the students with clones.

————. *Raven's Gate.* Gatekeepers series, book 1. Scholastic, 2005—QP 2006; Scholastic, 2006—PPYA 2008 (Magic in the Real World).
Sentenced to a probationary period helping out on a farm, Matt learns he is a Gatekeeper for Raven's Gate, a portal to evil.

————. *Scorpia.* An Alex Rider Adventure. Philomel, 2005. QP 2006.
The terrorist organization Scorpia almost succeeds in luring Alex away from M16, until he hears of its plan to kill thousands of English children.

————. *Skeleton Key.* An Alex Rider Adventure. Philomel, 2003. QP 2004.
Learning of General Sarov's plan to set off a nuclear attack and use the chaos to seize control of Russia, Alex befriends Sarov and employs all his gadgets to stop him.

————. *Stormbreaker.* An Alex Rider Adventure. Philomel, 2001—QP 2002; Penguin, 2002—PPYA 2003 (I've Got a Secret).
After Uncle Ian is killed, M16 asks Alex to assume Ian's work in investigating an unscrupulous businessman's offer of computers for every secondary school in England.

Hosler, Jay. *Clan Apis.* Active Synapse, 2000. PPYA 2002 (Graphic Novels).
Scientifically accurate black-and-white drawings tell of Nyuki the bee and his hive mates as they migrate, endure a woodpecker attack, and hibernate through the winter.

Howe, James, ed. *The Color of Absence: 12 Stories about Loss and Hope.* Simon Pulse, 2003. PPYA 2005 (Read 'Em and Weep).
A dozen portrayals of sadness reveal the rainbow that often follows gloomy times in these stories by noted YA authors.

————. *The Misfits.* Aladdin, 2003. PPYA 2005 (Own Your Freak).
Tired of being called names, four friends run losing campaigns for offices at their school, which calls attention to the harassment of demeaning name-calling.

Howe, Norma. *The Adventures of Blue Avenger.* HarperTempest, 2000. PPYA 2001 (Humor).
For years Blue draws a cartoon superhero, but suddenly he decides to become that hero, calls himself Blue Avenger, and rescues underdogs.

Hrdlitschka, Shelley. *Dancing Naked.* Orca, 2002. QP 2003; PPYA 2005 (Read 'Em and Weep).
Kia's family supports her decision to keep her baby after her first sexual experience leads to pregnancy and the baby's father wants her to obtain a secret abortion.

————. *Kat's Fall.* Orca, 2004. QP 2005.
Taking responsibility for raising his deaf, epileptic sister Kat while their mother

is in prison, Darcy worries he may have been responsible for his mother's sentence.

Hughes, Monica, ed. *What If . . . ? Amazing Stories.* Tundra, 1998. PPYA 2000 (Short Takes).
Talented Canadian writers fill this collection with short stories of science fiction, fantasy, and poetry, all written to reply to the question "What if?"

Hughes, Pat. *Open Ice.* Laurel-Leaf, 2007. PPYA 2008 (Anyone Can Play).
One too many concussions results in Nick being told it is too dangerous for him to ever again play ice hockey, but he is not sure how to adjust to a life without his favorite sport.

Hunter, Mollie. *The King's Swift Rider: A Novel on Robert the Bruce.* HarperTeen, 2000. PPYA 2002 (War).
Supporting Robert the Bruce after he escapes from the English, Martin is the "king's swift rider," acting as spy and courier in Scotland's fight for independence.

Huntington, Geoffrey. *Sorcerers of the Nightwing.* Ravenscliff series, book 1. Regan, 2003. PPYA 2005 (All Kinds of Creepy).
After his father dies, Devon is sent to live at Ravenscliff, where he learns he is a sorcerer, part of the Nightwing group that defends against the evil demons of the world.

Hurwin, Davida. *A Time for Dancing.* Puffin, 1997. PPYA 2005 (Read 'Em and Weep).
Once passionate about dancing, best friends Juliana and Samantha must now learn to say good-bye when one is diagnosed with advanced lymphoma.

Huth, Angela. *Land Girls: A Spirited Novel of Love and Friendship.* St. Martin's, 1998. PPYA 2002 (War).
With British men fighting during World War II, the Women's Land Army is formed and three women work on a Dorset farm, share an attic bedroom, and begin a lifelong friendship.

Hyde, Dayton O. *The Major, the Poacher and the Wonderful One-Trout River.* Boyds Mills, 1998. PPYA 1999 (Good Sports).
A 14-year-old poacher outwits a fanatical fly fisherman who is attempting to land a prize-winning trout.

Irwin, Jan. *Vogelein.* Clockwork Faerie series, book 1. Fiery Studios, 2003. PPYA 2005 (Gateway to Faerie).
Vogelein, a mechanical fairy constructed in the 17th century, must be wound daily; when her guardian dies, she has only five hours to find a replacement in this graphic novel.

Jacobs, Deborah Lynn. *Choices.* Roaring Brook, 2007. QP 2008.
After the accidental death of her brother, Kathleen enters alternate worlds where she can be Kay, Kathy, or Kate, but ultimately she must return to reality.

Jacobson, Jennifer Richard. *Stained.* Simon Pulse, 2006. PPYA 2007 (Religion).
Jocelyn's boyfriend is Benny, her dear friend and neighbor is Gabe, and the local priest is Father Warren. Gabe is missing, and she is sure the three males are linked somehow.

James, Mary. *Shoebag.* Scholastic, 1992. PPYA 1999 (Changing Dimensions).
In a reversal of Kafka's *Metamorphosis,* a happy cockroach named Shoebag is suddenly changed into a human boy.

Jemas, Bill. *Origin: The True Story of Wolverine.* Marvel Comics, 2002. QP 2003.
An orphan traveling with his childhood nanny, Wolverine tries to control his superhuman strength, but it is difficult when his past returns to complicate his life.

Jenkins, A. M. *Beating Heart: A Ghost Story.* HarperCollins, 2006. QP 2007.
Evan and his family renovate a Victorian house, which awakens Cora's ghost, who proceeds to fall in love with Evan.

——. *Breaking Boxes.* Laurel-Leaf, 2000. PPYA 2002 (Relationships).
Because Charlie and Brandon are friends who do everything together, Charlie is shocked when Brandon betrays his trust about his gay older brother.

Jett, Sarah. *Night of the Pompon.* Pocket, 2000. QP 2001.
Selected as school mascot by the head cheerleader, Jendra worships a pompon, which is connected to several missing persons including the principal.

Jimenez, Francisco. *The Circuit: Stories from the Life of a Migrant Child.* University of New Mexico Press, 1997. PPYA 2000 (Short Takes).
Now a professor, the author recounts episodes from his youth as he and his parents entered America illegally and then followed the grueling circuit of the migrant workers.

Johansen, Iris. *And Then You Die.* Bantam, 1998. PPYA 2000 (Page Turners).
When Bess and her sister arrive in Tenajo, Mexico, for a travel photography shoot, all the occupants of the quaint little town are dead.

Johns, Geoff. *A Kid's Game.* Teen Titans series, book 1. DC Comics, 2004. QP 2005.
This collection of the first seven issues of *Teen Titans* features teen superheroes Robin, Superboy, Wonder Girl, and Impulse as they are trained by Cyborg to use their powers.

Johnson, Angela. *The First Part Last.* Simon & Schuster, 2003—QP 2004; Simon Pulse, 2004—PPYA 2008 (What Makes a Family).
In this 2004 Printz Award winner and prequel to *Heaven,* Bobby learns to be a single father to Feather after her mother suffers brain damage.

——. *Heaven.* Simon & Schuster, 2000. PPYA 2003 (I've Got a Secret).
Angry at first to discover that her aunt and uncle aren't her real mother and father, Marley thinks about all the pluses in her life and realizes that living in Heaven is heaven.

——. *Toning the Sweep.* Scholastic, 1994. PPYA 2002 (Relationships).
Carrying on a family tradition, a mother and her daughter "tone the sweep" for their father and grandfather, hitting a plow with a hammer to ring the souls up to heaven.

Johnson, Kathleen Jeffrie. *Parallel Universe of Liars.* Roaring Brook, 2002. QP 2003.
Overweight, insecure Robin feels as though she lives in two parallel universes, the normal high school one and the abnormal one of lies, cheating, and sex.

Johnson, Maureen. *The Bermudez Triangle.* Razorbill, 2005. PPYA 2006 (GLBTQ).
Nina, Mel, and Avery are best friends, but when two of them fall in love, their friendship triangle is threatened.

———. *Devilish.* Razorbill, 2007. PPYA 2008 (Magic in the Real World). Excited that Lanalee has selected her as a "big sister," Ally doesn't realize that Lanalee is a demon and has just gained Ally's soul.

Johnson, Scott. *Safe at Second.* Philomel, 1999. QP 2000. Todd's dream of being a star pitcher is crushed when a ball strikes his eye during a game and blinds him.

Johnston, Jeffrey W. *Fragments.* Simon Pulse, 2006. QP 2008. Chase can't remember what led up to the automobile crash that killed four people, including his ex-girlfriend, partly because he is suppressing terrible secrets.

Jones, Diana Wynne. *Deep Secret.* Starscape, 2002. PPYA 2008 (Magic in the Real World). As a junior Magic who helps keep order in the Multiverse, when Rupert needs to replace his deceased mentor, he calls all the candidates to a sci-fi convention.

———. *Fire and Hemlock.* HarperTrophy, 2002. PPYA 2005 (Gateway to Faerie). Preparing for college, Polly thinks over her friendship with a musician and wonders if he was real or only a fantasy.

———. *Howl's Moving Castle.* Eos, 2001. PPYA 2003 (Flights of Fantasy). Since a curse turned her into an old woman, Sophia lives with a womanizing wizard named Howl aboard a castle that won't stay in one place.

Jones, Patrick. *Things Change.* Walker, 2004. QP 2005. By the time straight-A student Johanna realizes her charming boyfriend is abusive and controlling, she doesn't know where or who to ask for help in this first novel.

Jordan, Robert. *The Eye of the World.* The Wheel of Time series, book 1. Tor, 1990. PPYA 2003 (Flights of Fantasy). This first of an epic series introduces three frightened boys—Rand, Matrim, and Perrin—who are at a loss about who to trust as ancient forces of evil come ever closer.

Joseph, Lynn. *The Color of My Words.* HarperTrophy, 2001. PPYA 2003 (This Small World). Anna quickly learns the power of words when an article she writes condemning the government's plan to seize her village's land stirs up a revolt.

Juwell and Precious. *The Absolute Truth.* Platinum Teen series, book 2. Precioustymes Entertainment, 2005. QP 2007. Best friends Dymond, Kera, and Porsha worry when Porsha's boyfriend Abdul, a great student and basketball player, decides he needs to "tell all."

Kannagi, Satoru, and Hotaru Odagiri. *Only the Ring Finger Knows.* Digital Manga, 2004. PPYA 2006 (GLBTQ). Wearing matching rings is popular for couples in Waturu's school. Though single, he wears a ring, too, but is dismayed to discover that his ring matches one worn by another boy.

Kantor, Melissa. *If I Have a Wicked Stepmother, Where's My Prince?* Hyperion, 2007. PPYA 2008 (What Makes a Family?). In a contemporary Cinderella tale, Lucy thinks shes has found her prince when basketball star Connor dates her, but it is really rude, artistic Sam she enjoys being with.

Karr, Kathleen. *The Boxer.* Farrar, Straus, & Giroux, 2004. PPYA 2006 (Books That Don't Make You Blush).

Trying to earn extra money for his family, Johnny is arrested for fighting illegally, but six months in prison provides the training for him to become a professional boxer.

———. *The Great Turkey Walk*. Sunburst, 2000. PPYA 2001 (Western).
Out to make a profit on 1,000 turkeys he buys for 25 cents apiece and plans to sell in Denver for $5 each, Shane must figure out how to get the flock from Missouri to Denver.

Kass, Pnina Moed. *Real Time*. Graphia, 2006. PPYA 2007 (Religion).
The lives of a group of young and old people are forever fixed in tragedy when they meet a religious fanatic on a Jerusalem highway.

Kaye, Marilyn. *Amy, Number Seven*. Replica series. Bantam, 1998. QP 1999.
Learning she is the only survivor of a government experiment that created 13 clones, Amy now understands her enhanced mental and physical abilities.

———. *The Vanishing*. Last on Earth series, book 1. Avon, 1998. QP 1999.
Emerging from their basement geometry class, 25 seniors are met with silence as they look around and realize everything is deserted, from cars to stores, schools, and homes.

Kazumi, Maki. *Desire*. Digital Manga, 2004. PPYA 2008 (Sex Is . . .).
When Toru is caught in a love triangle with his two best friends, his plan to test Ryoji's love works so well that Kashiwazaki doesn't want to let Toru out of his embrace.

Kehret, Peg. *I'm Not Who You Think I Am*. Dutton, 1999. QP 2000.
With her parents out of town, Ginger is besieged by a mentally ill woman who claims to be her mother.

Keillor, Garrison. *Sandy Bottom Orchestra*. Hyperion, 1998. PPYA 2004 (On That Note).
Violinist Rachel studies at Interlochen for the summer, returns home, and earns a spot in her father's community orchestra.

Kemp, Kristen. *I Will Survive*. Push, 2002. QP 2003.
Her mother is having an affair, her sister is angry, and her boyfriend is cheating on her. Ellen decides that revenge may be the only solution to her problems.

Kennedy, Pagan. *The Exes*. Simon & Schuster, 1999. PPYA 2004 (On That Note).
In four chapters, the band members of the Exes, all ex-somethings of one another, reveal their take on music, touring, and fame in the indie music world.

Kerr, M. E. *Gentlehands*. HarperCollins, 1990. PPYA 2003 (I've Got a Secret).
It's hard for Buddy to believe that his favorite grandfather is also the Nazi war criminal known as "Gentlehands."

Kidd, Sue Monk. *The Secret Life of Bees*. Penguin, 2005. PPYA 2008 (What Makes a Family?).
Escaping her abusive father, Lily and the family cook move in with the Boatright sisters, who own the Black Madonna Honey Company, a possible link to Lily's mother.

Kightlinger, Laura. *Quick Shots of False Hope: A Rejection Collection*. Avon, 1999. PPYA 2000 (Short Takes).
Based on the author's life, these fictional stories relate the angst of being booed out of a school talent show and sharing her home with a live-in foreign exchange student.

Kimmel, Eric A. *Sword of the Samurai: Adventure Stories from Japan.* Harcourt Brace, 1999. QP 2000.

In medieval times in Japan, the knights were called samurai and their adventurous exploits were bound by strict tradition and culture, as shown in these 11 tales.

Kindl, Patrice. *Goose Chase.* Puffin, 2002. PPYA 2005 (Gateway to Faerie).

Goose girl Alexandria helps an old hag and in turn becomes beautiful, but then her loyal geese must try to save her from the king and the prince, who vie for her hand.

———. *Owl in Love.* Puffin, 1994. PPYA 1999 (Changing Dimensions).

By day a high school student, at night Owl shape-shifts into barn owl form and perches on a tree so she can watch her science teacher, on whom she has a healthy crush.

———. *Woman in the Wall.* Puffin, 1998. PPYA 1999 (Different Drummers).

For seven years shy Anna lives happily in a self-constructed lair hidden inside her family's rambling house, until she receives a mysterious love letter from Francis.

King, Stephen. *Carrie.* Signet, 1975. PPYA 1999 (Different Drummers).

Continually bullied and harassed in high school, Carrie exacts payback on prom night.

———. *It.* Signet, 1987. PPYA 2005 (All Kinds of Creepy).

Twenty-seven years earlier, seven teens discovered the evil source of a series of murders. Now another set of murders draws them back to the same town in Maine.

———. *Rose Madder.* Signet, 1996. PPYA 2000 (Page Turners).

After 14 years of an abusive marriage, Rose Daniels leaves her policeman husband, only to discover that psychopathic, obsessive Norman is following her.

———. *The Stand.* Random House, 1980. PPYA 2006 (What Ails You?).

A flu like no other arrives, and this supervirus kills 99 percent of the world's population, with the remnants left in two opposing forces.

Kingsolver, Barbara. *The Bean Trees.* HarperTorch, 1998. PPYA 2008 (What Makes a Family?).

Rather than end up "barefoot and pregnant," Taylor heads west, but when an abused child is left on the front seat of her VW she raises little Turtle in the Arizona desert.

Kinsella, W. P. *Shoeless Joe.* Ballantine, 1996. PPYA 1999 (Good Sports).

Fantasy, time travel, and one man's dream combine to create the ultimate baseball game.

Kirkman, Robert. *Invincible.* The Ultimate Collection series, vol. 1. Image Comics, 2005. QP 2006.

High school student and son of Omni-Man, Mark develops his superpowers in the first 13 issues of Kirkman's comic, which are collected in this initial volume.

Kishiro, Yukito. *Rusty Angel.* Battle Angel Alita series, vol. 1. VIZ, 1994. PPYA 2004 (Simply Science Fiction).

Doc Ido finds a badly damaged cyborg head in a trash heap, reconstructs the body, names her Alita, and discovers that her body remembers cyborg fighting techniques.

Klass, David. *Danger Zone.* Scholastic, 1998. PPYA 1999 (Good Sports).

A small-town basketball player, white Jimmy has to prove himself not only to his inner-city teammates but also to international fans at a tournament in Italy.

————. *Dark Angel.* Farrar, Straus, & Giroux, 2005. QP 2006.
When Jeff's older brother is released on a technicality from a prison sentence for murder, he returns home and Jeff's nearly perfect life becomes imperfect.

————. *You Don't Know Me.* HarperTempest, 2002. PPYA 2005 (Read 'Em and Weep).
John thinks that no one knows about the abuse he receives from his "almost stepfather," until he is severely beaten and his band teacher and community step forward to help him.

Klause, Annette Curtis. *Blood and Chocolate.* Laurel-Leaf, 1999. PPYA 2008 (Sex Is . . .); PPYA 2000 (Romance).
Teen werewolf Vivian falls in love with human Aiden, a quiet comfort after the rancorous, squabbling members of her pack, but should she show her wolf side to him?

————. *The Silver Kiss.* Laurel-Leaf, 1992. PPYA 1999 (Changing Dimensions).
When Simon captures Zoe's heart, she is not disturbed by the fact he is a 300-year-old vampire, for it is obvious he loves her.

Klise, Kate. *Trial by Journal.* Illustrated by M. Sarah Klise. HarperTrophy, 2002. PPYA 2003 (Lock It, Lick It, Click It).
When her teacher hears that Lily is the youngest person ever selected for jury duty, she requires her to keep a journal of her duties.

Kluger, Steve. *Last Days of Summer.* HarperCollins, 1999. PPYA 2003 (Lock It, Lick It, Click It).
Letters, news clippings, and diary entries

from the 1940s record the summer Joey set up a pen-pal acquaintance with Charlie Banks, a rookie New York Giants third baseman.

Knowles, Jo. *Lessons from a Dead Girl.* Candlewick, 2007. QP 2008.
When Leah dies, Laine is thankful that her former friend's blackmail also ends, a blackmail that began when the two experimented sexually.

Koertge, Ron. *The Brimstone Journals.* Candlewick, 2001. QP 2002; PPYA 2006 (Criminal Elements).
Short poems reveal the problems 15 students experience at Branston High School. Though Boyd is angriest of all, his plans are leaked before he can use his arsenal.

————. *Confess-o-Rama.* Laurel-Leaf, 1998. PPYA 2001 (Humor).
Tony's thoughts of keeping a low profile at his new school are spoiled when he wears an artichoke bra to call attention to a campaign against boys eyeballing girls' chests.

————. *Stoner and Spaz.* Candlewick, 2002—QP 2003; Candlewick, 2004—PPYA 2005 (Own Your Freak).
Embarrassed because of his cerebral palsy, reclusive, solitary Ben has a lifestyle change when befriended by tattooed, usually stoned Colleen.

————. *Strays.* Candlewick, 2007. QP 2008.
As Ted develops social skills while living in a foster home, he gradually loses his ability to converse with animals.

Koja, Kathe. *Buddha Boy.* Puffin, 2004. PPYA 2007 (Religion).
Justin's attempt to remain unnoticed fails when his partner for an economics project

is Jinsen, target of the school bullies for trying to live by Buddhist principles.

———. *Straydog*. Puffin, 2004. PPYA 2007 (Get Creative).
Rachel has two loves—writing and volunteering at an animal shelter—but her attachment to a feral collie proves her undoing.

Koller, Jackie French. *A Place to Call Home*. Simon Pulse, 1997. PPYA 2002 (Relationships).
Biracial Anna finally meets her white mother's family, but when she realizes how racist they are she gladly returns to her home in Connecticut.

Konigsburg, E. L. *Silent to the Bone*. Simon & Schuster, 2002. PPYA 2003 (I've Got a Secret).
Bran won't talk about the accident that hurt his sister, so his friend Connor devises flash cards to break his silence and prove his innocence.

Konomi, Takeshi. *Prince of Tennis*. Prince of Tennis series, vol. 1. VIZ, 2004. PPYA 2008 (Anyone Can Play).
Though an outstanding tennis player, seventh-grader Ryoma Echizen takes a big risk when he tries out for his school's tennis team, which is populated with upperclassmen.

Koontz, Dean. *Fear Nothing*. Bantam, 1998. PPYA 1999 (Different Drummers).
Because he has a rare genetic disorder, all of Chris's investigation into a government conspiracy involving rhesus monkeys occurs at night.

———. *Watchers*. Berkley, 1986. PPYA 2005 (All Kinds of Creepy).
Two animals that have been altered through genetic experimentation escape from their lab. One is an intelligent, lovable golden retriever and the other is a murderous baboon.

Korman, Gordon. *Abduction*. Kidnapped series, book 1. Scholastic, 2006. QP 2007.
After his wrongly convicted parents are finally released from prison, Aiden's life changes again when his sister Meg is kidnapped while walking home from school.

———. *Born to Rock*. Hyperion, 2006. QP 2007.
Needing money for college, Leo becomes a roadie and follows punk band Purge, hoping to elicit financial help from his biological father, Purge's lead singer King Maggot.

———. *The Chicken Doesn't Skate*. Scholastic, 1998. PPYA 2001 (Humor).
Once part of a science fair project, a formerly doomed chicken is resurrected to become the mascot for the school hockey team.

———. *Losing Joe's Place*. Scholastic, 1993. PPYA 2001 (Humor).
When older brother Joe lets Jason and his friends sublet his city apartment while he is in Europe, who knew they would drive the landlord crazy?

———. *No More Dead Dogs*. Hyperion, 2000. PPYA 2007 (What's So Funny?).
Tired of the dogs always dying in every book he reads, Wallace says so in his book report but then is made to rewrite the report while serving detention.

———. *Son of the Mob*. Hyperion, 2002—QP 2003; Hyperion, 2004—PPYA 2005 (Own Your Freak).
Son of a crime boss, Vince hides the family business when he falls for Kendra Bightly, daughter of the FBI agent who has chased his father for two years.

———. *Son of the Mob: Hollywood Hustle.* Hyperion, 2004. PPYA 2007 (What's So Funny?).
Vince Luca thinks he has escaped his mob family when he heads cross-country for college, but soon his "uncles" and brother show up, bringing trouble along with Mom's rigatoni.

———. *Toilet Paper Tigers.* Scholastic Apple, 1993. PPYA 1999 (Good Sports).
Embarrassed by his team's toilet paper logo and klutzy players, Corey is astounded when his coach's bossy granddaughter transforms his loser teammates into winners.

Koss, Amy Goldman. *The Girls.* Dial, 2000. QP 2001.
The thoughts of five girls are shared after their clique leader decides that one of the five doesn't belong and "the girls" are reduced to four.

Krovatin, Christopher. *Heavy Metal and You.* Push, 2005. QP 2006.
Used to drinking, smoking, and listening to heavy metal music, Sam changes when he dates "straightedge" Melissa but wonders if the new Sam is just an act.

Kudo, Kazuya. *Mai the Psychic Girl.* Mai the Psychic Girl series, book 1. Illustrated by Ryoichi Ikegami. VIZ, 1996. PPYA 2002 (Graphic Novels).
Inheriting her mother's psychic powers, Mai reluctantly accepts her own destiny as protector of the Earth.

Kunkel, Mike. *The Inheritance.* Herobear and the Kid series, vol. 1. Astonish Comics, 2003. PPYA 2004 (If It Weren't for Them).
When his grandfather dies, a young child inherits a beat-up, stuffed bear that comes magically to life as a ten-foot-tall superhero, the fulfillment of every little boy's dream.

Kyi, Tanya Lloyd. *Truth.* Orca, 2003. QP 2004; PPYA 2006 (Criminal Elements).
After a huge party attended by all her classmates, Jen learns of the murder of a local banker and investigates her friends for the school's television news.

Lackey, Mercedes. *Magic's Pawn.* Last Herald Mage trilogy, book 1. DAW, 1994. PPYA 2006 (GLBTQ).
When Vanyel's lover is killed, he vows to train as a bard rather than a warrior and embarks on his path to becoming a legendary Herald-Mage of Valdemar.

———. *The Oathbound.* Vows and Honor series, book 1. DAW, 1988. PPYA 2003 (Flights of Fantasy).
Swordswoman Tarma and sorceress Kathry join forces as mercenaries in the land of Valdemar, confronting demons who appear in human and not-so-human guise.

Lackey, Mercedes, and Ellen Guon. *Bedlam's Bard.* Baen, 2006. PPYA 2008 (Magic in the Real World).
Singing a doleful song after being jilted, Eric inadvertently releases the elf Korendil from years of imprisonment.

LaHaye, Tim, and Jerry Jenkins. *Left Behind: A Graphic Novel of Earth's Last Days.* Tyndale, 2002. QP 2003.
The illustrated version of the popular book of the same name tells of the seven dark years after Christ returns to Earth for the faithful and leaves behind the unfaithful.

L'Amour, Louis. *The Daybreakers.* The Sacketts series, book 5. Bantam, 1998. PPYA 2001 (Western).
After Tyrel kills a man in Tennessee, he and his brother Orrin head for the West, where they help maintain law and order, one with a badge and one without.

Lane, Dakota. *Johnny Voodoo.* Laurel-Leaf, 1997. PPYA 2000 (Romance).
A new student in a Louisiana bayou town, Deirdre is miserable until she meets high school dropout Johnny Vouchamps and falls in love for the first time.

———. *The Secret Life of It Girls.* Simon & Schuster, 2007. QP 2008.
This assortment of short stories from the "It Girls" relies on IM, diaries, and journals as they share anxieties and material concerns.

Lanier, Virginia. *Blind Bloodhound Justice.* HarperCollins, 1999. PPYA 2000 (Page Turners).
Jo Beth Sidden and her bloodhounds take on a seemingly dead trail of a 30-year-old murder and kidnapping that leads them into the Okefenokee Swamp of Georgia.

Larbalestier, Justine. *Magic or Madness.* Razorbill, 2006. PPYA 2008 (Magic in the Real World).
Rebelling against her grandmother's magical powers, Reason finally admits she has powers, too, when she unlocks a magic door and time-travels to New York City.

Larson, Gary. *There's a Hair in My Dirt: A Worm's Story.* HarperCollins, 1998—QP 1999; HarperCollins, 1999—PPYA 2001 (Humor).
A young worm receives a lesson in life and ecology from his wise worm father.

Lasky, Kathryn. *Alice Rose and Sam.* Hyperion, 1999. PPYA 2001 (Western).
While saving money to attend an eastern ladies' seminary, Alice teams up with news reporter Samuel Clemens to solve a murder in Virginia City, Nevada.

———. *Star Split.* Hyperion, 2001. PPYA 2004 (Simply Science Fiction).
When Darci meets her clone, she worries they'll both be incinerated because it is a crime to have a clone in 31st-century Bio Union.

Lassiter, Rhiannon. *Hex.* Archway, 2001. PPYA 2004 (Simply Science Fiction).
Raven, a computer hacker with a mutant mind, evades a powerful government agency seeking to destroy her and others with the powerful Hex gene, in 24th-century London.

Lawrence, Iain. *The Smugglers.* Delacorte, 1999. QP 2000.
Aboard his father's new ship as a company representative, John sails with a nefarious crew who delight in smuggling and will kill anyone who opposes them.

———. *The Wreckers.* Delacorte, 1998. QP 1999.
Fourteen-year-old John Spencer's 1799 sea voyage with his father ends in disaster when their ship wrecks on the Cornwall coast.

Laxalt, Robert. *Dust Devils.* University of Nevada Press, 1997. PPYA 2001 (Western).
A rodeo rider, aided by his Paiute friend, pursues the men who rustled his prize Arabian horse.

Lee, Lela. *Angry Little Girls.* Abrams, 2005. QP 2006.
With what began as an occasional cartoon starring Kim, the angry Asian girl, author Lee expands the comic to include girls of many races who offer edgy but true comments on friendship.

———. *Still Angry Little Girls.* Abrams, 2006. QP 2007.
In this sequel to the internationally popular *Angry Little Girls,* the girls are back as angry, engaging, and adorable as ever.

Lee, Marie G. *Necessary Roughness.* HarperTrophy, 1998. PPYA 2005 (Read 'Em and Weep).
Trying to acclimate to his school's culture, Korean American Chan plays football, though he dislikes his coach's motto of "necessary roughness."

Lee, Tanith. *Wolf Tower.* The Claidi Journals series, vol. 1. Puffin, 2001. PPYA 2003 (Lock It, Lick It, Click It).
Escaping from one harsh mistress, Claidi is dismayed when she and Naiman arrive at his town and discover she is supposed to be successor to his cruel grandmother.

LeGuin, Ursula K. *The Wind's Twelve Quarters: Seventeen Stories of Fantastic Adventure.* HarperPrism, 1991. PPYA 2000 (Short Takes).
This roundup of LeGuin's work features a foreword by the author, previously published short stories, and some that were later expanded into novels.

———. *A Wizard of Earthsea.* The Earthsea Cycle, book 1. Bantam, 2004. PPYA 2003 (Flights of Fantasy).
Ged/Sparrowhawk casts a spell to call up a spirit from the dead but never thinks the spirit will attack and leave him near death.

Lenhard, Elizabeth. *It's a Purl Thing.* Chicks with Sticks series, vol. 1. Puffin, 2006. PPYA 2007 (Get Creative).
Teens Scottie, Amanda, Bella, and Tay meet at KnitWit, where a shared love of knitting brings them together in other ways.

Lerangis, Peter. *Last Stop.* Watchers series, book 1. Scholastic, 1998. QP 1999.
Six months after his father disappears, David realizes that he still exists, but in a parallel world. To enter that world, David will have to join the Watchers.

Lester, Julius. *When Dad Killed Mom.* Harcourt, 2001. QP 2002.
Grief-stricken over their mother's murder, Jenna and Jeremy read their mother's diary, which reveals their father's affairs with his students.

Letts, Billie. *Where the Heart Is.* Warner, 1998. PPYA 2002 (Relationships).
Pregnant Novalee Nation flees her Tennessee trailer park and gives birth in a Wal-Mart in Oklahoma, surrounded by townspeople who rush to help her.

Levine, Gail Carson. *Ella Enchanted.* HarperTrophy, 1998. PPYA 2000 (Romance).
In this retelling of *Cinderella,* Ella meets Prince Charmant but won't marry him for fear her "gift" of obedience will endanger his kingdom.

Levithan, David. *Boy Meets Boy.* Knopf, 2003—QP 2004; Knopf, 2005—PPYA 2006 (GLBTQ).
This quirky first novel features teens Noah and Paul, who fall in love in a town where homophobia is nonexistent and the Boy Scouts are known as the Joy Scouts.

Levy, Marilyn. *Run for Your Life.* Putnam, 1997. PPYA 2002 (Tales of the Cities).
Running track for the first time helps Kisha escape the escalating division between her parents and becomes her solace when her father shoots her mother.

Limb, Sue. *Girl, 15, Charming but Insane.* Delacorte, 2005. PPYA 2007 (What's So Funny?).
Resigned to the fact that her friend Flora is more attractive than she is, Jess is also a failure at using her dry wit to attract boys.

Lipsyte, Robert. *The Contender.* HarperTeen, 1987. PPYA 1999 (Good Sports).

A high school dropout, Alfred learns from his boxing lessons that in life, as in boxing, being a contender is more important than being a winner.

————. *Raiders Night.* HarperTeen, 2007. PPYA 2008 (Anyone Can Play).
Caught in the midst of a sex and steroid use scandal at training camp, star football player Matt Rydek is afraid talking to the authorities will ruin his college chances.

Little, Jason. *Shutterbug Follies.* Doubleday, 2002. QP 2004.
When photo lab technician Bee notices a shot of a naked female corpse, she senses a possible murder and tails the photographer but is quickly outwitted.

Littman, Sarah Darer. *Confessions of a Closet Catholic.* Puffin, 2006. PPYA 2007 (Religion).
Wanting to be like her best friend, Justine gives up being Jewish for Lent, but when her beloved grandmother dies she fears her Lenten action caused the death.

Lockhart, E. *The Boyfriend List: 15 Guys, 11 Shrink Appointments, 4 Ceramic Frogs and Me, Ruby Oliver.* Delacorte, 2005. QP 2006.
After losing her best friends and boyfriend and now having no lunch companions, 15-year-old Ruby meets with her shrink Dr. Z to determine what causes her panic attacks.

————. *Fly on the Wall: How One Girl Saw Everything.* Delacorte, 2007. PPYA 2008 (Sex Is . . .).
Feeling like a misfit in the Manhattan School for the Arts, Gretchen dreams of being a fly on the wall in the boy's locker room, and suddenly she is buzzing around naked bodies.

Loeb, Jeph. *The Long Halloween.* Batman series. Illustrated by Tim Sale. DC Comics, 1999. PPYA 2002 (Graphic Novels).
Teaming up with the police and district attorney, Batman hunts for the serial killer Holiday before the month of October is up.

————. *Public Enemies.* Superman Batman series, vol. 1. DC Comics, 2004. QP 2006.
When evil Lex Luthor becomes U.S. president, he accuses Superman of a vile deed, which unites Batman and Superman to end Luthor's corrupt political career.

Logue, Mary. *Dancing with an Alien.* HarperCollins, 2000. QP 2001.
Two opposites meet when Tonia rescues nonswimmer Branko and falls in love with him.

Lott, Bret. *The Hunt Club.* Villard, 1998. QP 1999.
Huger's uncle owns 2,200 acres of hunting land, but some people will take any measure to get their hands on that land, including kidnapping Unc, Huger, and his mother.

Lowachee, Karin. *Warchild.* Aspect, 2002. PPYA 2004 (Simply Science Fiction).
When his family and their spaceship are destroyed, Jos is captured and trained by aliens to spy against humans, which leaves him conflicted.

Lowell, Pamela. *Returnable Girl.* Marshall Cavendish, 2006. QP 2007.
Abandoned by her drug-addicted mother, Ronnie bounces from one foster home to another. Now in a perfect home, she still dreams of living with her mother and brother.

Lubar, David. *Dunk.* Clarion, 2002. PPYA 2006 (Books That Don't Make You Blush).

Chad learns there is more to humor than being funny the summer he and Bozo the Clown become friends on the Jersey shore.

———. *Hidden Talents.* Tor, 1999—QP 2000; Starscape, 1999—PPYA 2005 (Own Your Freak).
Kicked out of several boarding schools, Martin's newest roommates display amazing powers of telekinesis and precognition, which help them oppose a ring of bullies.

———. *True Talents.* Tor, 2007. QP 2008.
On break from school, Martin and the rest of the talents respond to save Trashie when he is imprisoned in a research facility.

Lupica, Mike. *Heat.* Puffin, 2006. PPYA 2008 (Anyone Can Play).
An outstanding pitcher, Michael wants a shot at the Little League World Series, but he has no way to prove he is 12 years old because his birth certificate is in his native Cuba.

Lynch, Chris. *Iceman.* HarperTeen, 1995. PPYA 1999 (Good Sports).
Called the "Iceman" because of his cold ruthlessness when he plays ice hockey, Eric can begin to grow up only when he plays cleanly.

Lynch, Clam. *Ruby Gloom's Keys to Happiness.* Illustrated by Martin Hsu. Abrams, 2004. QP 2005.
Originally a best-selling accessory logo for goth teens and tweens, red-haired Ruby Gloom now shares her "little life lessons," including "misery loves company."

Lynn, Erin. *Demon Envy.* Berkley, 2007. QP 2008.
Accidentally dropping her acne lotion down the shower drain changes Kenzie's life when her lotion opens a portal and a demon named Levi appears in her shower.

Lynn, Tracy. *Snow.* Simon Pulse, 2003. PPYA 2005 (Gateway to Faerie).
Running away from her sinister step-mother, who wishes to use her heart to produce a male heir, Jessica seeks shelter with half-human creatures in a retelling of *Snow White.*

Lyons, Mary E. *Letters from a Slave Girl: The Story of Harriet Jacobs.* Simon Pulse, 1996. PPYA 2003 (Lock It, Lick It, Click It).
When her master Dr. Norcum makes sexual advances, Harriet runs away and hides for seven years in her grandmother's cramped storeroom; novel based on historical fact.

Mac, Carrie. *Charmed.* Orca, 2004. QP 2006.
Though Izzy dislikes her mother's boyfriend, she moves in with them anyway and becomes an unwilling partner in a dangerous prostitution ring.

———. *Crush.* Orca, 2006. QP 2007.
Arriving in New York City to stay with her sister, 17-year-old Hope takes a job as nanny for a lesbian couple, which leads to questions of her own sexuality.

MacDougal, Scarlett. Have a Nice Life series. Vol. 1, *Start Here;* vol. 2, *Play;* vol. 3, *Popover;* vol. 4, *Score.* Penguin Putnam, 2001. QP 2002.
Four girls have a chance to change their lives, thanks to the intervention of galactic angel Clarence Terence, but prom preparations cause them to ignore Clarence's advice.

Mackler, Carolyn. *Guyaholic: A Story of Finding, Flirting, Forgetting . . . and the Boy Who Changes Everything.* Candlewick, 2007. QP 2008.
Abandoned by her mother, V lives with her grandparents and bounces from one

guy's bed to another until she meets Sam, but she is scared to admit she cares for him.

————. *Love and Other Four Letter Words.* Delacorte, 2000. QP 2001.
Living in New York City with her depressed mother after her parents agree to a trial separation, Sammie sees things getting better when she meets Eli, the son of her mother's college roommate.

————. *Vegan Virgin Valentine.* Candlewick, 2004. QP 2005.
The "perfect" life of soon-to-be class valedictorian Mara is thrown into chaos with the arrival of her older sister's rebellious, 16-year-old daughter V.

Mancusi, Mari. *Boys That Bite.* Penguin, 2006. QP 2007.
Rayne wants to become a vampire, but it is her twin Sunshine who is bitten by vampire hunk Magnus, causing the twins and Magnus to try to reverse the process.

Manning, Sarra. *Guitar Girl.* Dutton, 2004. QP 2005.
Molly's all-girl band expands with the addition of Dean and his friend T, and suddenly the Hormones are popular and headed toward stardom.

Marchetta, Melina. *Saving Francesca.* Knopf, 2006. PPYA 2008 (What Makes a Family?).
To remove Francesca from her clique of girlfriends, her mother transfers her to an academic, formerly all-boys school, where she struggles to fit in.

Marsden, John. *Letters from the Inside.* Random House, 1996. PPYA 2002 (Relationships).
Two girls who have never met know everything about one another through their pen-pal letters—but do those letters hide more than they reveal?

————. *So Much to Tell You.* Fawcett, 1990. PPYA 1999 (Different Drummers).
Disfigured when an acid bath meant for her mother strikes her in the face, Anna attempts to understand the changes in her life by writing a journal.

Martin, Ann M. *Amalia.* California Diaries series, book 4. Scholastic, 1997. QP 1999.
Verbally assaulted with racial insults, Amalia turns to her family and friends to heal and regain her self-confidence.

Martinez, A. Lee. *Gil's All Fright Diner.* Tor, 2005. PPYA 2007 (What's So Funny?).
Earl the vampire and Duke the werewolf happen to stop at the All Night Diner and agree to help the owner fight zombies for a fee of $100.

Marunas, Nathaniel, and Erik Craddock. *The Blade of Kringle.* Manga Claus series. Razorbill, 2006. QP 2007.
The traditional Christmas story meets Japanese manga, with Santa a master of his samurai swords and nutcrackers masquerading as ninjas.

Marz, Ron, and Bart Sears. *The Path: Crisis of Faith.* The Path Traveler series. CrossGen, 2003. QP 2004.
When the monk Obo-san sees the gods he worships kill his brother, he vows revenge against them, eventually adding the mad emperor to those he targets.

Mass, Wendy. *A Mango-Shaped Space.* Little, Brown, 2003. PPYA 2006 (What Ails You?).
It isn't until she has trouble in Spanish and math that Mia tells her parents about seeing numbers and words in colors. A neurologist confirms that she is a synesthete.

Master's Choice: Mystery Stories by Today's Top Writers and the Masters Who Inspired Them, vol. 2. Berkley, 2001. PPYA 2004 (Guess Again).

A lucky 13 mystery writers each contribute an original, along with a story they enjoy reading, to compile a second collaboration of 26 tales.

Maxwell, Robin. *The Secret Diary of Anne Boleyn.* Touchstone, 1998. PPYA 2003 (Lock It, Lick It, Click It).

Queen Elizabeth I reads the diary of her mother, the executed second wife of Henry VIII of England, and always remembers the comment about not letting a man control your life.

Mayer, Melody. *The Nannies.* Delacorte, 2005. QP 2006.

Kylie, Lydia, and Esme, each working as a nanny for a different Hollywood star, become friends after meeting on the *Platinum Nanny* reality show.

Mazer, Anne, ed. *Walk in My World: International Short Stories about Youth.* Persea, 2000. PPYA 2003 (This Small World).

Stories by noted and lesser-known authors from Ireland, Antigua, Russia, Germany, India, and many other countries reveal their culture; includes biographical author sketches.

————. *Working Days: Short Stories about Teenagers at Work.* Persea, 1997. PPYA 2000 (Short Takes).

Working at a mind-numbing factory assembly line or a fast-food restaurant are only a few of the teen jobs written about in this collection.

Mazer, Harry. *The Last Mission.* Laurel-Leaf, 1981. PPYA 2002 (War).

Lying about his age, Jack enlists during World War II and is part of a crew flying missions over Germany. Shot down, the 16-year-old is taken to a German POW camp.

————, **ed.** *Twelve Shots: Outstanding Short Stories about Guns.* Laurel-Leaf, 1998. PPYA 2000 (Short Takes).

Original short works describe the relationships between teenagers and guns from a sensible, dangerous, and even humorous perspective.

McCafferty, Megan. *Sloppy Firsts.* Crown, 2001. QP 2003; PPYA 2003 (Lock It, Lick It, Click It).

Her only brother dies, her best friend moves away, and Jess copes with high school on her own, until a stint in journalism enables her to speak for all outsider students.

McCaffrey, Anne. *An Exchange of Gifts.* Illustrated by Pat Morrissey. Wildside, 1995. PPYA 2005 (Gateway to Faerie).

Princess Meanne runs away because she is not allowed to use her gift of plant growth. When she meets Wisp, the two begin a new life of shared magical skills.

McCants, William D. *Much Ado about Prom Night.* Browndeer, 1995. PPYA 2000 (Romance).

Dumped by Janet, T.J. attempts to win her back. He succeeds but quickly realizes that his childhood friend Vivian is the girl for him.

McClintock, Norah. *Bang!* Orca, 2007. QP 2008.

Quentin and JD have been friends for a long time, but when JD shoots someone during a robbery Quentin learns that he can trust no one but himself.

————. *Down.* Orca, 2007. QP 2008.

Having served time in juvie for beating up someone who insulted his girlfriend,

Remy doesn't want to choose sides when two groups argue over the local basketball court.

———. *Snitch.* Orca, 2005. PPYA 2006 (Criminal Elements).
Convicted of purse snatching, Josh agrees to take part in a program to retrain dogs for adoption, which helps him learn to control his anger.

———. *Tell.* Orca, 2006. QP 2007.
His avid card-playing stepfather is murdered and David must unearth long-buried truths about his family to locate the murderer and prove his own innocence.

McCormick, Patricia. *Cut.* Front Street, 2000. QP 2001.
In a mental health facility, Callie refuses to talk during group or to a therapist, until another cutter joins the facility and she finally opens up about her self-cutting.

———. *Sold.* Hyperion, 2006. QP 2007.
Thirteen-year-old Lakshmi is betrothed to Krishna, but her Nepalese stepfather sells her into sexual slavery and upends her peaceful life in this heartbreaking tale related in verse.

McDaniel, Lurlene. *Baby Alicia Is Dying.* Dell, 1993. PPYA 2005 (Read 'Em and Weep).
Searching for something unique to do, Desi volunteers at a home for babies with HIV, where she falls in love with five-month-old Alicia and is devastated when the baby dies.

———. *The Girl Death Left Behind.* Bantam, 1999. QP 2000.
After losing her entire family in a car accident when stomach flu prevented her attending a picnic with them, Beth eventually recovers in her new life with her aunt and uncle.

———. *I'll Be Seeing You.* Laurel-Leaf, 1996. PPYA 2000 (Romance).
Disfigured by removal of a facial tumor, Carley meets Kyle, blinded in a chemistry experiment, but worries he won't care for her when his bandages are removed.

———. *Six Months to Live.* Darby Creek, 2003. PPYA 2006 (What Ails You?).
Befriending one another in the hospital as they fight cancer together, Sandy and Dawn remain friends during remission. But when Sandy dies, Dawn wonders if she has a future.

———. *Till Death Do Us Part.* Bantam, 1997. QP 1999.
Diagnosed with an inoperable brain tumor, April can't believe her good fortune when she falls in love with Mark and he asks for her hand in marriage.

McDonald, Janet. *Twists and Turns.* Farrar, Straus, & Giroux, 2003. QP 2004.
Graduating from high school, sisters Keeba and Teesha have no career plans until a friend suggests they take out a loan and open a hair-braiding salon.

McDonald, Joyce. *Swallowing Stones.* Random House, 1999. PPYA 2003 (I've Got a Secret).
Michael fires a rifle in the air to celebrate his July 4th birthday, but when he hears that Jenna's father died he knows he is responsible.

McDonell, Nick. *Twelve.* Grove, 2002. QP 2003.
Harlem and the Upper East Side connect through White Mike, a wealthy teen whose drug sales to friends turn Christmas vacation into a nonstop party.

McKayhan, Monica. *Indigo Summer.* Harlequin, 2007. QP 2008.
Indigo gets a great date for homecoming,

but when she is dumped she turns to her reliable next-door neighbor, not realizing that he may no longer be available.

McKinley, Robin. *Beauty: A Retelling of the Story of Beauty and the Beast.* HarperTrophy, 1993. PPYA 2000 (Romance).
Though not the prettiest of the three sisters, Beauty meets the Beast and every night sits and talks with him in this magical, much-loved tale.

————. *The Blue Sword.* Puffin, 2000. PPYA 2003 (Flights of Fantasy).
Bored with her life, Harry doesn't mind being kidnapped by a king, especially when she discovers that she alone can control the legendary Blue Sword.

————. *Deerskin.* Ace, 1994. PPYA 2005 (Gateway to Faerie).
Raped by her father, Princess Lissar escapes with her dog Ash to the mountains to rebuild their spirits and bodies.

————. *The Hero and the Crown.* Penguin Putnam, 2000. PPYA 2004 (If It Weren't for Them).
Aerin's story is just beginning as she strives to become the hero who will claim the Blue Sword, eventually slaying the Black Dragon with the sword's help.

————. *Spindle's End.* Ace. 2001. PPYA 2005 (Gateway to Faerie).
Rosie has a special gift of communicating with animals, which helps her avoid the effects of her christening curse in this retelling of *Sleeping Beauty.*

McMurtry, Larry. *Lonesome Dove.* Pocket, 1988. PPYA 2001 (Western).
Two former Texas Rangers steal a herd of cattle from Mexico and then drive it to Montana to set up a ranch.

McNab, Andy, and Robert Rigby. *Avenger.* Penguin, 2007. QP 2008.
In this sequel to *Traitor* and *Payback,* Danny takes on another dangerous mission but must avoid being murdered when he completes the task.

McNamee, Graham. *Acceleration.* Random House, 2003. QP 2004.
A journal left in the subway's lost-and-found leads Duncan to suspect the writer wants to murder three women; when the police brush him off, what should he do?

————. *Hate You.* Delacorte, 1999. QP 2000.
Though her dad choked her when she tried to break up a parental fight, Alice learns to forgive him when he is dying of cancer.

McPhee, Phoebe. *The Alphabetical Hookup List A–J.* Simon & Schuster, 2002. QP 2003.
When three college roommates discover each has been dumped, a friendly competition is set up as they dare one another to kiss boys whose names begin with A through J.

Mead, Alice. *Adem's Cross.* Laurel-Leaf, 1998. PPYA 2002 (War).
Soldiers shoot his sister, beat his father, and carve an orthodox cross on Adem's chest, leaving the Albanian teen no choice but to flee from Kosovo.

Mead, Richelle. *Vampire Academy.* Razorbill, 2007. QP 2008.
Half-human Rose shares a psychic bond with, and the role of guardian for, vampire heiress Vasilisa, who is hunted by someone intent on destroying her Dragomir line.

Medina, Nico. *The Straight Road to Kylie.* Simon Pulse, 2007. PPYA 2008 (Sex Is . . .).

Thinking that gay Jonathan is suddenly available, popular Laura wants him as her pretend boyfriend, but he thinks returning to the closet might be less stressful for him.

Medley, Linda. *Castle Waiting: The Lucky Road.* Castle Waiting series, vol. 1. Cartoon Books, 2000. PPYA 2002 (Graphic Novels).
Sleeping Beauty's castle, populated by ghosts and goblins, becomes a safe haven and pregnant Jain is one of the first to seek refuge.

Metz, Melinda. Fingerprints series. Vol. 1, *Gifted Touch;* vol. 2, *Haunted;* vol. 3, *Trust Me;* vol. 4, *Secrets.* HarperCollins, 2001. QP 2002.
Rae has the unusual ability of touching an object and picking up the thoughts of the last person who held that object, which makes her a target for elimination.

Meyer, Adam. *The Last Domino.* Penguin Putnam, 2005. QP 2006.
An outcast at school and ignored at home in favor of the memory of his older, suicidal brother, Travis falls under the spell of manipulative Daniel.

Meyer, Stephenie. *New Moon.* Little, Brown, 2006. QP 2007.
When her beloved vampire Edward leaves to keep her safe, a saddened Bella befriends Jake but is surprised by his werewolf transformations.

————. *Twilight.* Little, Brown, 2005. QP 2006.
Bella Swan moves to rainy Forks and falls in love with the mysterious but enchanting Edward, a love that doesn't fade when he reveals his vampirism.

Michener, James A. *Centennial.* Fawcett, 1987. PPYA 2001 (Western).

A novel is built around the town of Centennial, Colorado, from its geological formation 136 million years ago to early settlement and finally life in the 1970s.

Mikaelsen, Ben. *Petey.* Hyperion, 1998. PPYA 2002 (Relationships).
When he is 70, Petey is finally diagnosed with cerebral palsy and moved to a nursing home, where he becomes friends with lonely Trevor, who saves him from bullies.

————. *Touching Spirit Bear.* HarperTrophy, 2002. PPYA 2006 (Criminal Elements).
Cole's mean, arrogant ways earn him the choice of prison time or spending a year on a remote Alaskan island. He chooses the island, where he meets the spirit bear.

Miklowitz, Gloria D. *Masada: The Last Fortress.* Eerdmans, 1999. PPYA 2002 (War).
The Roman army is determined to acquire the last stronghold of Judea, a mountaintop fortress near the Dead Sea, but the Jews commit mass suicide rather than be captured.

Millar, Mark. *Super-Human.* The Ultimates series, vol. 1. Marvel Comics, 2002. PPYA 2004 (If It Weren't for Them).
In this new series, Millar changes the Avengers into the Ultimates, who are still superheroes but exhibit human flaws.

————. *The Tomorrow People,* vol. 1. Ultimate X-Men series. Marvel Comics, 2001. QP 2002; PPYA 2002 (Graphic Novels).
The tension developing between humans and mutants is evident as the X-Men confront the terrorist Magneto.

Minter, J. *The Insiders.* Insiders series, book 1. Bloomsbury, 2004. QP 2005.

Five guys form the Insiders group and vow to never cheat with another member's girl, but things change when Jonathan's country cousin Kelli comes to town.

Mitchell, Margaret. *Gone with the Wind.* Avon, 1973. PPYA 2002 (War).
With her land and home destroyed during the Civil War, Scarlett O'Hara vows to do whatever is necessary to feed herself and her family in this American classic.

Miyazaki, Hayao. *Nausicaa of the Valley of Wind.* Tokuma's Magical Adventure series, vol. 1. Tokuma, 1993. PPYA 2002 (Graphic Novels).
Living in the far future when much of Earth has been devastated, gunship pilot Nausicaa is more interested in the ecology of her world.

Mlynowski, Sarah. *Bras and Broomsticks.* Delacorte, 2005. PPYA 2008 (Magic in the Real World).
Upset that her younger sister not only has the boobs but is also the witch in the family, Rachel wants to use Miri's witchy skills to become popular.

Moon, Elizabeth. *Once a Hero.* Heris Serrrano series. Baen, 1998. PPYA 2004 (If It Weren't for Them).
Esmay Suiza is the first person from her planet to attend Fleet Academy, but her career is almost destroyed when she takes part in a mutiny against a traitorous captain.

Moore, Alan. *Promethea.* Promethea series, book 1. DC Comics, 2001. PPYA 2002 (Graphic Novels).
College student Sophia Bangs becomes the latest in a long line of avatars for Promethea, a 2,000-year-old warrior woman with a fire-belching caduceus.

————. *Tom Strong.* Tom Strong series, book 1. DC Comics, 2001. QP 2001.
Raised by a robot after his parents die, Tom Strong, along with his wife and daughter, fights evil in the form of a Nazi superwoman and a monster.

Moore, Christopher. *Bloodsucking Fiends: A Love Story.* HarperCollins, 1995. PPYA 2007 (What's So Funny?).
While he is working as a night clerk, Tommy's shift brightens when sexy Jody walks in looking for a dark place to hide after being bitten by a vampire. It's love at first sight.

————. *Lamb: The Gospel According to Biff, Christ's Childhood Pal.* HarperPerennial, 2003. PPYA 2004 (If It Weren't for Them).
The resurrected Biff, who claims to be Christ's "best bud," offers a tongue-in-cheek account of Christ's teenage years.

Moore, Terry. *Strangers in Paradise: High School.* Strangers in Paradise series, vol. 1. Abstract Studios, 1999—PPYA 2002 (Graphic Novels); PPYA 2005 (Read 'Em and Weep); Abstract Studios, 2005—PPYA 2006 (GLBTQ).
Total opposites, Francine and Katchoo meet and become best friends in high school.

Moriarty, Jaclyn. *Feeling Sorry for Celia.* St. Martin's, 2002. PPYA 2003 (Lock It, Lick It, Click It).
Communicating with her mother via refrigerator notes, Elizabeth frets about her friend Celia, but when she rescues her from the circus Celia steals her boyfriend.

Morris, Gerald. *The Squire, His Knight, and His Lady.* The Squire's Tales series. Laurel-Leaf, 2001. PPYA 2003 (Flights of Fantasy).

Love, honor, battle, and magic are at stake as Squire Terence and his knight Sir Gawain of the Round Table prepare to meet the Green Knight.

Morrison, Grant. *JLA: Earth 2.* Justice League series. DC Comics, 2000. QP 2001.
In the parallel world of antimatter, JLA heroes such as Superman and Wonder Woman have similar adventures as Ultraman and Superwoman.

Moss, Steve, ed. *World's Shortest Stories: Murder, Love, Horror, and Suspense.* Illustrated by Glen Starkey. Running Press, 1998. PPYA 2000 (Short Takes).
With a maximum length of 55 words each, this assortment truly represents "short" stories.

Mowry, Jess. *Babylon Boyz.* Aladdin, 1999. PPYA 2002 (Tales of the Cities).
When Dante, Pook, and Wyatt find a suitcase filled with cocaine, their first thought is of its potential resale value, but their second is—who's the owner?

Murdock, Catherine Gilbert. *Dairy Queen.* Graphia, 2007. PPYA 2008 (Anyone Can Play).
Part of a football-loving family, D. J. Schwenk is unhappy when the rival quarterback works on her family's farm. Might she have a tiny crush on Brian Nelson?

Murphy, Claire. *To the Summit.* HarperTrophy, 1998. PPYA 1999 (Good Sports).
A climbing expedition to the top of Denali with her father takes 17-year-old Sarah on a journey of discovery deep within herself.

Murphy, Rita. *Night Flying.* Random House, 2002. PPYA 2003 (I've Got a Secret).
When Georgia questions the rules by which all the Hansen women fly unaided, family secrets tumble out.

Myers, Anna. *Ethan between Us.* Walker, 1998. QP 1999.
The relationship of best friends Clare and Liz changes when Ethan moves to town, but it is destroyed when Liz reads Clare's journal and tells the community a secret of Ethan's.

Myers, Walter Dean. *145th Street: Short Stories.* Delacorte, 2000—QP 2001; Laurel-Leaf, 2001—PPYA 2002 (Tales of the Cities).
Ten stories, from Joe enjoying his own funeral, to boxing for extra money for your family, to falling in love when you're a teenager, combine to reveal a community.

———. *Autobiography of My Dead Brother.* Illustrated by Christopher Myers. Amistad, 2006. PPYA 2007 (Get Creative).
Blood brothers Rise and Jesse become distant from one another, though Jesse continues to illustrate his promised autobiography of Rise.

———. *Hoops.* Laurel-Leaf, 1983. PPYA 1999 (Good Sports).
Lonnie's dreams of escaping Harlem through his basketball ability will shatter if his coach's old gambling problem resurfaces.

———. *Monster.* Illustrated by Christopher Myers. HarperCollins, 1999—QP 2000; HarperTempest, 2001—PPYA 2006 (Criminal Elements).
While sitting in jail awaiting trial, 16-year-old Steve Harmon describes his inadvertent involvement with a murder.

———. *The Righteous Revenge of Artemis Bonner.* HarperCollins, 1994. PPYA 2001 (Western).

Asked by his aunt to avenge his uncle's death, Artemis heads west and trails Catfish from Mexico to Alaska, aided by a half-Cherokee orphan named Frolic.

———. *Shooter.* HarperTempest, 2004. QP 2005.
Told through a variety of shifting points of view, the devastating aftermath of a high school shooting is examined to determine the spark that set the gunfire in motion.

———. *Slam!* Scholastic Point, 1998. PPYA 1999 (Good Sports).
Schoolwork and questionable friends combine to distract Slam from his basketball skills, until he learns to put his team and studies first.

———. *Somewhere in the Darkness.* Scholastic, 1997. PPYA 2002 (Relationships).
With one last chance to see his son Jimmy, prison escapee Crab and Jimmy have a memorable road trip from New York City to Crab's childhood home in Arkansas.

———. *Street Love.* HarperCollins, 2006. QP 2007.
Told through a series of short, lyrical poems, 17-year-old overachiever Damien falls in love with 16-year-old Junice, the daughter of a drug dealer.

———. *What They Found: Love on 145th Street.* Random House, 2007. QP 2008.
Poverty, drug use, and high unemploy-ment can't diminish the love neighbors feel for one another on 145th Street in Harlem.

Myracle, Lauren. *TTYL.* Abrams, 2004. QP 2005.
Instant messages written among best friends Zoe, Madigan, and Angela are enhanced by emoticons and IM lingo in this epistolary novel.

Naifeh, Ted. *Courtney Crumrin and the Night Things.* Courtney Crumrin series, book 1. Oni, 2003. PPYA 2005 (Own Your Freak).
Gloomy Courtney, along with her parents, moves in with her spooky uncle Aloysius, and she becomes entangled with wizards and the "night things" living at the foot of her bed.

Namioka, Lensey. *April and the Dragon Lady.* Browndeer, 1994. PPYA 2003 (This Small World).
When her traditional Chinese grandmother doesn't approve of her father's second wife, April gains an unexpected ally in her new stepmother.

———. *Ties That Bind, Ties That Break.* Laurel-Leaf, 2000. PPYA 2003 (This Small World).
Defying tradition, Ailin refuses to have her feet bound, attends an English school, babysits for a missionary family, and eventually leaves China with them.

Nance, Andrew. *Daemon Hall.* Illustrated by Colin Polhemus. Holt, 2007. QP 2008.
A ghost story session at Daemon Hall with horror author Ian Tremblin turns into real terror for five teen authors when some of them disappear.

Napoli, Donna Jo. *Beast.* Simon Pulse, 2004. PPYA 2005 (Gateway to Faerie).
A Persian prince angers a fairy, who turns him into a savage beast until he is redeemed by a French beauty named Belle in a reworking of *Beauty and the Beast.*

———. *Breath.* Simon Pulse, 2005. PPYA 2006 (What Ails You?).
Salz has always been the sickly one, until a strange disease breaks out in his medieval village and he is one of the few immune to it, in this retelling of the *Pied Piper of Hamelin.*

————. *Zel.* Puffin, 1998. PPYA 2005 (Gateway to Faerie); PPYA 2000 (Romance).

In this rendition of Rapunzel's story, her mother makes a pact with the devil and locks her daughter Zel in a tower to prevent her seeing Count Konrad.

Nash, Naomi. *You Are So Cursed.* Smooch, 2004. QP 2005.

In order to compete with the jocks and Queen B cliques, Vick adopts the persona of a powerful witch and enjoys her own set of groupies.

Naylor, Phyllis Reynolds. *Jade Green: A Ghost Story.* Atheneum, 2000—QP 2001; Simon & Schuster, 2001—PPYA 2003 (I've Got a Secret).

Judith bring a green-framed photo of her deceased mother to her uncle's home, which awakens the ghost of Jade Green, a servant who cut off her hand and bled to death.

Neenan, Colin. *Thick.* Brown Barn, 2006. QP 2007.

From his jail cell, Nick tells of his abusive father and a victimized friend, stories that tragically combine and lead to Nick's confession of murder.

Nelson, Blake. *Paranoid Park.* Viking, 2006. QP 2007.

A nameless skateboarding teen agonizes over his involvement in the accidental death of a railroad security guard.

————. *Rock Star, Superstar.* Viking, 2004. QP 2005.

After signing with a popular band that enjoys mainstream appeal, talented high school bass player Pete worries that he is selling out.

Neufeld, John. *Boys Lie.* DK, 1999. QP 2000.

Gina garners an unearned reputation at her new school, which encourages Eddie to attack her and then lie about what happened.

Newman, Leslea. *Jailbait.* Delacorte, 2005. QP 2006.

Andi walks home to avoid the teasing of her classmates on the school bus, which is how she meets and falls in love with the abusive drifter Frank.

Newton, Suzanne. *I Will Call It Georgie's Blues.* Puffin, 1990. PPYA 2004 (On That Note).

Two brothers have different reactions to their strict minister father: Neal doesn't tell anyone he is learning to play jazz, and Georgie finds a haven in his fantasy world.

Nickerson, Sara. *How to Disappear Completely and Never Be Found.* HarperTrophy, 2003. PPYA 2004 (Guess Again).

Margaret has three clues she is convinced are related to her father's mysterious death: a key, a swimming medal, and a handwritten comic book.

Niles, Steve. *30 Days of Night.* Illustrated by Ben Templesmith. Idea & Design Works, 2003. PPYA 2005 (All Kinds of Creepy).

The sun sets and for 30 days and nights darkness covers Barrow, Alaska—the perfect time for a group of vampires to arrive and sup until the sun comes up.

Nishiyama, Yuriko. *Harlem Beat.* Harlem Beat series, book 1. Tokyopop, 1999. PPYA 2002 (Graphic Novels).

Living in the big city, Nate Torres experiences pressure from gangs and a fast-paced lifestyle; now he adds the competitive world of street basketball.

Nix, Garth. *Sabriel.* The Abhorsen Trilogy, book 1. Eos, 1997. PPYA 2003 (Flights of Fantasy).
Sabriel journeys through the land of the Dead to save her necromancer father and her people from the greatest enemy ever faced, but how can she kill the Dead?

———. *Shade's Children.* HarperTrophy, 1997. PPYA 2004 (Simply Science Fiction).
The Overlords control Earth and "harvest" the brains and muscles of children when they reach the age of 14. Those who escape join Shade to fight against their oppressors.

Nixon, Joan Lowery. *The Haunting.* Delacorte, 1998. QP 1999.
When her mother inherits a pre–Civil War plantation and plans to fill it with foster children, Lia decides to thwart her mother's plans.

———. *The Name of the Game Was Murder.* Laurel-Leaf, 1994. PPYA 2004 (Guess Again).
After writing a "tell-all" book about his five houseguests, August promises that whoever locates his manuscript will have his secret removed, but then August is killed.

———. *Nightmare.* Delacorte, 2003. QP 2004.
Sent to a summer camp for under-achievers, Emily learns her recurring nightmare may be a warning that someone at camp wants to eliminate her.

———. *Whispers from the Dead.* Laurel-Leaf, 1991. PPYA 2004 (Guess Again).
Sarah moves to Houston, where she receives strange messages about a murder that was committed in her home.

———. *Who Are You?* Delacorte, 1999. QP 2000.
Discovering that Douglas Merson has kept a file on Kristi since her birth makes her want to meet him in the hopes he can explain why she doesn't look like her parents.

Nodelman, Perry. *Behaving Bradley.* Aladdin, 2000. PPYA 2001 (Humor).
At the end of the school year, Bradley ponders his unsuccessful attempts to end hypocrisy at Roblin Memorial High School by changing its conduct code.

Nolan, Han. *Born Blue.* Harcourt, 2003. PPYA 2004 (On That Note).
Abandoned by her heroin-addicted mother, Janie finds something she cares about when she is introduced to the great ladies who have sung the blues, like Aretha and Billie.

———. *If I Should Die before I Wake.* Harcourt, 1996. PPYA 1999 (Changing Dimensions).
While neo-Nazi wannabe Hilary Burke lies in a hospital bed, she slips into the horrific memories of her roommate, Holocaust survivor Chana Bergman.

———. *When We Were Saints.* Harcourt, 2005. PPYA 2007 (Religion).
Claire and Archie go on a pilgrimage to the Cloisters to determine if Archie really is a saint.

Nye, Naomi Shihab. *Habibi.* Simon & Schuster, 1999. PPYA 2002 (Relationships).
Leaving St. Louis so her father can return to his native Jerusalem, Liyana has difficulty adjusting to the tension between Jews and Arabs.

Oates, Joyce Carol. *Big Mouth and Ugly Girl.* HarperCollins, 2003. PPYA 2005 (Own Your Freak).
Matt teasingly says he will blow up the

school if his original play isn't accepted for the upcoming festival, and suddenly he's suspended and visited by the police.

O'Brien, Tim. *The Things They Carried.* Broadway, 1998. PPYA 2002 (War). O'Brien tells the stories behind the photos, moccasins, brandy, and M&Ms carried by his platoon mates in Vietnam along with their military gear.

O'Connell, Tyne. *Pulling Princes.* Bloomsbury, 2004. QP 2005. Calypso Kelly tries to become popular at her English boarding school, but she makes the girls jealous when she attracts too many boys, including Prince Freddie.

O'Connor, Barbara. *Beethoven in Paradise.* Farrar, Straus, & Giroux, 1997. PPYA 2004 (On That Note). His father thinks music is for sissies and that Martin should play baseball, but Martin hates baseball, so he teaches himself to play the violin when he visits his grandmother.

Ohba, Tsugumi. *Death Note,* vol. 1. Illustrated by Takeshi Obata. VIZ, 2005. QP 2006. High school student Light uses Death Note to rid the world of criminals in this first volume of a manga series.

Olin, Sean. *Killing Britney.* Simon Pulse, 2005. QP 2006. Britney's new popularity changes after her mother is killed, then her boyfriend and best friend. Could there be a serial killer loose in her hometown?

Oppel, Kenneth. *Airborn.* HarperCollins, 2004—QP 2005; Eos, 2005—PPYA 2006 (Books That Don't Make You Blush). In an alternate world of flying airships, cabin boy Matt hears the dying words of a lone balloonist, confronts pirates, and

spots a new species of "flying beasts," the Cloud Cats.

Orlev, Uri. *The Man from the Other Side.* Puffin, 1995. PPYA 2002 (War). Marek travels through the sewers to bring food to Warsaw ghetto occupants, but when he leads Josek to fight in the uprising tragedy awaits; based on a true story.

O'Shea, Pat. *The Hounds of the Morrigan.* HarperTeen, 1999. PPYA 2003 (Flights of Fantasy). Pidge and Brigit are unlikely heroes in this humorous, action-packed quest to triumph over the Morrigan and her evil forces in a book inspired by Celtic myth and lore.

Pagliarulo, Antonio. *A Different Kind of Heat.* Delacorte, 2006. QP 2007. When a cop's bullet kills her brother, Luz's angry reaction sends her to a probationary group home, where she learns to deal with her rage.

Parker, Daniel, and Lee Miller. Watching Alice series. Vol. 1, *Break the Surface;* vol. 2, *Walk on Water.* Razorbill, 2004. QP 2005. Moving from Vermont to Manhattan to escape his past, Tom meets secretive Alice. Just as they become more than friends, she disappears.

Pascal, Francine. *Fearless.* Fearless series, book 1. Pocket, 1999. QP 2001. Lacking the gene for fear, Gaia has extra speed and strength that enable her to excel in self-defense and become a dangerous opponent.

Paterson, Katherine. *Come Sing, Jimmy Jo.* Puffin, 1995. PPYA 2004 (On That Note). James doesn't like being part of his family's traveling band, as he misses his grandmother, has no friends in school, and is now called Jimmy Jo.

———. *Jip: His Story.* Puffin, 1998. PPYA 1999 (Different Drummers).
Abandoned as a baby, Jip learns about his mother when a slave catcher comes to town.

Patterson, James. *Along Came a Spider.* Warner, 1993. PPYA 2000 (Page Turners).
Black DC police detective Alex Cross and white Secret Service agent Jezzie Flanagan work together to capture a serial killer who murders for the recognition.

———. *Maximum Ride: School's Out— Forever.* Little, Brown, 2007. PPYA 2008 (What Makes a Family?).
Escaping from the lab where they were bred, Max and five other avian-American teens are adopted by an FBI agent.

———. *Maximum Ride: The Angel Experiment.* Little, Brown, 2005. QP 2006.
Led by 14-year-old Max, genetically engineered teens put their wings to use and take to the skies to battle against half-humans and rescue members of their "flock."

Patterson, Richard North. *Eyes of a Child.* Ballantine, 1996. PPYA 2000 (Page Turners).
Young lawyer Teresa Peralta wants to escape from her creepy husband, but when he is found dead with a gun wedged in his mouth her boss is accused of the crime.

Paulsen, Gary. *Brian's Return.* Delacorte, 1999. QP 2000.
When it's difficult to return to pizzas, MTV, and his classmates after his ordeal in *Hatchet,* a properly supplied Brian returns to the site of the plane crash.

———. *The Haymeadow.* Illustrated by Ruth Wright Paulsen. Yearling, 1994. PPYA 2001 (Western).
Living on the Three Bar S ranch, John spends the summer in the haymeadow guarding 6,000 sheep, two horses, and four dogs against coyotes, bears, and a flood.

———. *The Schernoff Discoveries.* Yearling, 1998. PPYA 2001 (Humor).
The unnamed narrator's best friend, science whiz Harold Schernoff, strikes out in the nonscientific areas of kissing, dating, skiing, and dealing with bullies.

———. *Soldier's Heart: Being the Story of the Enlistment and Due Service of the Boy Charley Goddard in the First Minnesota Volunteers.* Delacorte, 1998—QP 1999; Laurel-Leaf, 2000— PPYA 2002 (War).
Facing real fighting in the Civil War makes Charlie realize that war truly is "Hell on Earth."

———. *The Transall Saga.* Delacorte, 1998. QP 1999.
While on a solo backpacking trip in the desert, Mark is transported to a primitive Earth where just surviving becomes more important than trying to return home.

Pausewang, Gudrun. *Final Journey.* Puffin, 1998. PPYA 2002 (War).
After her cattle car trip to Auschwitz, Alice is glad to shower off the trip's grime, not knowing it will be her "final journey."

Payne, C. D. *Frisco Pigeon Mambo.* Aivia, 2000. PPYA 2007 (What's So Funny?).
Released from a lab, the now-free pigeons think they're human and cadge bar drinks by dancing the mambo, until they meet cars and cats and want to return to the lab.

Pearsall, Shelley. *All of the Above.* Illustrated by Javaka Steptoe. Little, Brown, 2006. QP 2007.
Challenged by their seventh-grade math teacher to construct the world's largest

tetrahedron, four misfits exceed his expectations and build friendships along with their structure.

Pearson, Ridley. *No Witnesses.* Dell, 1996. PPYA 2000 (Page Turners).
A crazed killer murders people by poisoning supermarket food in a case that stymies police detective Lou Boldt and police psychologist Daphne Matthews.

Peck. Richard. *A Long Way from Chicago: A Novel in Stories.* Puffin, 2000. PPYA 2001 (Humor).
Joey and his sister Mary Alice spend seven memorable summers with their "respectable" grandmother, who's not above cheating to win the County Fair pie contest.

Peck, Robert Newton. *Cowboy Ghost.* HarperCollins, 2000. PPYA 2001 (Western).
Sixteen-year-old Titus comes of age the year he drives 500 head of cattle across Florida, aided by a ghost who helps fend off attacks by Seminole Indians and cattle rustlers.

Peel, John. *Doomsday.* Fear the Year 2099 series, vol. 1. Scholastic, 1999. QP 2000.
Living when everything is controlled by technology, Tristan hacks into a computer that houses the Doomsday virus, not realizing his clone Devon plans to release that virus.

Peretti, Frank. *Hangman's Curse.* Veritas Project series, vol. 1. Thomas Nelson, 2002. PPYA 2004 (Guess Again).
When three teens lie in comas, supposedly because of the Abel Frye curse, Elijah and Elisha go undercover to investigate.

———. *Nightmare Academy.* Veritas Project series, vol. 2. Thomas Nelson, 2002. QP 2004.
Commissioned by the president to look

into unusual occurrences involving the supernatural, teens Elijah and Elisha search a school for runaways.

Perez, Marlene. *Unexpected Development.* Roaring Brook, 2004. QP 2005.
An essay about how she spent her summer vacation reveals Megan's concern that her bust size is the only reason her longtime crush Jake wants to date her.

Perkins, Mitali. *Monsoon Summer.* Laurel-Leaf, 2006. PPYA 2008 (What Makes a Family?).
When Jazz, spending the summer in India, learns that their cook faces an arranged marriage, she helps Danita start a business so she will be self-supporting.

Peters, Julie Anne. *Define "Normal."* Little, Brown, 2000—QP 2001; Little, Brown, 2003—PPYA 2005 (Own Your Freak).
Peer counselor Antonia is surprised to see her new counselee Jazz in punk attire, black lipstick, and an asymmetrical haircut, but each learns to look beyond the other's façade.

———. *Keeping You a Secret.* Little, Brown, 2005. PPYA 2006 (GLBTQ).
With her life on the prescribed course of boyfriend, college, and marriage, Holland is dismayed when she falls madly in love with lesbian Cece.

———. *Luna.* Little, Brown, 2005. PPYA 2006 (GLBTQ).
At night Regan's brother Liam secretly dons his female identity of Luna, but when he decides to come out of the closet Regan worries about her family accepting him as Luna.

Peters, Kimberly Joy. *Painting Caitlyn.* Lobster, 2006. QP 2007.
Feeling lonely and ignored by friends and

family, Caitlyn eagerly gravitates to Tyler, not realizing she is giving up her identity to an abusive, controlling boyfriend.

Petrie, Doug. *Ring of Fire.* Buffy the Vampire Slayer series, book 1. Illustrated by Ryan Sook. Dark Horse, 2000. PPYA 2002 (Graphic Novels).
When baddies attempt to resurrect the demon samurai Kelgor, Buffy has her hands full trying to avert disaster.

Philbrick, Rodman. *Freak the Mighty.* Scholastic, 2001. PPYA 2002 (Relationships).
Best friends Max and Freak make use of their handicaps as they form a partnership of brains and brawn.

Picoult, Jodi. *My Sister's Keeper.* Simon & Schuster, 2005. PPYA 2006 (What Ails You?).
Conceived in vitro to help her older sister fight leukemia, Anna finally rebels against the bone marrow and blood transfers and sues for control of her body.

———. *The Pact: A Love Story.* HarperTrade, 1998. PPYA 2006 (Criminal Elements).
Chris and Emily are high school lovers, but when pregnant Emily commits suicide Chris is charged with her murder.

Pierce, Meredith Ann. *The Darkangel.* The Darkangel Trilogy, vol. 1. Magic Carpet, 1998. PPYA 2003 (Flights of Fantasy).
Aeriel is kidnapped to serve the Dark-angel's 13 brides, but she stands in his way as he prepares for the 14th, who will bring him the power of a vampire.

Pierce, Tamora. *Alanna.* Song of the Lioness series, book 1. Random House, 1997. PPYA 2003 (Flights of Fantasy).
Alanna is an adventurous girl who swaps places with her scholarly brother and trains to become a knight.

———. *Tris's Book.* Circle of Magic series, book 2. Scholastic, 1998. QP 1999.
Tris and three other young mages at Winding Circle Temple must unite their powers to defend the temple against pirates.

Pines, Tonya, ed. *Thirteen: 13 Tales of Horror by 13 Masters of Horror.* Scholastic, 2004. PPYA 2005 (All Kinds of Creepy).
Stine, Pike, Windsor, and Bennett are a few of the authors whose shivery short stories are included in this grouping.

Pinkwater, Jill. *Buffalo Brenda.* Aladdin, 1992. PPYA 2001 (Humor).
Kicked off the school newspaper for their reporting, Brenda and India Ink launch their own underground newspaper and acquire a real bison for their school mascot.

Plummer, Louise. *Finding Daddy.* Delacorte, 2007. QP 2008.
Determined to meet her father, Mira contacts him and quickly realizes the reason her mother divorced him: he's a psychopath intent on revenge.

———. *The Unlikely Romance of Kate Bjorkman.* Laurel-Leaf, 1997. PPYA 2000 (Romance).
While writing a love story, Kate unexpectedly stars in her own romance.

Plum-Ucci, Carol. *The Body of Christopher Creed.* Hyperion, 2001. PPYA 2004 (Guess Again).
When Christopher Creed goes missing, Torey organizes a search for him, which in turn unlocks a lot of secrets from the town's past.

———. *The Night My Sister Went Missing.* Harcourt, 2006. QP 2007.
At a party on an abandoned pier, Kurt sees his sister pitch backward into the ocean just as he hears a gunshot.

————. *What Happened to Lani Garver?*
Harcourt, 2002. PPYA 2005 (Own Your
Freak).
Claire has no trouble befriending Lani
Garver, who offers her advice and
consolation in her struggle against
leukemia, leading Claire to wonder if Lani
is really an angel.

Pope, Elizabeth Marie. *The Perilous Gard.*
Houghton Mifflin, 2001. PPYA 2003
(Flights of Fantasy).
In the mid-1500s, Kate Sutton is exiled to
a remote castle by Queen Mary Tudor, but
she finds an underground world populated
by Fairy Folk.

Porter, Connie. *Imani All Mine.* Houghton
Mifflin, 2000. PPYA 2005 (Read 'Em and
Weep).
Only 14, Tasha doesn't have much in this
world to call her own except her beloved
daughter Imani, and their time together is
only temporary.

Pow, Tom. *Captives.* Roaring Brook, 2007.
QP 2008.
While vacationing in the Caribbean,
two families are suddenly captured by
guerrillas, blindfolded, and shoved into
trucks to be taken to the island's interior.

Powell, Randy. *Tribute to Another Dead
Rock Star.* Sunburst, 2003. PPYA 2004
(On That Note).
After his rocker mother dies and his
grandmother remarries, Grady needs
a place to live but will have to alter
his lifestyle when it clashes with his
stepmother's Christian views.

Pratchett, Terry. *Carpe Jugulum.*
Discworld series. HarperCollins, 2000.
PPYA 2003 (Flights of Fantasy).
The king of Lancre makes a big mistake
when he invites a family of vampires
to celebrate his daughter's birth, but

Granny Weatherwax and her witches
intervene.

————. *Maskerade.* HarperPrism, 1998.
PPYA 2000 (Page Turners).
Agnes Nitt wants to sing arias in a haunted
opera house, but Nanny Ogg and Granny
Weatherwax want her to be the third witch
in their coven.

————. *Men at Arms.* HarperTorch, 1997.
PPYA 2001 (Humor).
In this spoof of the hard-boiled detective
novel, a ragtag band of trolls, dwarfs, and
"humans" solve a series of murders in
Discworld.

Preston, Douglas, and Lincoln Child. *Relic.*
Tor, 1996. PPYA 2000 (Page Turners).
A beast haunts the halls of New York's
Museum of Natural History and preys on
good and bad guys alike.

Preston, Richard. *The Cobra Event.*
Random House, 1997. QP 1999.
The bodies of a student and a homeless
man are both cannibalized, sending Dr.
Austen on a search for a mad scientist
with a biological weapon.

Price, Susan. *The Sterkarm Handshake.*
Eos, 2000. PPYA 2004 (Simply Science
Fiction).
When scientists build a time tunnel to raid
Scotland of gold and then build a resort,
they underestimate the native Sterkarmers,
who regularly hassle time travelers.

Pullman, Philip. *Clockwork, or All
Wound Up.* Illustrated by Leonid Gore.
Scholastic, 1998. QP 1999.
This story within a story links an
apprentice clock maker with a prince who
has a clock for a heart.

————. *The Golden Compass.* His Dark
Materials series, book 1. Random House,
1999. PPYA 2003 (Flights of Fantasy).
Lyra hears of a plot to steal children and

send them north, but trying to rescue them involves her in a clash of universes.

———. *The Subtle Knife.* His Dark Materials series, book 2. Del Rey, 1998. PPYA 1999 (Changing Dimensions).
Will joins Lyra in an alternate world where she has gone in pursuit of the mysterious Dust. Together they continue the journey, discovering an ancient weapon in their travels.

Putney, Mary Jo. *One Perfect Rose.* Fawcett, 1998. PPYA 2000 (Romance).
Believing he has a fatal illness, the Duke of Ashburton gives up his ducal duties, joins up with a family of traveling actors, and falls in love with their adopted daughter.

Qualey, Marsha. *Close to a Killer.* Delacorte, 1999—QP 2000; Laurel-Leaf, 2000—PPYA 2004 (Guess Again).
After Barrie's mother Daria is released from prison, she sets up a beauty salon with other former inmates but becomes the first suspect when two of her clients are murdered.

Quintana, Anton. *The Baboon King.* Laurel-Leaf, 2001. PPYA 2003 (This Small World).
Caught between the Kikuyu and Masai tribes, Morengaru is kicked out of the Kikuyu, joins a baboon troop, and becomes its leader, though he longs to return to humanity.

Rabb, M. E. The Missing Persons series. Vol. 1, *The Rose Queen;* vol. 2, *The Chocolate Lover;* vol. 3, *The Venetian Policeman;* vol. 4, *The Unsuspecting Gourmet.* Penguin Speak, 2004—QP 2005 (vols. 1–4); PPYA 2006 (vol. 1) (Books That Don't Make You Blush).
When their father dies, sisters Sam and Sophie run away from their stepmother and settle in Venice, Indiana, where they help solve cases involving missing persons.

Rallison, Janette. *All's Fair in Love, War, and High School.* Walker, 2005. PPYA 2006 (Books That Don't Make You Blush).
When her SATs tank, Samantha knows she needs a hook for college, so she decides to run for student body president, a task that necessitates her being nice for two weeks.

———. *Life, Love and the Pursuit of Free Throws.* Walker, 2006. PPYA 2007 (What's So Funny?).
Best friends Josie and Cami compete on the basketball court to play with a star from the WNBA, but they vie in a romantic triangle when Ethan enters their realm.

Randle, Kristin. *The Only Alien on the Planet.* Scholastic, 1995. PPYA 1999 (Different Drummers).
New student Ginny is drawn to loner Smitty, kisses him at a party, and listens to his dreadful account of the abuse he receives from his brother.

Raskin, Ellen. *The Westing Game.* Puffin, 1992. PPYA 2004 (Guess Again).
The will of wealthy industrialist Samuel Westing requires the 16 heirs to pair up and solve his murder to claim the inheritance, but the murderer is one of the 16.

Reaver, Chap. *A Little Bit Dead.* Dell, 1994. PPYA 2001 (Western).
Trapper Reece saves the life of Indian Shanti Ma Teck but later needs Teck to vouch for him when Reece is accused of murder.

Rees, Celia. *The Soul Taker.* Hodder, 2003. PPYA 2005 (All Kinds of Creepy).
Lewis tells his boss, the toy shop owner, about his crush on popular Jennie, not realizing that he is promising his soul to his employer in return for Jennie's love.

———. *Witch Child.* Candlewick, 2002. PPYA 2003 (Lock It, Lick It, Click It).
After her grandmother is executed as a witch, Mary is sent to America for protection, but her herbal skills create concern among the colonists.

Rees, Douglas. *Vampire High.* Delacorte, 2003—QP 2004; Laurel-Leaf, 2005—PPYA 2007 (What's So Funny?).
Cody is one of the few non-vampire students at his high school and is accepted only because his swimming prowess aids the school's water polo team.

Reinhardt, Dana. *A Brief Chapter in My Impossible Life.* Random House, 2007. PPYA 2008 (What Makes a Family?).
Meeting her biological mother begins an amazing year for Simone as she gains then loses her mother to cancer, acquires a boyfriend, and learns about her Jewish heritage.

———. *Harmless.* Random House, 2007. QP 2008.
Caught at a party where they're not supposed to be, three friends claim one of them was attacked, but that "harmless" lie to escape punishment grows out of control.

Reiss, Kathryn. *Paperquake: A Puzzle.* Harcourt, 1998. PPYA 2004 (Guess Again).
An earthquake shakes an old wall and letters and a diary hinting at murder tumble out, sending Violet time-traveling to solve the mystery.

———. *Time Windows.* Harcourt, 2000. PPYA 2001 (Paranormal).
In the attic Mandy discovers a dollhouse that is an exact replica of her own home, and when she looks through its windows she can watch the former inhabitants.

Remarque, Erich-Maria. *All Quiet on the Western Front.* Fawcett, 1978. PPYA 2002 (War).
Paul Baumer and three of his friends enlist in World War I and join the other soldiers in trench warfare, but only Paul survives in this classic.

Rennison, Louise. *Angus, Thongs, and Full-Frontal Snogging.* Confessions of Georgia Nicolson series, vol. 1. HarperCollins, 2000—QP 2001; HarperTeen, 2001—PPYA 2003 (Lock It, Lick It, Click It).
Georgia's diary is filled with hilarious details of a stuffed olive costume, her wacky, vicious cat Angus, and her obsession with snogging the "Sex God" Robbie.

———. *Knocked Out by My Nunga Nungas.* Confessions of Georgia Nicolson series, vol. 3. HarperCollins, 2002. QP 2003.
Surviving a family vacation to Scotland, Georgia returns to her "Sex God" boyfriend, enjoys a snog with an ex-boyfriend, and parents an egg as part of a biology project.

———. *On the Bright Side, Now I'm the Girlfriend of a Sex God.* Confessions of Georgia Nicolson series, vol. 2. HarperCollins, 2001. QP 2002.
Thoughts of moving to New Zealand for her father's new job send Georgia into a tizzy, for she's finally landed SG, also known as "Sex God."

Reuter, Bjarne. *The Boys from St. Petri.* Translated by Anthea Bell. Penguin, 1996. PPYA 2002 (War).
Meeting in the St. Petri church, sons of the local minister lead other Danish teens in harassment of German soldiers during World War II.

Revoyr, Nina. *The Necessary Hunger.* St. Martin's, 1998. PPYA 2006 (GLBTQ).
Nancy's crush on basketball teammate Raina accelerates when her Japanese American father falls in love with Raina's African American mother.

Reynolds, Marilyn. *Beyond Dreams.* Morning Glory, 1995. PPYA 2000 (Short Takes).
In this cluster of stories, teens at Hamilton High School face one crisis after another, from drunk driving to changes in family dynamics when an elderly relative moves in.

Riefe, Barbara. *Against All Odds: The Lucy Scott Mitchum Story.* Tor, 2000. PPYA 2001 (Western).
Accompanying her husband on an 1849 wagon train destined for Sacramento, Baltimorean Lucy meets Indians and buffalo, shoes an ox, and survives a massacre.

Rinaldi, Ann. *The Coffin Quilt: The Feud between the Hatfields and the McCoys.* Gulliver, 2001. PPYA 2002 (Relationships).
When a Hatfield elopes with a McCoy, the legendary feud intensifies and Roseanna stitches the necessary coffin quilt to record the deaths.

———. *The Second Bend in the River.* Scholastic, 1999. PPYA 2000 (Romance).
As a young girl, Rebecca meets the noted Indian Tecumseh and enjoys his friendship, but when he asks her to marry him she worries that their backgrounds are too different.

———. *The Staircase.* Harcourt, 2002. PPYA 2007 (Religion).
While the students at her Catholic boarding school in 1870s Santa Fe pray to St. Joseph to build a staircase to the choir loft, Lizzie finds an elderly carpenter to do the work.

Riordan, Rick. *The Lightning Thief.* Miramax, 2006. PPYA 2008 (Magic in the Real World).
When his algebra teacher turns into a monster, it's Percy's first clue that he's about to become better acquainted with the gods of Mount Olympus, including his father.

Roberts, Nora. *Born in Fire.* Born In trilogy, book 1. Jove, 1994. PPYA 2000 (Romance).
Talented glassmaker Maggie is as fiery as her work and argues with gallery owner Rogan, as often occurs when opposites attract, in this first book about three Irish sisters.

Roberts, Willo Davis. *Twisted Summer.* Aladdin, 1998. PPYA 2004 (Guess Again).
Ceci investigates when she hears a friend of the family has been accused of murdering a summer visitor, but she is dismayed when the trail implicates her stepgrandfather.

Robinson, James. *Sins of the Father.* Starman series, vol. 1. DC Comics, 1996. PPYA 2004 (If It Weren't for Them).
When his brother David is killed, Jack Knight reluctantly dons the mantle of superhero to continue the tradition begun by their father, the original Starman.

Rodowsky, Colby. *Lucy Peale.* Farrar, Straus, & Giroux, 1994. PPYA 2000 (Romance).
Pregnant after a date rape, Lucy leaves home rather than stand in front of her father's fundamentalist church and "confess" that she's a "Jezebel."

Rose, Malcolm. Traces (Luke Harding, Forensic Investigator) series. Book 1, *Framed;* book 2, *Lost Bullet;* book 3, *Roll Call.* Kingfisher, 2005. QP 2006.
Teen forensic scientist Luke Harding solves homicides with the help of Malc, his laser-equipped robot sidekick.

Rostkowski, Margaret L. *After the Dancing Days.* HarperCollins, 1988. PPYA 2002 (War).
Helping at a convalescent center for soldiers sent home during World War I, Annie befriends a badly scarred man and wonders why America is involved in this way.

Roth, Matthue. *Never Mind the Goldbergs.* Push, 2005. PPYA 2007 (Religion).
Hava's spiked hair and punk look hide her observant Jewish ways. When she spends the summer as the lead in a sitcom about a Jewish family, she reexamines her beliefs.

Rottman, S. L. *Head above Water.* Peachtree, 2003. PPYA 2008 (Anyone Can Play).
A star swimmer, Skye is a busy high school student whose brother Sunny has Down syndrome and doesn't understand that his beloved sister is finally enjoying a social life.

———. *Hero.* Puffin, 2000. PPYA 2004 (If It Weren't for Them).
Coming from a troubled family, Sean always seems to be in a predicament, until a stint at community service introduces him to someone who cares about him.

———. *Rough Waters.* Peachtree, 1997. QP 1999.
Orphaned after their parents die, Gregg and Scott move to Colorado to live with their uncle and quickly learn to help with his white-water rafting business.

———. *Shadow of a Doubt.* Peachtree, 2003. PPYA 2008 (What Makes a Family?).
Shadow's perfect school year and calm family life dissolve when his long-absent brother Daniel calls from jail to say he's being held on a murder charge.

Rovin, Jeff. *Vespers.* St. Martin's, 1999. PPYA 2000 (Page Turners).
Two giant bats and droves of smaller ones attack the residents of New York City as the bats search for a nesting place.

Ruby, Laura. *Good Girls.* HarperCollins, 2006. QP 2007.
Breaking up with Luke to concentrate on school, Audrey gives him one final "gift" at a party, but a photo of their private act leads to horrible consequences.

Rucka, Greg. *Half a Life.* Gotham Central series, vol. 2. Illustrated by Michael Lark. DC Comics, 2005. PPYA 2006 (GLBTQ).
Detective Renee Montoya of Gotham's police force is outed and must deal with the fallout while she continues to battle supervillains.

Ruditis, Paul. *Rainbow Party.* Simon Pulse, 2005. PPYA 2008 (Sex Is . . .).
A promise of oral sex from a rainbow of lipsticked mouths titillates, but the party is a nonevent when the hostess's father arrives home unexpectedly.

Ryan, Darlene. *Responsible.* Orca, 2007. QP 2008.
As the new kid in school, Kevin goes along with his bullying friend, until Nick starts picking on Erin.

Ryan, Pam Muñoz. *Esperanza Rising.* Blue Sky, 2002. PPYA 2003 (This Small World).
When Esperanza and her mother lose

their farm, they leave Mexico for the San Joaquin Valley, where Esperanza works to pay for her beloved grandmother to join them.

Rylant, Cynthia. *I Had Seen Castles.* Harcourt, 1995. PPYA 2002 (War).
As an old man, John remembers when he was young and fell in love with Ginny but left to serve in World War II. Now he wonders whatever happened to her.

Sachar, Louis. *Holes.* Farrar, Straus, & Giroux, 1998—QP 1999; Random House, 2003—PPYA 2006 (Criminal Elements).
A one-legged gypsy curses Stanley's great-great-grandfather for stealing a pig, and now every day Stanley must dig a new hole at the correctional camp.

Sakai, Stan. *Duel at Kitanoji.* Usagi Yojimbo series, vol. 17. Dark Horse, 2003. PPYA 2004 (If It Weren't for Them).
The lone samurai rabbit prepares to witness a duel between his former teacher and his teacher's rival in feudal Japan.

———. *Grasscutter.* Usagi Yojimbo series, vol. 12. Dark Horse, 1999. PPYA 2002 (Graphic Novels).
Usagi Yojimbo, a ronin warrior rabbit, is responsible for Kusanagi, a legendary blade forged by the gods.

Salinger, J. D. *The Catcher in the Rye.* Little, Brown, 1991. PPYA 2005 (Own Your Freak).
Holden Caulfield is expelled from school and roams around New York City, looking for something real in a world of phoniness.

Sanchez, Alex. *Rainbow Boys.* Simon Pulse, 2003. PPYA 2006 (GLBTQ).
Seniors Jason, Kyle, and Nelson make some life-changing decisions as they deal with their sexual identity.

Saul, John. *The Presence.* Fawcett, 1997. QP 1999.
Studying primitive bones on Maui, Katherine's son Michael spots a strange geode while diving and suddenly can't breathe oxygen, leaving Katherine frantic to help him.

Schaefer, Jack. *Shane.* Bantam, 1983. PPYA 2001 (Western).
No one is aware that Shane, a ranch hand on the Starrett farm in the late 1880s, is a gunfighter escaping his past.

Schindler, Nina. *An Order of Amelie, Hold the Fries.* Translated by Rob Barrett. Annick, 2004. PPYA 2006 (Books That Don't Make You Blush).
Tim meets and falls in love with Amelie in a tale told through IMs, texting, and phone messages.

Schraff, Anne. *Lost and Found.* Bluford series. Scholastic, 2007. PPYA 2008 (What Makes a Family?).
Darcy's younger sister enters a defiant, argumentative stage, but when she disappears Darcy seeks help from new friends and her long-lost father to search for her.

Schreiber, Ellen. *Vampire Kisses.* HarperCollins, 2003. QP 2004.
When Alexander's family moves into the supposedly haunted Sterling mansion, Raven feels her chances of becoming a vampire have bumped up a step.

Schreiber, Mark. *Starcrossed.* Llewellyn, 2007. QP 2008.
Meeting in a plastic surgeon's office where each is having the tattoo of an ex's name removed, Ben and Christy are like Romeo and Juliet as they seek a happy ending.

Scott, Elizabeth. *Bloom.* Simon Pulse, 2007. PPYA 2008 (Sex Is . . .).

When her old boyfriend Evan returns to town, Lauren turns her attention from her devoted but deeply religious boyfriend to someone who offers a little more affection.

Scott, Kieran. *I Was a Non-blonde Cheerleader.* Puffin, 2007. PPYA 2008 (Anyone Can Play).
Moving to Florida from New Jersey, Annisa is surprised to see that the female students are blond and wonders if her black hair will prevent her from becoming a cheerleader.

Scrimger, Richard. *The Nose from Jupiter.* Tundra, 1998. PPYA 1999 (Changing Dimensions).
Usually picked on by his classmates, Alan suddenly attracts girls, improves his soccer skills, and scares away the bullies when an alien named Norbert lives in his nose.

Sebold, Alice. *The Lovely Bones.* Back Bay, 2004. PPYA 2005 (All Kinds of Creepy).
Lured to a neighbor's hideaway in a cornfield, Susie Salmon is murdered, but in her heaven she is able to observe and relate the effect of her death on her family and town.

Sewell, Earl. *Keysha's Drama.* Harlequin, 2007. QP 2008.
About to be assigned to foster care, Keysha is instead sent to live with her middle-class father, but she rebels against this lifestyle.

Shakespeare, William. *Manga Shakespeare: Romeo and Juliet.* Adapted by Richard Appignanesi; illustrated by Sonia Leong. Abrams, 2007. QP 2008.
Set in Tokyo with rival gang families portraying the Montagues and the Capulets, this graphic novel presents Shakespeare's play in a more accessible format for young teens.

Shan, Darren. *A Living Nightmare.* Cirque du Freak: The Saga of Darren Shan, book 1. Little, Brown, 2001. PPYA 2005 (All Kinds of Creepy).
After sneaking out to a freak show, Steve wants to join the vampire Mr. Crepsley, and Darren steals the huge spider Madame Octa to teach her tricks.

———. *Lord Loss.* The Demonata series, vol. 1. Little, Brown, 2005. QP 2006.
Grubbs Grade arrives home to find his parents and sister killed by "demon master" Lord Loss, whose grotesque appearance is revealed only to Grubbs in this grim series.

Shaw, Susan. *The Boy from the Basement.* Dutton, 2004. QP 2006.
Kept in the basement by his father, Charlie sneaks outside when his parents are sleeping but doesn't know how to act outdoors.

———. *Safe.* Dutton, 2007. QP 2008.
Raped by an older boy on the last day of seventh grade, Tracy feels she'll never again be safe and withdraws from everyone and everything, except for her father and piano playing.

Shaw, Tucker. *Confessions of a Backup Dancer.* Simon Pulse, 2004. QP 2005.
Kelly's magical summer of dancing backup for pop diva Darcy is exciting but grueling, especially when Kelly is caught between Darcy and her controlling mother.

———. *Flavor of the Week.* Hyperion, 2005. PPYA 2006 (Books That Don't Make You Blush).
Part of a romantic triangle, overweight, talented chef Cyril loves Rose, but Rose loves his best friend Nick, who passes himself off as a great cook.

Sheffield, Charles. *Higher Education.*
Jupiter Novel series, vol. 1. Tor, 1997.
PPYA 2004 (Simply Science Fiction).
After being expelled from school, Rick
faces a dead-end future but seizes the
opportunity of asteroid mining training to
become an interplanetary space miner.

Sheldon, Dyan. *Confessions of a Teenage
Drama Queen.* Candlewick, 1999—QP
2000; Candlewick, 2005—PPYA 2006
(Books That Don't Make You Blush).
Determined to be noticed in a dull New
Jersey suburb, Lola lies and boasts about
herself, but when she lands the lead in the
school play she meets her match in Carla
Santini.

Shepard, Jim. *Project X: A Novel.* Vintage,
2005. PPYA 2006 (Criminal Elements).
Edwin Hanratty is a miserable eighth-
grader who is so bullied and harassed
by students and teachers that he and his
friend Flake plot revenge.

Shetterly, Will. *Elsewhere.* Harcourt,
2004—PPYA 2005 (Own Your Freak);
Tor, 1992—PPYA 1999 (Changing
Dimensions).
A runaway from the World, Ron meets
humans, elves, and halvies in Bordertown,
where magic and technology do not, and
cannot, coexist.

Showalter, Gena. *Oh My Goth.* MTV, 2006.
QP 2008.
When a goth and a Barbie are trapped
in an alternate reality game, both learn
about conformity and stereotyping before
working together to escape.

Shusterman, Neal. *The Dark Side of
Nowhere.* Tor, 1999. PPYA 2003 (I've
Got a Secret).
When he reaches his teen years, Jason
learns that he's an alien in human form
who's been left behind after a failed
invasion of Earth.

———. *Downsiders.* Simon & Schuster,
1999—QP 2000; Simon Pulse, 1999—
PPYA 2002 (Tales of the Cities).
Searching for medicine for his sister,
underground dweller Talon meets
aboveground teen Lindsay and the
two are drawn to one another.

———. *Dread Locks.* Dark Fusion series,
book 1. Dutton, 2005. QP 2006.
In this retelling of the Medusa myth,
Parker comes under the magnetic sway
of Tara, whose golden curls conceal her
ability to turn his friends into statues.

———. *Full Tilt.* Simon Pulse, 2004. PPYA
2005 (All Kinds of Creepy).
Entering a special amusement park, Blake
discovers that his soul will be retained
unless he tries seven rides, each of which
reflects a terrifying moment from his life.

———. *Red Rider's Hood.* Dark Fusion
series, book 2. Dutton, 2005. QP 2006.
Seeking revenge after the Wolves mug his
grandmother, Red is surprised to discover
that they are werewolves and he needs
special training to kill them.

———. *The Schwa Was Here.* Puffin, 2006.
PPYA 2007 (What's So Funny?).
Antsy befriends Calvin Schwa, the
"invisible" kid in class, and together
they pull off some paid stunts until one
involves mean Mr. Crawley, who has no
trouble seeing Calvin.

———. *Unwind.* Simon & Schuster, 2007.
QP 2008.
Three teens scheduled to be "unwound,"
with their body parts used for transplants
or appearance upgrades, avoid the
"Harvest Camps" after they run away.

Sinclair, April. *Coffee Will Make You
Black.* HarperCollins, 1995. PPYA 2002
(Tales of the Cities).

This first novel tells of Stevie's attempts to be "cool" in high school as she grows up in south Chicago amid the racial turmoil of the 1960s.

Singer, Marilyn. *Stay True: Short Stories for Strong Girls.* Scholastic, 1999. PPYA 2000 (Short Takes).
Eleven noted young adult authors share stories of girls who learn to be independent and able to stand up for themselves.

Singleton, L. J. (Linda Joy). Regeneration series. Book 1, *Regeneration;* book 2, *The Search;* book 3, *The Truth.* Berkley, 2000. QP 2001.
A crazed doctor wants to eliminate products of a secret cloning experiment, but one of the five clones starts searching, intent on locating and warning the others.

———. *Witch Ball.* The Seer series, vol. 3. Llewellyn, 2006. QP 2007.
Finally accepted at her new high school, Sabine acknowledges her psychic abilities when the mysterious crystal Witch Ball reappears in her life in this continuing series.

Sitomer, Alan L. *Homeboyz.* Jump at the Sun, 2007. QP 2008.
Arrested when he seeks revenge on his sister's killers, Teddy must mentor 12-year-old gangster wannabe Micah as punishment, a task more difficult than serving jail time.

Skurzynski, Gloria. *Virtual War.* Aladdin, 1999. PPYA 2004 (Simply Science Fiction).
Genetically engineered to be a soldier, Corgan is poised to fight a virtual war against two other world powers to claim land recently cleared for habitation.

Sleator, William. *Boltzmon!* Dutton, 1999. QP 2000.
Chris is told by a powerful subatomic particle about a deadly accident caused by Lulu, which can be averted if Chris heals his relationship with her.

———. *The Boxes.* Dutton, 1998—QP 1999; Puffin, 2000—PPYA 2001 (Paranormal).
Warned by weird Uncle Marco not to open two boxes, Anne does so anyway and releases a strange crab from one and a time-controlling clock from the other.

———. *The Boy Who Couldn't Die.* Abrams, 2004. QP 2005.
Afraid of death, Ken gives his mortal soul to a voodoo priestess for safety, which leaves him invulnerable to pain but enables a black magic priest to use his soul for murder.

———. *Oddballs.* Puffin, 1995. PPYA 2001 (Humor).
Though everyone thinks his or her own family is weird, the madcap adventures of this family earn them the title of "oddballs" in a work based loosely on the author's life.

———. *Rewind.* Dutton, 1999. QP 2000.
Struck and killed by a car, Peter learns that he is not "permanently dead" but must alter events leading to the accident. It's only changing his behavior that prevents his demise.

———. *Strange Attractors.* Puffin, 1991. PPYA 1999 (Changing Dimensions).
Teen science genius Max is hunted by two time-traveling scientists from parallel worlds who both want the time-travel phaser he accidentally picked up from a lab.

Sloan, Brian. *A Really Nice Prom Mess.* Simon & Schuster, 2005. QP 2006.
Shane and Cameron take girls to the prom

to hide their gay relationship, but the night goes downhill for Cameron after his date throws up in a fish tank.

Smith, Betty. *A Tree Grows in Brooklyn.* Trumpet, 1989. PPYA 2002 (Tales of the Cities).
Just like the tree of heaven that grows in the gutters of 19th-century Brooklyn, so too does Francie Nolan bloom despite her dysfunctional family in this American classic.

Smith, Charles R., Jr. *Tall Tales: Six Amazing Basketball Dreams.* Dutton, 2000. QP 2001.
Special shoes that help in jumping, a girl playing pickup who can stuff it, and descriptions of the funkiest smelling clothes are a few highlights of these street-smart, fantastic tales.

Smith, Greg Leitich. *Ninjas, Piranhas, and Galileo.* Little, Brown, 2005. PPYA 2006 (Books That Don't Make You Blush).
Three seventh-graders, two boys and a girl, conclude that their romantic triangle impedes completion of their science fair projects.

Smith, Jeff. *Bone: Out from Boneville.* Bone series, book 1. Graphix, 2005— PPYA 2007 (What's So Funny?); Cartoon Books, 1996—PPYA 2002 (Graphic Novels).
Leaving their home of Boneville, the Bone cousins Fone, Phoney, and Smiley are lost for a while in a desert but eventually arrive in a valley filled with wonderful creatures.

Smith, Kevin. *Guardian Devil.* Daredevil Visionaries series, vol. 1. Marvel Comics, 2001. PPYA 2002 (Graphic Novels).
The crime fighter known as Daredevil searches for answers in a case involving a mysterious child left in his care.

Smith, Roland. *Peak.* Harcourt, 2007. QP 2008.
Accompanying his estranged father on a Mount Everest climb rather than serve jail time for illegally scaling a building, Peak prepares for the adventure of his life.

———. *Sasquatch.* Hyperion, 1998. QP 1999.
When Dylan's father joins the Bigfoot International Society to prevent its members from killing a sasquatch, Dylan decides to follow and offer him some help.

———. *Zach's Lie.* Hyperion, 2001. QP 2002.
As part of the Witness Protection Program, Jack becomes Zach but records what happened to his family in a journal. When the journal is stolen, his family's safety is threatened.

Smith, Sherri L. *Lucy the Giant.* Laurel-Leaf, 2003. PPYA 2005 (Own Your Freak).
Tired of being tall, being called "Giant," and dragging her father out of bars, Lucy lands a job on a crabbing boat out of Kodiak and is finally judged by what she accomplishes.

Sniegoski, Tom. *Sleeper Agenda.* The Sleeper Conspiracy series, book 2. Razorbill, 2006. QP 2007.
Trusting no one but his neighbor Madison, Tom struggles to regain control of himself so he can locate and destroy his enemy, the corrupt government agent Brandon Kavanagh.

———. *Sleeper Code.* The Sleeper Conspiracy series, book 1. Razorbill, 2006. QP 2007.
Tom discovers that his rare narcolepsy is a cover for the assassin personality Tyler Garrett, who awakens in his body whenever Tom thinks he's sleeping.

Sones, Sonya. *One of Those Hideous Books Where the Mother Dies.* Simon & Schuster, 2004—QP 2005; Simon Pulse, 2005—PPYA 2008 (What Makes a Family?).
After her mother dies, Ruby gradually becomes accustomed to living with her movie star father, though Los Angeles is worlds away from her former home in Boston.

————. *Stop Pretending: What Happened When My Big Sister Went Crazy.* HarperCollins, 1999—QP 2000; HarperTeen, 2001—PPYA 2002 (Relationships).
Her sister's mental breakdown leads to other family problems as Cookie watches her parents' marriage dissolve in this novel in verse.

————. *What My Girlfriend Doesn't Know.* Simon & Schuster, 2007. QP 2008.
Robin worries that Sophie will tire of him and return to her popular friends, but when they go away to college it's Robin who almost ends their relationship.

————. *What My Mother Doesn't Know.* Simon & Schuster, 2001. QP 2002.
Finally falling in love with a "Mr. Right" who's also in her art class, Sophie has a big problem convincing her friends that Robin is not a jerk in this novel written in verse.

Sonnenblick, Jordan. *Drums, Girls and Dangerous Pie.* Scholastic, 2006. PPYA 2007 (Get Creative).
When Steven's little brother Jeffrey is diagnosed with leukemia, his mother lives at the hospital, his father cries, and Steven throws himself into playing his drums.

Sorrells, Walter. *Fake ID.* The Hunted series, book 1. Dutton, 2005. QP 2006.
Before she is sent to foster care,

Chass must unravel the mysterious disappearance of her mother, which is just one of many strange events in her life.

Soto, Gary. *The Afterlife.* Harcourt, 2003. QP 2004.
Stabbed in the men's room while on a date, Chuy watches his friends carry on without him until he befriends another ghost who helps him fade.

————. *Buried Onions.* HarperTrophy, 1999. PPYA 2002 (Tales of the Cities).
Life seems stacked against Eddie, with poverty and gangs in Fresno, the murder of his cousin, and then loss of his job, making the army seem the only viable option for him.

————. *Pacific Crossing.* Harcourt, 1992. PPYA 2003 (This Small World).
An exchange student to Japan, Lincoln discovers that there is much more to Japan than martial arts as he works in the fields and even cooks a Mexican meal for his host family.

————. *Petty Crimes.* Harcourt Brace, 1998. QP 1999.
Young teens dealing with everyday life, from Alma who grieves over her mother's death to young Rudy the boxer, can be found in this assortment of stories.

Sparks, Beatrice, ed. *Kim: Empty Inside; The Diary of an Anonymous Teenager.* Avon, 2002. QP 2003.
Kim hid her anorexia from her family and friends in high school, but her secret finally surfaces when she becomes a gymnast at UCLA.

————. *Treacherous Love: The Diary of an Anonymous Teenager.* Avon, 2000. QP 2001.
Feeling abandoned by her not-at-home father, her pill-popping mother, and her

best friend, Jennie accepts the comfort substitute teacher Mr. Johnstone offers.

Spears, Britney, and Lynne Spears. *A Mother's Gift.* Delacorte, 2001. QP 2002.
Feeling out of place as a scholarship student at the Haverty School of Music, Holly Faye gets a confidence boost by being selected to sing at the school's Talent Hour.

Spinelli, Jerry. *Stargirl.* Random House, 2004. PPYA 2005 (Own Your Freak).
Stargirl wows the students at Mica High School but is unprepared for the fickle rise and fall of popularity when she becomes an outcast.

————. *Who Put That Hair in My Toothbrush?* Little, Brown, 2000. PPYA 2000 (Humor).
Told in alternating chapters, Megan and her older brother have a long-standing feud that simmers continually, until a crisis shows them the advantage of having a sibling.

Springer, Nancy. *Blood Trail.* Holiday House, 2003. QP 2004.
When Jeremy's best friend Aaron is found covered with blood from 70 stab wounds, Jeremy wonders if the police will ever track down the killer.

————, ed. *Prom Night.* DAW, 1999. PPYA 2000 (Short Takes).
This combination of science fiction, fantasy, and realistic fiction includes zombies, alternate worlds, and misfit teens as they relate to the prom.

St. James, James. *Freak Show.* Dutton, 2007. QP 2008.
Beaten up for his drag queen ways, Billy stands up for all his outcast classmates when he runs for homecoming queen with the slogan "Tease hair, not homos."

Standiford, Natalie. The Dating Game series. Book 1, *The Dating Game;* book 2, *Breaking Up Is Really, Really Hard to Do.* Little, Brown, 2005. QP 2006.
The Dating Game website created by Madison, Holly, and Lina for a class becomes popular on campus as both matchmaker and forum for student views on sex, love, and dating.

Staples, Suzanne Fisher. *Haveli.* Laurel-Leaf, 1995. PPYA 2003 (This Small World).
Shabanu, the fourth wife of Pakistani Rahim, and her daughter are picked on by his other wives. When he dies, Shabanu hides in a secret room in Rahim's ancestral home.

————. *Shiva's Fire.* HarperTrophy, 2001. PPYA 2003 (This Small World).
Shiva studies classical Indian dance at a *gurukulan*, which brings honor and wealth to her parents.

Stephens, J. B. The Big Empty series. Vol. 1, *The Big Empty;* vol. 2, *Paradise City.* Razorbill, 2004. QP 2005.
After the decimation of three-quarters of the world's population by a virus, seven teens band together and search for a safe refuge in the empty heartland of America.

Stewart, Mary. *Nine Coaches Waiting.* Fawcett, 1983. PPYA 2000 (Romance).
Arriving at Chateau Valmy as governess to the young count, Linda is initially thrilled but soon realizes that her charge is in danger.

Stewart, Sean. *Nobody's Son.* Illustrated by Tristan Elwell. Magic Carpet, 2000. PPYA 2005 (Gateway to Faerie).
Entering a haunted forest, Mark becomes a hero when he breaks a curse on a kingdom and wins the hand of the princess in marriage, but is this his "happily ever after"?

Stewart, Sean, Jordan Weisman, and others. *Cathy's Book: If Found Call 650-266-8233.* Running Press, 2006. QP 2007.

Cathy's boyfriend breaks up with her and she is determined to learn why in this interactive mystery that includes actual websites, phone numbers, drawings, and letters.

Stine, R. L. *Dangerous Girls.* Dangerous Girls series, book 1. HarperCollins, 2003—QP 2004; Avon, 2003—PPYA 2005 (All Kinds of Creepy).

When a vampire attempts to convert Destiny to full vampire status, she impales him with a tent pole before he can transform her, but nothing can undo her twin Livy's vampirism.

Stoehr, Shelley. *Crosses.* Laurel-Leaf, 1998. PPYA 1999 (Different Drummers).

Attempting to block the emotional pain of her alcoholic parents, Nancy smokes, does drugs, and cuts herself, leaving cross marks on her body.

Stolarz, Laurie Faria. *Blue Is for Nightmares.* Llewellyn, 2003. QP 2005; PPYA 2007 (Religion).

Stacey employs spells she learned from her grandmother to discover who intends to kill her boarding school roommate Drea.

Stone, Jeff. *Crane.* The Five Ancestors series, book 4. Random House, 2007. QP 2008.

Hiding from her rogue brother, crane-style kung fu master Hok abandons her disguise as a boy and tries to understand what devilment Ying plans.

———. *Monkey.* The Five Ancestors series, book 2. Random House, 2005. QP 2006.

Five orphaned monk boys study kung fu until an elder monk destroys the monastery and kills their teacher in this volume that focuses on the youngest monk, Monkey.

Stone, Tanya Lee. *A Bad Boy Can Be Good for a Girl.* Random House, 2006. QP 2007.

High school students Josie, Nicolette, and Viv all succumb to the charms of the same senior guy, but some schoolwide "girl talk" on their part halts any further conquests.

Straczynski, J. Michael. *Born in Fire.* Rising Stars series, vol. 1. Image Comics, 2001. PPYA 2003 (I've Got a Secret).

Born after a mysterious "flash" hits their small Illinois town, 133 children have supernatural powers and townspeople worry how the "rising stars" will use that power.

———. *Coming Home.* Amazing Spider-Man series, vol. 1. Marvel Comics, 2001. QP 2003.

Spider-Man is warned to beware a being named Morlun who feeds off animal-emulating powers such as those exhibited by Peter Parker/Spider-Man.

Strasser, Todd. *Boot Camp.* Simon & Schuster, 2007. QP 2008.

Hoping to end his romance with an older woman, Garrett's parents overreact and send him to a school specializing in behavior modification, where he's beaten and abused.

———. *Can't Get There from Here.* Simon & Schuster, 2004. QP 2005.

Maybe, the youngest of a group of kids homeless by choice rather than living with their abusive families, finally trusts an adult enough to ask for help.

———. *Give a Boy a Gun.* Simon & Schuster, 2000. PPYA 2006 (Criminal Elements).

Facts about shootings and guns are interspersed with interviews of students when two unhappy boys shoot classmates and teachers at their school dance.

———. *How I Spent My Last Night on Earth*. Aladdin, 2000. PPYA 2000 (Humor).
Brilliant "Legs" stargazes with a handsome surfer as they enjoy their last perfect day before the rumor of a giant asteroid destroying Earth comes true.

———. *Slide or Die*. DriftX series. Simon Pulse, 2006. QP 2007.
Skilled at the illegal form of auto racing called drifting, Japanese American Kennin longs to race head-to-head against a racist classmate.

Stratton, Allan. *Chanda's Secrets*. Annick, 2004. PPYA 2005 (Read 'Em and Weep).
In Africa, Chanda's family has been ravaged by the unspoken-of disease AIDS, so she makes sure all her siblings are tested for it.

———. *Leslie's Journal*. Annick, 2000. QP 2001; PPYA 2003 (Lock It, Lick It, Click It).
When new student Jason winks at her, Leslie is thrilled and eager to date him, not realizing until almost too late that he is abusive and controlling.

Sutcliff, Rosemary. *Tristan and Iseult*. Farrar, Straus, & Giroux, 1991. PPYA 2004 (If It Weren't for Them).
After Tristan defeats Ireland's greatest warrior, he is sent by his king in search of a queen in this retelling of a 5th-century Celtic legend.

Swanson, Julie A. *Going for the Record*. Eerdmans, 2004. PPYA 2005 (Read 'Em and Weep).
Even after her father is diagnosed with pancreatic cancer, soccer continues to occupy all Leah's attention, until he dies and she realizes that soccer is just a game.

Sweeney, Joyce. *Headlock*. Holt, 2006. QP 2008.
Dreaming of becoming a professional wrestler, Kyle surprises everyone after graduation when he enrolls in a wrestler training school and develops his signature frog splash move.

———. *Players*. Winslow, 2000. QP 2001.
Senior captain Corey prepares for a great year of basketball but doesn't realize that new student Noah is setting up players to fail so that he can rise up the roster.

———. *Takedown*. Marshall Cavendish, 2004. QP 2005.
When he opens the door for pizza delivery, Joe and his friends are taken hostage and only Joe's fantasy hero, an aging wrestler, offers any help.

Swendson, Shanna. *Enchanted, Inc.* Ballantine, 2005. PPYA 2008 (Magic in the Real World).
Excited to be in New York City, Katie accepts a job with MSI—or Magic, Spells, and Illusions—where her lack of magic helps detect fake spells and disguised intruders.

Takahashi, Rumiko. *Ranma ½*. Ranma ½ series, vol. 1. VIZ, 1993. PPYA 2002 (Graphic Novels).
Martial artist Ranma once fell into the "spring of the drowned girl," and now when struck with cold water he turns into a girl.

Takanashi, Mitsuba. *Crimson Hero*. Crimson Hero series, vol. 1. VIZ, 2005. PPYA 2008 (Anyone Can Play).
Nobara defies her parents and enrolls in Crimson High School to play volleyball,

discovering too late that only the boys have a team.

Takaya, Natsuki. Fruits Basket series, vols. 1–5. Tokyopop, 2004. QP 2005 (vols. 1–5); PPYA 2006 (vol. 1) (Books That Don't Make You Blush).
In this popular manga series, orphan Tohru Honda must save the Sohmas from the evil curse that haunts the entire family.

Talbot, Bryan. *The Tale of One Bad Rat.* Dark Horse, 1995. PPYA 2007 (Get Creative).
Escaping her abusive father, Helen Potter and her pet rat flee a London squat and begin a healing journey to places her namesake Beatrix Potter might have visited.

Tan, Maureen. *AKA Jane.* Warner, 1999. PPYA 2000 (Page Turners).
Eager to leave MI5 after infiltrating terrorist groups, Jane accepts her literary agent's offer to attend a conference in Georgia but ironically meets a former enemy there.

Tanzman, Carol M. *Shadow Place.* Roaring Brook, 2002. QP 2003.
Though Lissa's friends ostracize her neighbor Rodney, she cares about him and puts her life at risk to talk to him after he steals several guns from his abusive father.

Tashjian, Janet. *The Gospel According to Larry.* Laurel-Leaf, 2003. PPYA 2005 (Own Your Freak).
Wanting to make the world a less materialistic place, Josh starts a website listing his ideas and instantly becomes famous, though no one knows his name isn't Larry.

———. *Tru Confessions.* Scholastic, 1999. PPYA 2003 (Lock It, Lick It, Click It).
Once Trudy accepts that her twin brother

is handicapped, she makes a video of Eddie's life for a television studio's contest—and wins!

Taylor, William. *The Blue Lawn.* Alyson, 1999. PPYA 2000 (Romance).
Rugby star David and sophisticated Theo grapple with their intense attraction for each other but are unsure about acting on their feelings.

Tenapel, Douglas. *Creature Tech.* Top Shelf, 2002. PPYA 2004 (Simply Science Fiction).
The ghost of Dr. Jameson steals the Shroud of Turin from Dr. Ong, resurrects his own body, and then sets out to gain control of the world in a tale of good and evil.

Tezuka, Osamu. *Kapilavastu.* Buddha series, vol. 1. Vertical, 2006. PPYA 2007 (Religion).
This first of a projected eight-volume set is a graphic novelization of the life of Siddhartha, the prince who becomes Buddha.

———. *Two-Fisted Surgeon.* Black Jack series, vol. 1. VIZ, 1999. QP 2000.
Distrustful of the medical community, a trained but unlicensed surgeon performs brilliantly, charges large fees, and secretly donates his income to aid others.

Thomas, Rob. *Doing Time: Notes from the Undergrad.* Simon Pulse, 1999. PPYA 2000 (Short Takes).
Nine tales illustrate the role of community service projects and their effect on the lives of many high school students.

———. *Rats Saw God: A Comic Emotionally Charged Tale.* Simon & Schuster, 1996. PPYA 2002 (Relationships).
One credit shy of graduating, Steve is assigned a 100-page essay about his life.

Writing it helps him understand his relationship with his father and a former girlfriend.

Thompson, Craig. *Blankets: An Illustrated Novel.* Top Shelf, 2003. PPYA 2005 (Read 'Em and Weep).
Thompson's journey from fundamentalist roots through first love and the earned wisdom of young adulthood is enhanced by his black-and-white drawings.

Thompson, Kate. *Midnight's Choice.* Hyperion, 1999. QP 2000.
Approaching the age when she will have to decide whether to remain human or choose a permanent animal form, Tess realizes she is attracted to the world of vampires.

Thomson, Celia. The Nine Lives of Chloe King series. Vol. 1, *The Fallen;* vol. 2, *The Stolen.* Simon Pulse, 2004. QP 2005.
Chloe survives a fall from San Francisco's Coit Tower but is left with claws and the ability to see in the dark. Now someone wants to kill her.

Tiernan, Cate. Balefire series. Book 1, *A Chalice of Wind;* book 2, *A Circle of Ashes.* Razorbill, 2005. QP 2006.
After Thais Allard's father dies in a car accident, she discovers she has an identical twin, Clio, and the two must unite to complete a ritual for themselves and their witch's coven.

————. Sweep series. Book 1, *Book of Shadows;* book 2, *Coven;* book 3, *Blood Witch;* book 4, *Dark Magick;* book 5, *Awakening.* Penguin Putnam, 2001. QP 2002.
When new student Cal Blaire arrives, he quickly pulls some classmates into his Wiccan coven, including Morgan, who exhibits signs of being a blood witch.

Tingle, Rebecca. *Edge on the Sword.* Penguin Putnam, 2003. PPYA 2004 (If It Weren't for Them).
Trained in defensive techniques, Flaed and her bodyguard Red use them to stand against Danish raiders while on her wedding journey to marry Ethelred.

Tolan, Stephanie. *Surviving the Applewhites.* HarperTrophy, 2004. PPYA 2005 (Own Your Freak).
When no other school will take him, Jake enrolls at the Applewhites' home school, where he is supposed to design his own education plan, but a detention home might be easier.

————. *Welcome to the Ark.* HarperTrophy, 1998. PPYA 1999 (Different Drummers).
Four gifted but troubled kids connect in an experimental, paranormal program at a psychiatric institution where the goal is to reduce, or stop, worldwide violence.

Tomey, Ingrid. *Nobody Else Has to Know.* Delacorte, 1999. QP 2000.
After being involved in a traffic accident that paralyzes a young girl, Webber discovers that his grandfather lies to protect him, and now the police think his grandfather was the driver.

Torres, J., and Scott Chantler. *Days like This.* Oni, 2003. PPYA 2004 (On That Note).
Three girl singers discovered at a high school talent show become Tina and the Tiaras and climb in popularity in this graphic novella set in the early 1960s.

Townsend, Sue. *The Secret Diary of Adrian Mole, Aged 13¾.* Avon, 1987. PPYA 1999 (Different Drummers).
Adrian Mole, who feels continually criticized, records his thoughts in the diary he begins the day his chin sprouts its first zit.

Triana, Gaby. *Cubanita.* Rayo, 2006. PPYA 2008 (What Makes a Family?).
Locked in constant battle with her Cuban immigrant mother, Isabel just wants to be a regular American teen and can hardly wait to leave Miami for college in Minnesota.

Trottier, Maxine. *Sister to the Wolf.* Kids Can, 2004. PPYA 2006 (Books That Don't Make You Blush).
When Cecile sees a young Pawnee Indian slave being branded in Quebec, she buys him. In turn, the Indian swears to protect Cecile and her father on their journey to Fort Detroit.

Trueman, Terry. *Inside Out.* HarperCollins, 2003. QP 2004.
Held hostage by two brothers inside a coffee shop, Zach calls his shrink to act as a mediator and the hostage situation ends, but not Zach's wish to commit suicide.

———. *Stuck in Neutral.* HarperCollins, 2000. QP 2001.
Cerebral-palsied teen Shawn wishes he could tell his dad how much he wants to live, but he can't speak or control his body and hopes his dad's pity doesn't lead to euthanasia.

Tucker, Lisa. *The Song Reader.* Pocket, 2003. PPYA 2004 (On That Note).
Orphaned Leeann lives with her older sister Mary Beth, who supports them by waiting tables and "reading" songs that become stuck in your head and reveal your psyche.

Tullson, Diane. *The Darwin Expedition.* Orca, 2007. QP 2008.
Avoiding a traffic backup, Liam and Tej take an old logging road over a mountain, but their truck flips, Tej's leg breaks, and Liam must cross through grizzly territory for help.

Turnbull, Ann. *No Shame, No Fear.* Candlewick, 2006. PPYA 2007 (Religion).
In 1662 England, young Anglican William analyzes his own faith after meeting devout Quaker Suzanne.

Turner, Megan Whalen. *The Thief.* Penguin, 1998. PPYA 2003 (Flights of Fantasy).
In jail for stealing the king's seal, Gen is offered his freedom if he will steal a mythical stone from a temple, a treasure that confers the right to rule on its wearer.

Turning Seventeen series. Vol. 1, *Any Guy You Want* by Rosalind Noonan; vol. 2, *More Than This* by Wendy Corsi Staub; vol. 3, *For Real* by Christa Roberts; vol. 4, *Show Me Love* by Elizabeth Craft. HarperCollins, 2000. QP 2001.
Kerri, Jessica, Maya, and Erin are ready for whatever life brings them, from new boyfriends to school life, and make plans for the future the year they turn 17.

Tyler, Anne. *A Slipping-Down Life.* Ivy, 1992. PPYA 2004 (On That Note).
When dowdy Evie Decker hears an interview with musician Drumstrings Casey, she becomes obsessed with him, attends all his concerts, and carves his name on her forehead.

Ullman, James Ramsey. *Banner in the Sky.* HarperTrophy, 1995. PPYA 2004 (If It Weren't for Them).
A young boy is determined to conquer the Citadel, the mountain that claimed his father.

van Diepen, Allison. *Snitch.* Simon Pulse, 2007. QP 2008.
Resolving to stay clear of the gang life that surrounds her at Brooklyn High School, straight-A student Julia DeVino changes plans when she falls in love.

——. *Street Pharm.* Simon Pulse, 2006. QP 2007.

With his father in prison, Ty takes over his drug business, but the advice of a single mother and a drive-by shooting help him rethink the family dealings.

Van Draanen, Wendelin. *Flipped.* Knopf, 2003. PPYA 2006 (Books That Don't Make You Blush).

In second grade, Juli loved Bryce and he ignored her. Now in eighth grade their feelings flip, but it takes a conversation with Bryce's grandfather for Juli to reconsider him.

——. *Sammy Keyes and the Hotel Thief.* Random House, 1998. PPYA 2004 (Guess Again).

Living illegally with her grandmother in a seniors-only building, Sammy can't report the hotel thievery she witnesses, so she is forced to delve into the theft on her own.

Van Meter, Jen, Christine Norrie, and Chynna Clugston-Major. *Hopeless Savages.* Oni, 2002. PPYA 2004 (On That Note).

Born to parents who were punk rock's most vicious couple, Rat Hopeless-Savage has few rebellious outlets, so he becomes a normal citizen with a nine-to-five job.

Vande Velde, Vivian. *Being Dead.* Harcourt, 2003. PPYA 2005 (All Kinds of Creepy).

The dead don't always stay dead, as shown by the ones in these stories who leave their graves and travel into the human world.

——. *Companions of the Night.* Laurel-Leaf, 1996. PPYA 2000 (Romance).

Attracted to Ethan, Kerry helps save him when he is attacked by a vigilante committee, but she unwittingly places her family in harm's way because of Ethan's vampirism.

——. *Ghost of a Hanged Man.* Marshall Cavendish, 1998. QP 1999.

Ben needs his deceased mother's ghost to keep his sheriff father safe from the spirit of Jake, an outlaw hanged just the previous year.

——. *Never Trust a Dead Man.* Harcourt Brace, 1999. QP 2000.

Accused of murder, innocent Selwyn is thrown into the burial chamber with the decomposing body, but a witch helps him track down the real murderer.

——. *Now You See It . . .* Magic Carpet, 2006. PPYA 2008 (Magic in the Real World).

When Wendy's glasses break, she dons a pair of sunglasses and suddenly sees witches disguised as classmates and portals to other worlds.

——. *Remembering Raquel.* Harcourt, 2007. QP 2008.

Raquel dies in an automobile accident, and the memories and thoughts expressed by various family members, friends, and classmates paint a complex portrait of her.

——. *The Rumpelstiltskin Problem.* Scholastic, 2002. PPYA 2005 (Gateway to Faerie).

Rather than the miller's daughter spinning gold for the king, these stories offer six humorous alternatives to the original *Rumpelstiltskin.*

Vankin, Jonathan. *Big Book of Grimm.* Illustrated by Alec Stevens. DC Comics, 1999. QP 2000.

Capturing the original dark gruesomeness of the Grimm fairy tales, this graphic novel illustrates the horrors found in such favorites as *Snow White* and *Little Red Riding Hood.*

Vaughan, Brian K. *Pride and Joy.* Runaways series, book 1. Illustrated by Adrian Alphona. Marvel Comics, 2005—QP 2007; Marvel Comics, 2004—PPYA 2006 (Books That Don't Make You Blush).
Learning that their parents are mass murdering supervillains, six childhood friends strike out on their own to retaliate against evil.

———. *Unmanned.* Y: The Last Man series, vol. 1. Illustrated by Pia Guerra. DC Comics, 2003. PPYA 2006 (What Ails You?).
Yorick discovers that being the last man left alive in a world filled with women is not exactly a dream come true.

Vazquez, Diego. *Growing through the Ugly.* Holt, 1998. PPYA 1999 (Changing Dimensions).
Seventeen-year-old Buzzy, who had one of the first numbers to be called in the draft lottery, tells his life story while being flown back from Vietnam in his coffin.

Velez, Ivan. *Dead High Yearbook.* Dutton, 2007. QP 2008.
Eight grisly stories describe the death of students who are killed by explosions, encounters with vampires and zombies, and mundane car accidents in this graphic novel.

Viguie, Debbie. *Midnight Pearls.* Once upon a Time series. Simon Pulse, 2003. PPYA 2005 (Gateway to Faerie).
Plucked from the sea, Pearl and Prince James become friends, until rumors threaten that relationship in this variation of *The Little Mermaid.*

Vijayaraghavan, Vineeta. *Motherland.* Soho, 2002. PPYA 2003 (This Small World).
Maya spends the summer with relatives in the south of India, where she learns more about her family and how to balance her American and Indian cultures.

Vizzini, Ned. *Be More Chill.* Hyperion, 2004—QP 2005; Miramax, 2005—PPYA 2007 (What's So Funny?).
Desperate to impress Christine, nerdy Jeremy swallows a pill-size computer, which lodges in his brain and instructs him about what to wear or say to be cool.

Voigt, Cynthia. *Izzy, Willy-Nilly.* Fawcett Juniper, 1991. PPYA 2002 (Relationships).
The friends of pretty cheerleader Izzy desert her after she loses her leg in a car accident, but blunt, unattractive Rosamunde fills the void and helps her return to school.

———. *A Solitary Blue.* Aladdin, 2003. PPYA 2005 (Read 'Em and Weep).
Abandoned by his mother, Jeff is raised by his seemingly distant professor father. When his mother returns and he must decide with whom to live, he makes the right choice.

Volponi, Paul. *Black and White.* Viking, 2005—QP 2006; Puffin, 2006—PPYA 2008 (Anyone Can Play).
Best friends black Marcus and white Eddie jeopardize their futures in basketball, along with their friendship, when they stage a series of armed robberies.

———. *Rooftop.* Viking, 2006. QP 2007.
Cousins Clay and Addison reconnect when they're in the same drug treatment facility, but a rooftop meeting with police leads to tragedy.

———. *Rucker Park Setup.* Viking, 2007. QP 2008.
The death of his longtime friend and teammate J.R. during the legendary Rucker Park tournament leaves Mackey bereft and worried that he is at fault.

Von Ziegesar, Cecily. *Gossip Girl.* Gossip Girl series, book 1. Little, Brown, 2002. QP 2003.

A gossip website records the actions of wealthy teens who live on New York City's Upper East Side and cluster together for school, parties, shopping, and gossip.

———. *You Know You Love Me.* Gossip Girl series, book 2. Little, Brown, 2002. QP 2003.

With her mother preparing to marry a "tacky" boyfriend and her own boyfriend cheating on her, Blair is extremely nervous and distracted during her Yale interview.

Vrettos, Adrienne Maria. *Sight.* Margaret K. McElderry, 2007. QP 2008.

Since she was young, Dylan has aided the sheriff with her visions of dead children. Now she forces herself to watch the entire vision to save a special child.

———. *Skin.* Margaret K. McElderry, 2006. QP 2007.

Donnie and his sister Karen take different approaches to the domestic discord in their family; Donnie tries for invisibility while Karen chooses starvation.

Waid, Mark. *JLA: Tower of Babel.* DC Comics, 2001. QP 2003.

Ancient enemy Ra's al Ghul lures Justice League members into traps where one by one he eliminates them.

Wallace, Rich. *Playing without the Ball: A Novel in Four Quarters.* Random House, 2000. QP 2001.

Cut by his basketball coach to allow more playing time for younger team members, Jay signs up for a church league, where he meets a special girl.

———. *Wrestling Sturbridge.* Laurel-Leaf, 1997. PPYA 2008 (Anyone Can Play); PPYA 1999 (Good Sports).

Though his coach wants him to be his friend's workout partner, Ben wants to win the state championship wrestling title himself so he can escape from Sturbridge, Pennsylvania.

Wallington, Aury. *Pop!* Razorbill, 2006. PPYA 2008 (Sex Is . . .).

Convinced she needs to lose her virginity, Marit invites her good friend Jamie to lose his with her, but that plan leads to disaster.

Walters, Eric. *Overdrive.* Orca, 2004. QP 2005.

On the first day of his driver's license, Jake is driving his brother's souped-up Chevy and is goaded into a street race.

Warner, Sally. *Sort of Forever.* Knopf, 1998. QP 1999.

Cady's best friend Nana is diagnosed with terminal cancer, which makes her feel guilty about a new friend at school.

Wasserman, Robin. *The Awakening.* Chasing Yesterday series, book 1. Scholastic, 2007. QP 2008.

JD, short for Jane Doe, knows she's in danger—but why or from whom is lost to her after an explosion erases her memory.

Watase, Yuu. *Absolute Boyfriend.* Absolute Boyfriend series, vol. 1. VIZ, 2006. PPYA 2008 (Sex Is . . .).

Wishing for a boyfriend, Riko orders a "lover figurine" and a cute, naked guy arrives. Now she must decide whether to return him in three days or pay his $1,000,000 price tag.

Watson, Andi. *Geisha.* Oni, 1999. PPYA 2002 (Graphic Novels).

As an android, artist Jomi Sohodo is considered less than human, so no one buys her paintings. Needing rent money, she enters the family bodyguard business.

Watson, Carrie Gordon. *Quad.* Razorbill, 2007. QP 2008.
Within each school there are cliques that avoid one another. Now six students from different groups are trapped in the school store while a shooter is loose on the quad.

Watson, Larry. *Montana 1948.* Pocket, 1993. PPYA 2001 (Western).
The summer David becomes 12, he learns the importance of doing what's right when his sheriff father has to arrest his uncle Frank for abusing several Indian women.

Weaver, Will. *Memory Boy.* HarperTrophy, 2003. PPYA 2006 (Books That Don't Make You Blush).
Miles invents a fantastic vehicle that enables his family to escape from a worldwide ecological disaster.

Weber, Lori. *Klepto.* Lorimer, 2004. PPYA 2006 (Criminal Elements).
Hannah is the bad sister who is sent away for running drugs. Kat doesn't miss her, but she turns to shoplifting for the feeling of power it gives her.

Wells, Ken. *Meely LaBauve.* Random House, 2001. PPYA 2002 (Relationships).
When his father escapes to drink and hunt alligators, Meely is left on his own and spends a lot of time fending off those alligators, as well as the police.

Welter, John. *I Want to Buy a Vowel: A Novel of Illegal Alienation.* Berkley, 1997. PPYA 2001 (Humor).
Eleven-year-old Eva Galt comments on small town life, a teen who's a wannabe satanist, and an illegal immigrant she meets while exploring a haunted house.

Werlin, Nancy. *Black Mirror.* Puffin, 2003. PPYA 2005 (Own Your Freak).
To learn the truth about her brother's supposed suicide, Frances confronts her school's powerful charity club and her own distorted reflection.

——. *Double Helix.* Puffin, 2005. PPYA 2006 (What Ails You?).
The summer Eli works for a transgenics lab seems the perfect opportunity to be tested for the gene for Huntington's disease, which killed his mother.

——. *The Killer's Cousin.* Delacorte, 1998—QP 1999; Random House, 2000—PPYA 2003 (I've Got a Secret).
Acquitted of murder, 17-year-old David moves to another town and lives with his aunt and uncle, but his new home feels a lot less safe and secure than he'd hoped for.

——. *The Rules of Survival.* Dial, 2006. QP 2007.
Seventeen-year-old Matt protects his two younger sisters, Callie and Emmy, from the chaotic violence created by their manic, abusive mother.

Westall, Robert. *Demons and Shadows: The Ghostly Best Stories of Robert Westall.* Farrar, Straus, & Giroux, 1997. PPYA 2000 (Short Takes).
A posthumous collection of stories from a noted writer features churchyards, cats, and antiques, all with his characteristic tinge of terror.

Westerfeld, Scott. *The Last Days.* Razorbill, 2006. QP 2007.
As the peeps spread their destruction across the city, Moz and Zahler start up a band, and their music calls the giant worms from the ground so they can be destroyed.

——. *The Secret Hour.* Midnighters series, book 1. Eos, 2004. QP 2005; PPYA 2008 (Magic in the Real World).
Moving to Bixby, Oklahoma, Jessica is one

of a few midnighters who can move about during the 25th hour, when the rest of the townspeople are frozen in their beds.

———. *The Uglies.* Simon Pulse, 2005. PPYA 2006 (Books That Don't Make You Blush).
In Tally's world everyone is an Ugly, until they are turned into Pretties on their 16th birthday.

Weyn, Suzanne. *Bar Code Tattoo.* Scholastic, 2004. QP 2005.
Everyone now has a bar code tattoo, which acts as credit card or driver's license, but Kayla's refusal to get one sets her apart.

Whedon, Joss. *Fray.* Dark Horse, 2003. QP 2005.
Against her will, teen Melaka Fray is drawn into the battles against vampires when told that she is to become a vampire hunter.

Whelan, Gloria. *Homeless Bird.* HarperTrophy, 2001. PPYA 2002 (Tales of the Cities).
Widowed after an arranged marriage at 13, young Koly pays for her food and shelter by embroidering.

White, Ruth. *Weeping Willow.* Farrar, Straus, & Giroux, 1994. PPYA 2005 (Read 'Em and Weep).
Tiny enjoys high school, where she has friends and a chance to sing, but her homelife is dreadful, with a stepfather who rapes her and threatens to kill her dog if she tells on him.

Whitney, Kim Ablon. *See You down the Road.* Laurel-Leaf, 2005. PPYA 2006 (Criminal Elements).
Bridget's family was good at being like everyone else except when it came to one thing—obeying the law.

Whyman, Matt. *Boy Kills Man.* HarperCollins, 2005. QP 2006.
Sonny and Alberto help a local mobster in drug-ravaged Medellin, earning Alberto a gun and leaving Sonny jealous, until the day Alberto doesn't return home.

Wieler, Diana. *Drive.* Groundwood, 2001. PPYA 2004 (On That Note).
A busker and his brother embark on an impromptu concert tour to pay off a $5,000 debt for demo tapes.

———. *RanVan: The Defender.* RanVan trilogy, book 1. Groundwood, 1998. PPYA 1999 (Changing Dimensions).
Fifteen-year-old Rhan Van's dreams of saving damsels in distress and conquering evil come true when his world of video games overlaps with reality.

Wiess, Laura. *Such a Pretty Girl.* MTV, 2007. QP 2008.
After being raped by her father, Meredith thinks she will have more time before he is released from prison, but now he's coming home and she's scared.

Wilhelm, Kate. *The Good Children.* Fawcett, 1999. PPYA 2000 (Page Turners).
When the McNair siblings lose their last parent, they fear being split up and sent to foster homes, so they bury their mother and tell no one that she is dead.

Williams, Lori Aurelia. *Broken China.* Simon & Schuster, 2005. QP 2006.
Taking good care of a daughter she didn't want, 14-year-old China Cup is grief-stricken when Amina dies and she must perform in a strip club to pay for the funeral.

———. *When Kambia Elaine Flew in from Neptune.* Simon & Schuster, 2001. PPYA 2005 (Read 'Em and Weep).

Though Shayla's home life is filled with troubles, she realizes that Kambia Elaine's life is worse and that her imaginative stories cover up the sexual abuse she endures.

Williams-Garcia, Rita. *Fast Talk on a Slow Track.* Puffin, 1998. PPYA 2002 (Tales of the Cities).
Not doing well in Princeton's summer program, Denzel is ready to attend community college, but time with a street dude makes him realize his world lies with Princeton.

————. *Like Sisters on the Homefront.* Avon, 1987. PPYA 1999 (Different Drummers).
Sent to live with her cousins in a small Georgia town, 14-year-old Gayle brings both her baby and her New York City attitude, but her grandmother melts her tough façade.

Willingham, Bill. *Animal Farm.* Fables series, vol. 2. DC Comics, 2003. QP 2004.
Rose Red and Snow White visit the farm in upstate New York and learn that the nonhuman residents resent those living in Fabletown and are ready to revolt.

————. *Legends in Exile.* Fables series, vol. 1. DC Comics, 2002. QP 2004; PPYA 2005 (Gateway to Faerie).
Favorite human characters from fairy tales live in Fabletown in New York City while nonhuman ones live in upstate New York.

Willis, Connie. *The Doomsday Book.* Bantam, 1993. PPYA 2004 (Simply Science Fiction).
By mistake a time-traveling graduate student winds up at the wrong date in the Middle Ages, just as the Black Plague strikes.

————. *To Say Nothing of the Dog.* Bantam, 1998. PPYA 1999 (Changing Dimensions).
Sent to retrieve an artifact from Victorian England, time-traveling Oxford students accidentally alter the past and can't quite fix their mistakes.

Wilson, Jacqueline. *Girls in Love.* Delacorte, 2002. QP 2003.
Returning to school and discovering that her best friends all have boyfriends, Ellie decides she needs one, too, though hers is a composite of several guys she met over the summer.

Windling, Terri, and Delia Sherman, eds. *The Essential Bordertown.* Tor, 1999. PPYA 2005 (Gateway to Faerie).
Thirteen noted fantasy writers, from McKillip to Brust and de Lint, tell about Bordertown, the city where humans and fairy folk interact.

Windsor, Patricia. *The Blooding.* Scholastic, 1999. PPYA 2001 (Paranormal).
Maris's summer as an au pair takes a terrifying turn when she discovers she is working for a werewolf.

Winick, Judd. *The Adventures of Barry Ween, Boy Genius.* Oni, 2000. PPYA 2002 (Graphic Novels).
When you're only ten years old and have an IQ of 350, you're allowed to be cranky when you're continually bothered and kept from completing your experiments.

————. *Brother's Keeper.* Green Lantern series, vol. 3. Illustrated by Dale Eaglesham. DC Comics, 2003. PPYA 2006 (GLBTQ).
When his best friend is brutally gay-bashed, Kyle Rayner, aka the Green Lantern, accepts that his powers can't change everything.

Wister, Owen. *The Virginian.* Forge, 1998. PPYA 2001 (Western).
First published in 1902, this classic romance features the tough but fair cowpuncher called the Virginian, who loses his heart to a young Vermont schoolteacher.

Wittlinger, Ellen. *Hard Love.* Simon & Schuster, 1999—QP 2000; Simon & Schuster, 2001—PPYA 2002 (Relationships).
Though Marisol warns him that she is a lesbian, lonely John allows himself to move past friendship into love, only to have his heart broken on prom night.

———. *The Long Night of Leo and Bree.* Simon & Schuster, 2002. QP 2003.
Angry that his sister died in a car accident, Leo kidnaps Bree with the intention of killing her, but he discards that idea after a night of talking and sharing personal demons.

———. *Razzle.* Simon Pulse, 2003. PPYA 2005 (Own Your Freak).
Ken almost chooses a self-centered sexpot intent on a modeling career rather than tall, independent Razzle, who doesn't care that she is different.

———. *Zigzag.* Simon Pulse, 2003. PPYA 2008 (What Makes a Family?).
With her boyfriend in Rome for the summer, Robin joins her aunt and cousins on a trip to the Southwest and finally discovers her relatives' good qualities.

Wolff, Virginia. *Make Lemonade.* Scholastic, 1994. PPYA 2002 (Tales of the Cities).
Though living amid poverty and crime, LaVaughn works hard to keep up her grades and earn money for college.

———. *The Mozart Season.* Scholastic, 1991. PPYA 2004 (On That Note).
Preparing for a music competition, Allegra brings all facets of her life into her interpretation of the Mozart concerto she is practicing.

———. *Probably Still Nick Swansen.* Scholastic, 1997. PPYA 1999 (Different Drummers).
Sweet, sensitive Nick musters his courage and invites Shana to the prom. She says yes, but prom night turns disastrous for Nick.

Woods, Brenda. *Emako Blue.* Penguin Putnam, 2004. QP 2005.
Monterey, Jamal, and Eddie know that Emako's beautiful voice will lead her to stardom, but then comes the day she is mistaken for her brother and killed in a drive-by shooting.

Woodson, Jacqueline. *Behind You.* Penguin Putnam, 2004. QP 2005.
Jeremiah's family and friends struggle to deal with his accidental death while he watches and tries to let them know how much he loves them.

———. *From the Notebooks of Melanin Sun.* Scholastic, 2003. PPYA 2006 (GLBTQ).
Melanin can't understand why his mother, once his best friend, has to fall in love with some white lady and destroy the relationship they used to have.

———. *The House You Pass on the Way.* Puffin, 2003. PPYA 2006 (GLBTQ).
Once Staggerlee kissed a girl, and she and her cousin Tyler really like one another, which leaves her confused about her sexual identity and wondering if she is a lesbian.

———. *If You Come Softly.* Putnam, 2000. PPYA 2002 (Tales of the Cities).

Black Jeremiah and white Ellie are in love, but it seems that racism and prejudice will forever haunt their relationship.

———. *Miracle's Boys*. Puffin, 2006. PPYA 2008 (What Makes a Family?).
After their mother Milagro dies, it will be a miracle if newly orphaned Lafayette, Charlie, and Ty'ree Bailey can survive as a family with the obstacles they face.

Wrede, Patricia. *Dealing with Dragons.* Scholastic, 1992. PPYA 2001 (Humor).
Running away from her castle, Princess Cimorene discovers that being captured by a dragon is preferable to meeting more boring suitors.

Wynne-Jones, Tim. *The Boy in the Burning House.* Farrar, Straus, & Giroux, 2000. PPYA 2004 (Guess Again).
Investigating his father's disappearance leads Jim to suspect the minister, whose stepdaughter claims he was involved in another murder 30 years earlier.

Yamanaka, Lois-Ann. *Name Me Nobody.* Hyperion, 2000. PPYA 2005 (Read 'Em and Weep); PPYA 2003 (This Small World).
When Emi-Lou, raised in Hawaii, realizes that her friend Von likes girls, her grandmother helps her understand the need to accept people as they are.

Yazawa, Ai. *Paradise Kiss.* Paradise Kiss series, vol. 1. Tokyopop, 2002. PPYA 2007 (Get Creative).
Bookworm Yukari is kidnapped by fashion school students who turn her life upside down when they want her to be their model.

Yolen, Jane. *Boots and the Seven Leaguers: A Rock-and-Troll Novel.* Magic Carpet, 2003. PPYA 2004 (On That Note).
While attending the concert of his favorite rock-and-troll band, Gog's brother Magog is kidnapped and Gog uses more than magic to free his squirmy brother.

———. *Briar Rose.* Tor, 2002. PPYA 2003 (I've Got a Secret).
The fairy tale of Briar Rose and the reality of the Jewish Holocaust intertwine in Becca's grandmother's stories. Later, Becca travels to Poland to locate her grandmother's castle.

———. *Dragon's Blood.* Pit Dragon trilogy, book 1. Harcourt, 1996. PPYA 2003 (Flights of Fantasy).
Dreaming of being a dragon trainer, a stable boy steals an egg, knowing that if the dragon flies successfully he'll be able to earn enough money to buy his freedom.

Yolen, Jane, and Bruce Coville. *Armageddon Summer.* Harcourt Brace, 1998. QP 1999.
Marina and Jed meet at a mountain retreat, dragged there by their parents to await the end of the world, as predicted by Reverend Beelson.

Yolen, Jane, and Adam Stemple. *Troll Bridge: A Rock 'n' Roll Fairy Tale.* Starscape, 2007. PPYA 2008 (Magic in the Real World).
County fair princesses and three teen brothers from a rock-and-roll band meet on the Trollholm Bridge and enter a world where a fox and a troll are locked in battle.

Yoshizumi, Wataru. *Ultra Maniac.* Ultra Maniac series, vol. 1. VIZ, 2005. PPYA 2008 (Magic in the Real World).
Shy Ayu befriends Nina, not realizing that she is a witch whose spells and potions never work quite right in this manga tale.

Yukimura, Makoto. *Planetes.* Planetes series, vol. 1. Tokyopop, 2003. PPYA 2004 (Simply Science Fiction).

Yuri, Hachimaki, and Fee each have their own reason for taking a job as a space junker.

Yumoto, Kazumi. *The Friends.* Yearling, 1998. PPYA 2003 (This Small World).
Curious about death, three Japanese boys select an old man they are sure will die soon and follow him around, but the old man is so pleased by their attention that he perks up.

Zarr, Sara. *Story of a Girl.* Little, Brown, 2007. QP 2008.
Deanna has to live with the wrath of her father and the horrid nickname "school slut" because of her one mistake in the back of Tommy's Buick.

Zeises, Lara M. *Anyone but You.* Laurel-Leaf, 2007. PPYA 2008 (What Makes a Family?).
Stepsiblings Critter and Seattle have always been close until this summer when Critter falls for a rich, pretty girl, which makes Seattle jealous.

Zindel, Paul. *Night of the Bat.* Hyperion, 2001. QP 2002.
In the Amazon to help his father's research project on echolocation in bats, Jake helps catch a giant mutated bat that has already eaten several project members.

———. *Rats.* Hyperion, 1999—QP 2000; Hyperion, 2000—PPYA 2002 (Tales of the Cities).
Asphalting a landfill drives out the rats and sends them into toilets, water parks, and even people's beds until Michael and his white rat Surfer figure out a way to stop them.

———. *Reef of Death.* HarperCollins, 1998. QP 1999.
Trying to help his uncle recover a sea treasure off the Great Barrier Reef, PC must defeat the wicked scientist who controls the carnivorous sea monster guarding the treasure.

CHAPTER 7

THEME-ORIENTED BOOKLISTS
Pam Spencer Holley

T he books in the themed lists are selected from the 1999–2008 Quick Picks and Popular Paperbacks lists. The lists in this chapter were selected on the basis of teen interests, which were evident from the original selections. In addition to these thematic lists, the original PPYA and QP lists are available on the YALSA website at www.ala.org/yalsa/booklists/.

Well-liked topics, as judged by the number of titles within various subject areas, determined which lists were developed. The popularity of tattoos, hip-hop music, vampires, and witches is readily evident from just glancing over some of the original lists, but other subjects also proved of interest to teens. Do-it-yourself projects were common in the areas of crafts, fashion, and beauty, as were books on fashion and beauty advice from experts. Some other popular topics in the area of creativity were cartooning, drawing, and photography. Works by teens for teens, anime and manga, and popular culture reflect changing interests in the teen world from a decade ago, but some standard themes remain popular, including school life, romance, sports, and automobiles and motorcycles. And how could one not include a list of disgusting things or amazing facts or some of those books about really odd and unusual subjects such as human stupidity?

Some of the titles selected for QP or PPYA are among YALSA award winners from the Alex, Edwards, or Printz lists (for more about these awards, visit www.ala.org/yalsa/booklists/). In this chapter, these books are grouped under a Multiple-Award Winners section, and a display of them would interest a wide variety of teens as well as other library patrons. Many of the selections also appeared on more than one PPYA or QP list; these are grouped under Overlapping Titles.

These lists are intended for readers' advisory work, displays, or bookmarks and can be added to or edited to reflect library holdings. The lists vary in length depending upon the number of titles on the original lists. Because all the annotations are provided in chapters 5 and 6, no further annotations are provided here. Several of the lists can be downloaded from the book's website, at www.ala.org/editions/extras/holley35774.

Whether the teens in your library devour books, read only when they have to, or avoid reading as much as possible, there are enough titles on these lists to provide everyone with something fun to read.

ABUSE (FICTION)

Atkins, Catherine. *When Jeff Comes Home.*

Glovach, Linda. *Beauty Queen.*

Goobie, Beth. *Something Girl.*

Gould, Stephen. *Jumper.*

Hopkins, Ellen. *Crank.*

———. *Glass.*

Jones, Patrick. *Things Change.*

Neenan, Colin. *Thick.*

Neufeld, John. *Boys Lie.*

Newman, Leslea. *Jailbait.*

Peters, Kimberly Joy. *Painting Caitlyn.*

Shaw, Susan. *The Boy from the Basement.*

Werlin, Nancy. *The Rules of Survival.*

AMAZING FACTS (NONFICTION)

Ash, Russell. *Firefly's World of Facts.*

———. *The Top 10 of Everything 1998.*

Boese, Alex. *Hippo Eats Dwarf: A Field Guide to Hoaxes and Other B.S.*

Buckley, James, Jr. *Scholastic Book of Firsts: More Than 1000 of the Coolest, Biggest, and Most Exciting First Facts You'll Ever Read.*

Leslie, Jeremy, and David Roberts. *Pick Me Up.*

Meserole, Mike. *Ultimate Sports Lists.*

Morse, Jenifer Corr. *Scholastic Book of World Records 2004.*

Perel, David, and the editors of the Weekly World News. *Bat Boy Lives! "The Weekly World News" Guide to Politics, Culture, Celebrities, Alien Abductions, and the Mutant Freaks That Shape Our World.*

Ripley's Believe It or Not.

ANIME AND MANGA (FICTION AND NONFICTION)

Araki, Hirohito. *Jojo's Bizarre Adventure.* (F)

Aranzo, Aronzi. *The Bad Book.* (NF)

Azuma, Kiyohiko. *Yotsuba&!* series. (F)

Greatest Stars of the NBA series. Vol. 1, *Shaquille O'Neal;* vol. 2, *Tim Duncan;* vol. 3, *Jason Kidd;* vol. 4, *Kevin Garnett.* (NF)

Hart, Christopher. *Anime Mania: How to Draw Characters for Japanese Animation.* (NF)

———. *Manga Mania Chibi and Furry Characters: How to Draw the Adorable Mini-Characters and Cool Cat Girls of Japanese Comics,* and many more by this author. (NF)

Hirano, Kohta. *Hellsing* series. (F)

Japanese Comickers: Draw Anime and Manga like Japan's Hottest Artists. (NF)

Marunas, Nathaniel, and Erik Craddock. *The Blade of Kringle.* (F)

Nagatomo, Haruno. *Draw Your Own Manga: All the Basics.* (NF)

Ohba, Tsugumi. *Death Note.* (F)

Shakespeare, William. *Manga Shakespeare: Romeo and Juliet.* (NF)

Sugiyama, Rika. *Comics Artists—Asia: Manga Manhwa Manhua.* (NF)

Takaya, Natsuki. Fruits Basket series. (F)

Yoshizumi, Wataru. *Ultra Maniac.* (NF)

BEAUTY ACCORDING TO EXPERTS (NONFICTION)

Banks, Tyra. *Tyra's Beauty Inside and Out.*

Bressler, Karen W., and Susan Redstone. *D.I.Y. Beauty.*

Brous, Elizabeth. *How to Be Gorgeous: The Ultimate Beauty Guide to Hair, Makeup and More.*

Brown, Bobbi, and Annemarie Iverson. *Bobbi Brown Teenage Beauty: Everything You Need to Know to Look Pretty, Natural, Sexy and Awesome.*

Cooke, Kaz. *Real Gorgeous: The Truth about Body and Beauty.*

Fornay, Alfred. *Born Beautiful: The African American Teenager's Complete Beauty Guide.*

Irons, Diane. *Teen Beauty Secrets: Fresh, Simple and Sassy Tips for Your Perfect Look.*

Knowles, Tina. *Destiny's Style: Bootylicious Fashion, Beauty, and Lifestyle Secrets from Destiny's Child.*

Odes, Rebecca, Esther Drill, and Heather McDonald. *The Looks Book: A Whole New Approach to Beauty, Body Image, and Style.*

Pratt, Jane. *Beyond Beauty: Girls Speak Out on Looks, Style and Stereotypes.*

Teen People magazine, ed. *"Teen People" Celebrity Beauty Guide: Star Secrets for Gorgeous Hair, Makeup, Skin and More!*

Thalia, with Belen Atanda-Alvarado. *Thalia: Belleza! Lessons in Lipgloss and Happiness.*

Yoshinaga, Masayuki. *Gothic and Lolita.*

BLACK HISTORY MONTH (FICTION)

Adoff, Jaime. *Jimi and Me.*

Booth, Coe. *Tyrell.*

Brooks, Bruce. *The Moves Make the Man.*

Curtis, Christopher Paul. *The Watsons Go to Birmingham—1963.*

Davidson, Dana. *Jason and Kyra.*

Draper, Sharon M. *Forged by Fire.*

Frost, Helen. *Keesha's House.*

Hamilton, Virginia. *The House of Dies Drear.*

Johnson, Angela. *The First Part Last.*

Kidd, Sue Monk. *The Secret Life of Bees.*

Lyons, Mary E. *Letters from a Slave Girl: The Story of Harriet Jacobs.*

Myers, Walter Dean. *Hoops.*

———. *The Righteous Revenge of Artemis Bonner.*

———. *What They Found: Love on 145th Street.*

Sinclair, April. *Coffee Will Make You Black.*

Stratton, Allan. *Chanda's Secrets.*

Volponi, Paul. *Black and White.*

———. *Rucker Park Setup.*

Williams-Garcia, Rita. *Fast Talk on a Slow Track.*

Woodson, Jacqueline. *If You Come Softly.*

———. *Miracle's Boys.*

BLACK HISTORY MONTH (NONFICTION)

Adoff, Arnold, ed. *I Am the Darker Brother: An Anthology of Modern Poems by African Americans.*

Beals, Melba Pattillo. *Warriors Don't Cry: A Searing Memoir of the Battle to Integrate Little Rock's Central High.*

Bell, Janet Chatman, and Lucille Usher Freeman, eds. *Stretch Your Wings: Famous Black Quotations for Teens.*

Carroll, Rebecca. *Sugar in the Raw: Voices of Young Black Girls in America.*

Forman, Ruth. *We Are the Young Magicians.*

Fornay, Alfred. *Born Beautiful: The African American Teenager's Complete Beauty Guide.*

Okutoro, Lydia Omolola, ed. *Quiet Storm: Voices of Young Black Poets.*

Patterson, Lindsay, ed. *A Rock against the Wind: African American Poems and Letters of Love and Passion.*

Shakur, Tupac. *The Rose That Grew from Concrete.*

Wallace, Terry. *Bloods: An Oral History of the Vietnam War by Black Veterans.*

BODY ADORNMENT (FICTION AND NONFICTION)

Barnes, Jennifer Lynn. *Tattoo.* (F)

Gerard, Jim. *Celebrity Skin: Tattoos, Brands, and Body Adornments of the Stars.* (NF)

Gottlieb, Andrew. *In the Paint: Tattoos of the NBA and the Stories behind Them.* (NF)

Hogya, Bernie, and Sal Taibi. *Milk Mustache Mania.* (NF)

Miller, Jean-Chris. *The Body Art Book: A Complete Illustrated Guide to Tattoos, Piercings, and Other Body Modifications.* (NF)

Polhemus, Ted. *Hot Bodies, Cool Styles: New Techniques in Self-Adornment.* (NF)

Saltz, Ina. *Body Type: Intimate Messages Etched in Flesh.* (NF)

Schreiber, Mark. *Starcrossed.* (F)

Schulberg, Jay. *The Milk Mustache Book.* (NF)

Tattoo Nation: Portraits of Celebrity Body Art. (NF)

Weyn, Suzanne. *Bar Code Tattoo.* (F)

Yoshinaga, Masayuki. *Gothic and Lolita.* (NF)

BY TEENS, FOR TEENS (NONFICTION)

Writings by teens range from poetry to recipes and offer a look at what is important to them.

Canfield, Jack, Mark Victor Hansen, and Kimberly Kirberger. *Chicken Soup for the Teenage Soul II: 101 More Stories of Life, Love, and Learning.*

Carle, Megan, and Jill Carle. *Teens Cook: How to Cook What You Want to Eat.*

Carroll, Rebecca. *Sugar in the Raw: Voices of Young Black Girls in America.*

Diary of a Junior Year.

Franco, Betsy, ed. *Things I Have to Tell You: Poems and Writings by Teenage Girls.*

———. *You Hear Me? Poems and Writing by Teenage Boys.*

Friedman, Linda, and Dana White, eds. *Teen People: Real Life Diaries; Inspiring True Stories from Celebrities and Real Teens.*

Gootman, Marilyn E. *When a Friend Dies: A Book for Teens about Grieving and Healing.*

Hear Me Out: True Stories of Teens Educating and Confronting Homophobia.

Johnson, Dave, ed. *Movin': Teen Poets Take Voice.*

Kalergis, Mary Motley, ed. *Seen and Heard: Teenagers Talk about Their Lives.*

Paint Me like I Am: Teen Poems.

Patnaik, Gayatri, and Michelle T. Shinseki. *The Secret Life of Teens: Young People Speak Out about Their Lives.*

Pletka, Bob, ed. *My So-Called Digital Life: 2,000 Teenagers, 300 Cameras, and 30 Days to Document Their World.*

Pratt, Jane. *Beyond Beauty: Girls Speak Out on Looks, Style and Stereotypes.*

Seventeen magazine, ed. *Seventeen Presents . . . Traumarama! Real Girls Share Their Most Embarrassing Moments Ever.*

Tom, Karen, and Kiki, eds. *Angst! Teen Verses from the Edge.*

Watson, Esther Pearl, and Mark Todd, eds. *The Pain Tree, and Other Teenage Angst-Ridden Poetry.*

CARTOONING AND DRAWING (NONFICTION)

Caldwell, Ben. *Fantasy! Cartooning.*

Hart, Christopher. *Anime Mania: How to Draw Characters for Japanese Animation.*

———. *Manga Mania Chibi and Furry Characters: How to Draw the Adorable Mini-Characters and Cool Cat Girls of Japanese Comics.*

———. *Manga Mania Fantasy Worlds: How to Draw the Amazing World of Japanese Comics.*

———. *Manga Mania: How to Draw Japanese Comics.*

———. *Manga Mania Villains: How to Draw the Dastardly Characters of Japanese Comics.*

———. *Manhwa Mania: How to Draw Korean Comics.*

———. *Mecha Mania. How to Draw the Battling Robots, Cool Shapeships, and Military Vehicles of Japanese Comics.*

Japanese Comickers: Draw Anime and Manga like Japan's Hottest Artists.

Miller, Steve, and Bryan Baugh. *Scared! How to Draw Fantastic Horror Comic Characters.*

Nagatomo, Haruno. *Draw Your Own Manga: All the Basics.*

Scott, Damion, and Kris Ex. *How to Draw Hip Hop.*

Sugiyama, Rika. *Comics Artists—Asia: Manga Manhwa Manhua.*

CRAFTS (NONFICTION)

Aranzo, Aronzi. *The Bad Book.*

Blakeney, Faith, Justina Blakeney, and Ellen Schultz. *99 Ways to Cut, Sew, and Deck Out Your Denim.*

Bonnell, Jennifer. *D.I.Y. Girl: The Real Girl's Guide to Making Everything from Lip Gloss to Lamps.*

CosmoGirl, ed. *CosmoGirl! Make It Yourself: 50 Fun and Funky Projects.*

Haab, Sherri. *The Hip Handbag Book: 25 Easy-to-Make Totes, Purses and Bags.*

Knapp, Jennifer. *Cheap Frills: Fabulous Facelifts for Your Clothes.*

Murillo, Kathy Cano. *Crafty Chica's Art de la Soul: Glittery Ideas to Liven Up Your Life.*

Naylor, Caroline. *Beauty Trix for Cool Chix: Easy-to-Make Lotions, Potions, and Spells to Bring Out a Beautiful You.*

Nicolay, Megan. *Generation T: 108 Ways to Transform a T-Shirt.*

Okey, Shannon. *Knitgrrl: Learn to Knit with 15 Fun and Funky Projects.*

Rannels, Melissa, Melissa Alvarado, and others. *Sew Subversive: Down and Dirty DIY for the Fabulous Fashionista.*

Rogge, Hannah. *Hardware: Jewelry from a Toolbox.*

———. *Save This Shirt: Cut It, Stitch It, Wear It Now!*

Traig, Jennifer. *Makeup: Things to Make and Do.*

———. *Slumber Parties: Things to Make and Do.*

Vitkus, Jessica. *AlternaCrafts: 20+ Hi-Style Lo-Budget Projects to Make.*

DATING (FICTION)

Barnes, Derrick. *The Making of Dr. Truelove.*

Black, Jonah. The Black Book: Diary of a Teenage Stud series. Vol. 1, *Girls, Girls, Girls;* vol. 2, *Stop, Don't Stop.*

Bradley, Alex. *24 Girls in 7 Days.*

Brian, Kate. *The Princess and the Pauper.*

Clarke, Miranda. *Night of a Thousand Boyfriends.*

Cray, Jordan. *Gemini7.*

Davidson, Dana. *Jason and Kyra.*

Eberhardt, Thom. *Rat Boys: A Dating Experiment.*

Grant, Vicki. *Dead-End Job.*

Jones, Patrick. *Things Change.*

McKayhan, Monica. *Indigo Summer.*

McPhee, Phoebe. *The Alphabetical Hookup List A–J.*

Perez, Marlene. *Unexpected Development.*

Peters, Kimberly Joy. *Painting Caitlyn.*

Standiford, Natalie. The Dating Game series. Book 1, *The Dating Game;* book 2, *Breaking Up Is Really, Really Hard to Do.*

Stewart, Sean, Jordan Weisman, and others. *Cathy's Book: If Found Call 650-266-8233.*

Stone, Tanya Lee. *A Bad Boy Can Be Good for a Girl.*

EEEWWW! ALL MANNER OF DISGUSTING THINGS (NONFICTION)

Handy, Roger, and Karin Elsener, eds. *Found Photos: Rear Ends.*

Holt, David, and Bill Mooney. *Spiders in the Hairdo: Modern Urban Legends.*

Jillette, Penn, and Teller. *Penn and Teller's How to Play with Your Food.*

Masoff, Joy. *Oh, Yuck! The Encyclopedia of Everything Nasty.*

Meglin, Nick, and John Ficarra, eds. *The "Mad" Gross Book.*

Menzel, Peter, and Faith D'Aluisio. *Man Eating Bugs: The Art and Science of Eating Insects.*

O'Donnell, Kerri. *Inhalants and Your Nasal Passages: The Incredibly Disgusting Story.*

Roach, Mary. *Stiff: The Curious Lives of Human Cadavers.*

Shaw, Tucker. *"What's That Smell?" (Oh, It's Me): 50 Mortifying Situations and How to Deal.*

Szpirglas, Jeff. *Gross Universe: Your Guide to All Disgusting Things under the Sun.*

FRIENDSHIP (FICTION)

Acito, Marc. *How I Paid for College: A Novel of Sex, Theft, Friendship, and Musical Theater.*

Block, Francesca Lia. *Violet and Claire.*

Brooks, Bruce. *The Moves Make the Man.*

Chambers, Veronica. *Marisol and Magdalena: The Sound of Our Sisterhood.*

Danziger, Paula, and Ann M. Martin. *P.S. Longer Letter Later.*

————. *Snail Mail No More.*

Dessen, Sarah. *Someone like You.*

Griffin, Adele. *Amandine.*

Harazin, S. A. *Blood Brothers.*

Juwell and Precious. *The Absolute Truth.*

Lubar, David. *Hidden Talents.*

McDaniel, Lurlene. *Six Months to Live.*

Minter. J. *The Insiders.*

Myers, Anna. *Ethan between Us.*

Myers, Walter Dean. *Autobiography of My Dead Brother.*

Myracle, Lauren. *TTYL.*

Tanzman, Carol M. *Shadow Place.*

Turning Seventeen series. Vol. 1, *Any Guy You Want* by Rosalind Noonan; vol. 2, *More Than This* by Wendy Corsi Staub; vol. 3, *For Real* by Christa Roberts; vol. 4, *Show Me Love* by Elizabeth Craft.

Warner, Sally. *Sort of Forever.*

GLBTQ (FICTION)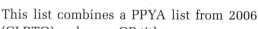

This list combines a PPYA list from 2006 (GLBTQ) and some QP titles.

Acito, Marc. *How I Paid for College: A Novel of Sex, Theft, Friendship, and Musical Theater.*

De Oliveira, Eddie. *Lucky.*

Ferris, Jean. *Eight Seconds.*

Freymann-Weyr, Garret. *My Heartbeat.*

Hartinger, Brent. *The Geography Club.*

Johnson, Maureen. *The Bermudez Triangle.*

Kannagi, Satoru, and Hotaru Odagiri. *Only the Ring Finger Knows.*

Lackey, Mercedes. *Magic's Pawn.*

Levithan, David. *Boy Meets Boy.*

Moore, Terry. *Strangers in Paradise: High School.*

Peters, Julie Anne. *Define "Normal."*

————. *Keeping You a Secret.*

Revoyr, Nina. *The Necessary Hunger.*

Rucka, Greg. *Half a Life.*

Sanchez, Alex. *Rainbow Boys.*

Sloan, Brian. *A Really Nice Prom Mess.*

St. James, James. *Freak Show.*

Winick, Judd. *Brother's Keeper.*

Wittlinger, Ellen. *Hard Love.*

Woodson, Jacqueline. *From the Notebooks of Melanin Sun.*

————. *The House You Pass on the Way.*

Yamanaka, Lois-Ann. *Name Me Nobody.*

GOT WHEELS? (NONFICTION)

Armstrong, Lance, and Sally Jenkins. *It's Not about the Bike: My Journey Back to Life.*

Burgess-Wise, David. *The Ultimate Race Car Book.*

Coombs, Davey, and the editors of Racer X Illustrated. *MX: The Way of the Motocrosser.*

Flaherty, Mike. *American Chopper: At Full Throttle.*

Genat, Robert. *Funny Cars.*

————. *Lowriders.*

Hayhurst, Chris. *Bicycle Stunt Riding! Catch Air.*

————. *Mountain Biking: Get on the Trail.*

Johnstone, Mike. *NASCAR: The Need for Speed.*

Klancher, Lee. *Monster Garage: How to Customize Damn Near Anything.*

Lane, Billy. *Billy Lane Chop Fiction: It's Not a Motorcycle Baby, It's a Chopper!*

Lord, Trevor. *Big Book of Cars.*

Miller, Timothy, and Steve Milton. *NASCAR Now!*

Rohrer, Russ. *Ten Days in the Dirt: The Spectacle of Off-Road Motorcycling.*

Seate, Mike. *Choppers: Heavy Metal Art.*

———. *Jesse James: The Man and His Machines.*

———. *Streetbike Extreme.*

Smedman, Lisa. *From Boneshakers to Choppers: The Rip-Roaring History of Motorcycles.*

HIP-HOP MUSIC AND MUSICIANS (NONFICTION)

Ashanti. *Foolish/Unfoolish: Reflections on Love.*

Coker, Cheo Hodari. *Unbelievable: The Life, Death and Afterlife of the Notorious B.I.G.*

Eleveld, Mark, ed. *The Spoken Word Revolution: Slam, Hip Hop and the Poetry of a New Generation.*

Farley, Christopher John. *Aaliyah: More Than a Woman.*

Fricke, Jim. *Yes Yes Y'all: The Experience Music Project Oral History of Hip-Hop's First Decade.*

Hip Hop Divas.

Kenner, Rob, and George Pitts. *VX: 10 Years of Vibe Photography.*

Kramer, Nika. *We B*Girlz.*

Malone, Bonz. *Hip-Hop Immortals: The Remix.*

Oh, Minya. *Bling Bling: Hip Hop's Crown Jewels.*

Powell, Kevin. *Who Shot Ya? Three Decades of Hiphop Photography.*

Scott, Damion, and Kris Ex. *How to Draw Hip Hop.*

Steffans, Karrine. *Confessions of a Video Vixen.*

Thigpen, David E. *Jam Master Jay: The Heart of Hip-Hop.*

Vibe magazine, ed. *Tupac Shakur.*

Westbrook, Alonzo. *Hip Hoptionary: The Dictionary of Hip Hop Terminology.*

MULTIPLE-AWARD WINNERS (FICTION AND NONFICTION) 🌐

Anderson, Laurie Halse. *Speak.* Printz Honor 2000; QP 2000. (F)

Barry, Lynda. *One Hundred Demons.* Alex 2003; PPYA 2007. (NF)

Block, Francesca Lia. *Cherokee Bat and the Goat Guys.* Edwards 2005; PPYA 2004. (F)

———. *Missing Angel Juan.* Edwards 2005; PPYA 2002. (F)

———. *Witch Baby.* Edwards 2005; PPYA 1999. (F)

Blume, Judy. *Forever.* Edwards 1996; PPYA 2008. (F)

Bradley, James, and Ron Powers. *Flags of Our Fathers: Heroes of Iwo Jima.* Alex 2001; PPYA 2004. (NF)

Card, Orson Scott. *Ender's Game.* Edwards 2008; PPYA 2000. (F)

———. *Ender's Shadow.* Alex 2000; Edwards 2008; PPYA 2004. (F)

Carroll, Rebecca. *Sugar in the Raw: Voices of Young Black Girls in America.* Alex 1998; PPYA 2000. (NF)

Colton, Larry. *Counting Coup: A True Story of Basketball and Honor on the Little Big Horn.* Alex 2001; PPYA 2008. (NF)

Cook, Karin. *What Girls Learn: A Novel.* Alex 1998; PPYA 2006. (F)

Crutcher, Chris. *Athletic Shorts: Six Short Stories.* Edwards 2000; PPYA 2000. (F)

———. *Staying Fat for Sarah Byrnes.* Edwards 2000; PPYA 1999. (F)

Davis, Amanda. *Wonder When You'll Miss Me.* Alex 2004; PPYA 2005. (F)

Duncan, Lois. *I Know What You Did Last Summer.* Edwards 1992; PPYA 2005. (F)

Freymann-Weyr, Garret. *My Heartbeat.* Printz Honor 2003; PPYA 2006. (F)

Frost, Helen. *Keesha's House.* Printz Honor 2004; PPYA 2008. (F)

Gaiman, Neil. *Stardust.* Alex 2000; PPYA 2003. (F)

Gantos, Jack. *Hole in My Life.* Printz Honor 2003; PPYA 2006. (NF)

Going, K. L. *Fat Kid Rules the World.* Printz Honor 2004; PPYA 2005. (F)

Green, John. *Looking for Alaska.* Printz Winner 2006; QP 2006. (F)

Haddon, Mark. *The Curious Incident of the Dog in the Night-Time.* Alex 2004; PPYA 2006. (F)

Hamill, Pete. *Snow in August.* Alex 1998; PPYA 2002. (F)

Hinton, S. E. *The Outsiders.* Edwards 1988; PPYA 2006. (F)

Johnson, Angela. *The First Part Last.* Printz Winner 2004; QP 2004. (F)

Kerr, M. E. *Gentlehands.* Edwards 1993; PPYA 2003. (F)

Kluger, Steve. *Last Days of Summer.* Alex 1999; PPYA 2003. (F)

LeGuin, Ursula K. *A Wizard of Earthsea.* Edwards 2004; PPYA 2003. (F)

Lipsyte, Robert. *The Contender.* Edwards 2004; PPYA 1999. (F)

Martinez, A. Lee. *Gil's All Fright Diner.* Alex 2006; PPYA 2007. (F)

Myers, Walter Dean. *Hoops.* Edwards 1994; PPYA 1999. (F)

———. *Monster.* Printz Winner 2000; PPYA 2006. (F)

Oppel, Kenneth. *Airborn.* Printz Honor 2005; PPYA 2006. (F)

Picoult, Jodi. *My Sister's Keeper.* Alex 2005; PPYA 2006. (F)

Plum-Ucci, Carol. *The Body of Christopher Creed.* Printz Honor 2001; PPYA 2004. (F)

Porter, Connie. *Imani All Mine.* Alex 2000; PPYA 2005. (F)

Rennison, Louise. *Angus, Thongs, and Full-Frontal Snogging.* Printz Honor 2001; QP 2001. (F)

Roach, Mary. *Stiff: The Curious Lives of Human Cadavers.* Alex 2004; PPYA 2007. (NF)

Salzman, Mark. *True Notebooks: A Writer's Year at Juvenile Hall.* Alex 2004; PPYA 2007. (NF)

Santiago, Esmeralda. *Almost a Woman.* Alex 1999; PPYA 2002. (NF)

Satrapi, Marjane. *The Story of a Childhood.* Alex 2004; PPYA 2007. (NF)

Shepard, Jim. *Project X: A Novel.* Alex 2005; PPYA 2006. (F)

Stratton, Allan. *Chanda's Secrets.* Printz Honor 2005; PPYA 2005. (F)

Trueman, Terry. *Stuck in Neutral.* Printz Honor 2001; QP 2001. (F)

Vijayaraghavan, Vineeta. *Motherland.* Alex 2002; PPYA 2003. (F)

Voigt, Cynthia. *A Solitary Blue.* Edwards 1995; PPYA 2005. (F)

Walls, Jeannette. *The Glass Castle: A Memoir.* Alex 2006; PPYA 2008. (NF)

Willis, Connie. *To Say Nothing of the Dog.* Alex 1998; PPYA 1999. (F)

Wittlinger, Ellen. *Hard Love.* Printz Honor 2000; QP 2000. (F)

Woodson, Jacqueline. *From the Notebooks of Melanin Sun.* Edwards 2006; PPYA 2006. (F)

———. *If You Come Softly.* Edwards 2006; PPYA 2002. (F)

———. *Miracle's Boys.* Edwards 2006; PPYA 2008. (F)

OVERLAPPING TITLES (FICTION AND NONFICTION)

Alphin, Elaine Marie. *Counterfeit Son.* QP 2001; PPYA 2003. (F)

Anderson, Laurie Halse. *Speak.* QP 2000; PPYA 2003. (F)

Atwater-Rhodes, Amelia. *In the Forests of the Night.* QP 2000; PPYA 2001. (F)

———. *Shattered Mirror.* QP 2002; PPYA 2005. (F)

Barnes, Derrick. *The Making of Dr. Truelove.* QP 2007; PPYA 2008. (F)

Barnes, Jennifer Lynn. *Tattoo.* QP 2008; PPYA 2008. (F)

Bauer, Cat. *Harley, like a Person.* QP 2001; PPYA 2002; PPYA 2008. (F)

Bauer, Joan. *Rules of the Road.* QP 1999; PPYA 2001. (F)

———. *Thwonk.* PPYA 1999; PPYA 2007. (F)

Beale, Fleur. *I Am Not Esther.* QP 2003; PPYA 2007. (F)

Bechard, Margaret. *Hanging On to Max.* QP 2003; PPYA 2005. (F)

Bendis, Brian Michael. *Power and Responsibility.* QP 2002; PPYA 2002. (F)

Black, Holly. *Valiant: A Modern Tale of Faerie.* QP 2006; PPYA 2008. (F)

Black, Jonah. The Black Book: Diary of a Teenage Stud series. QP 2002; PPYA 2003. (F)

Bunting, Eve. *Blackwater.* QP 2000; PPYA 2003. (F)

Cabot, Meg. *All-American Girl.* QP 2003; PPYA 2006. (F)

———. *The Princess Diaries,* vol. 1. QP 2001; PPYA 2003. (F)

Chbosky, Stephen. *The Perks of Being a Wallflower.* QP 2000; PPYA 2002. (F)

Cohn, Rachel, and David Levithan. *Nick and Norah's Infinite Playlist.* QP 2007; PPYA 2008. (F)

Conford, Ellen. *Crush.* QP 1999; PPYA 2000. (F)

Cormier, Robert. *Heroes.* QP 1999; PPYA 2004. (F)

———. *Tenderness.* PPYA 1999; PPYA 2005. (F)

Daldry, Jeremy. *The Teenage Guy's Survival Guide: The Real Deal on Girls, Growing Up, and Other Guy Stuff.* QP 2000; PPYA 2000. (NF)

Danziger, Paula, and Ann M. Martin. *P.S. Longer Letter Later.* QP 1999; PPYA 2003. (F)

Davidson, Dana. *Played.* QP 2007; PPYA 2008. (F)

Davis, James. *Skateboarding Is Not a Crime: 50 Years of Street Culture.* QP 2006; PPYA 2007. (NF)

Dee, Catherine, and Ali Douglas, eds. *The Girl's Book of Wisdom: Empowering, Inspirational Quotes from 400 Fabulous Females.* QP 2000; PPYA 2000. (NF)

de la Peña, Matt. *Ball Don't Lie.* QP 2006; PPYA 2008. (F)

Drill, Esther, Heather McDonald, and Rebecca Odes. *Deal with It! A Whole New Approach to Your Body, Brain and Life as a gURL.* QP 2001; PPYA 2000. (NF)

Eminem. *Angry Blonde.* QP 2002; PPYA 2004. (NF)

Ewing, Lynne. *Party Girl.* QP 1999; PPYA 2002. (F)

Ferris, Jean. *Bad.* QP 1999; PPYA 2006. (F)

Flinn, Alex. *Breathing Underwater.* QP 2002; PPYA 2003. (F)

———. *Nothing to Lose.* QP 2005; PPYA 2006. (F)

Frank, E. R. *America.* QP 2003; PPYA 2005. (F)

Fujishima, Kosuke. *Oh My Goddess! Wrong Number.* QP 2003; PPYA 2002. (F)

Gaiman, Neil. *Neverwhere.* PPYA 1999; PPYA 2008. (F)

Genat, Robert. *Lowriders.* QP 2002; PPYA 2007. (NF)

Giles, Gail. *Shattering Glass.* QP 2003; PPYA 2005. (F)

Grimes, Nikki. *Bronx Masquerade.* QP 2003; PPYA 2007. (F)

Haddix, Margaret Peterson. *Among the Hidden.* QP 2000; PPYA 2003. (F)

———. *Just Ella.* QP 2000; PPYA 2007. (F)

Hart, Christopher. *Manga Mania: How to Draw Japanese Comics.* QP 2002; PPYA 2007. (NF)

Hartinger, Brent. *Last Chance Texaco.* QP 2005; PPYA 2006. (F)

Hesser, Terry Spencer. *Kissing Doorknobs.* QP 1999; PPYA 2006. (F)

Hobbs, Will. *The Maze.* QP 1999; PPYA 2002. (F)

Holt, David, and Bill Mooney. *Spiders in the Hairdo: Modern Urban Legends.* QP 2000; PPYA 2000. (NF)

Hopkins, Ellen. *Crank.* QP 2005; PPYA 2005. (F)

Horowitz, Anthony. *Raven's Gate.* QP 2006; PPYA 2008. (F)

———. *Stormbreaker.* QP 2002; PPYA 2003. (F)

Hoye, Jacob, and Karolyn Ali, eds. *Tupac: Resurrection 1971–1996.* QP 2004; PPYA 2007. (NF)

Hrdlitschka, Shelley. *Dancing Naked.* QP 2003; PPYA 2005. (F)

Irwin, Cait. *Conquering the Beast Within: How I Fought Depression and Won . . . and How You Can, Too.* QP 2001; PPYA 2000. (NF)

Jacobs, Thomas. *They Broke the Law, You Be the Judge: True Cases of Teen Crime.* QP 2005; PPYA 2006. (NF)

———. *What Are My Rights? 95 Questions and Answers about Teens and the Law.* QP 1999; PPYA 2000. (NF)

Klancher, Lee. *Monster Garage: How to Customize Damn Near Anything.* QP 2005; PPYA 2007. (NF)

Klause, Annette Curtis. *Blood and Chocolate.* PPYA 2000; PPYA 2008. (F)

Koertge, Ron. *The Brimstone Journals.* QP 2002; PPYA 2006. (F)

———. *Stoner and Spaz.* QP 2003; PPYA 2005. (F)

Kool Moe Dee. *There's a God on the Mic: The True 50 Greatest MCs.* QP 2005; PPYA 2007. (NF)

Korman, Gordon. *Son of the Mob.* QP 2003; PPYA 2005. (F)

Kyi, Tanya Lloyd. *Truth.* QP 2004; PPYA 2006. (F)

Larson, Gary. *There's a Hair in My Dirt: A Worm's Story.* QP 1999; PPYA 2001. (NF)

Levithan, David. *Boy Meets Boy.* QP 2004; PPYA 2006. (F)

Lubar, David. *Hidden Talents.* QP 2000; PPYA 2005. (F)

McCafferty, Megan. *Sloppy Firsts.* QP 2003; PPYA 2003. (F)

Miller, Timothy, and Steve Milton. *NASCAR Now!* QP 2005; PPYA 2008. (NF)

Moore, Terry. *Strangers in Paradise: High School.* PPYA 2002; PPYA 2005; PPYA 2006. (F)

Myers, Walter Dean. *145th Street: Short Stories.* QP 2001; PPYA 2002. (F)

Napoli, Donna Jo. *Zel.* PPYA 2000; PPYA 2005. (F)

Naylor, Phyllis Reynolds. *Jade Green: A Ghost Story.* QP 2001; PPYA 2003. (F)

Oppel, Kenneth. *Airborn.* QP 2005; PPYA 2006. (F)

Owen, David. *Hidden Evidence: Forty True Crime Stories and How Forensic Science Helped to Solve Them.* QP 2001; PPYA 2007. (NF)

Packer, Alex. *How Rude! The Teenager's Guide to Good Manners, Proper Behavior, and Not Grossing People Out.* QP 1999; PPYA 2000. (NF)

Palmer, Chris. *Streetball: All the Ballers, Moves, Slams and Shine.* QP 2006; PPYA 2007. (NF)

Pardes, Bronwen. *Doing It Right: Making Smart, Safe and Satisfying Choices about Sex.* QP 2008; PPYA 2008. (NF)

Paulsen, Gary. *Soldier's Heart: A Novel of the Civil War.* QP 1999; PPYA 2002. (F)

Perel, David, and the editors of the Weekly World News. *Bat Boy Lives! The Weekly World News Guide to Politics, Culture, Celebrities, Alien Abductions, and the Mutant Freaks That Shape Our World.* QP 2006; PPYA 2007. (NF)

Peters, Julie Anne. *Define "Normal."* QP 2001; PPYA 2005. (F)

Pfetzer, Mark, and Jack Galvin. *Within Reach: My Everest Story.* QP 1999; PPYA 2003. (NF)

Pratt, Jane. *Beyond Beauty: Girls Speak Out on Looks, Style and Stereotypes.* QP 1999; PPYA 1999. (NF)

Qualey, Marsha. *Close to a Killer.* QP 2000; PPYA 2004. (F)

Rees, Douglas. *Vampire High.* QP 2004; PPYA 2007. (F)

Rennison, Louise. *Angus, Thongs, and Full-Frontal Snogging.* QP 2001; PPYA 2003. (F)

Riley, Andy. *The Book of Bunny Suicides.* QP 2005; PPYA 2007. (NF)

Rothbart, Davy. *Found: The Best Lost, Tossed and Forgotten Items from around the World.* QP 2005; PPYA 2007. (NF)

Rylant, Cynthia. *God Went to Beauty School.* QP 2004; PPYA 2007. (NF)

Sachar, Louis. *Holes.* QP 1999; PPYA 2006. (F)

Shaw, Maria. *Maria Shaw's Star Gazer: Your Soul Searching, Dream Seeking, Make Something Happen Guide to the Future.* QP 2005; PPYA 2007. (NF)

Sheldon, Dyan. *Confessions of a Teenage Drama Queen.* QP 2000; PPYA 2006. (F)

Shetterly, Will. *Elsewhere.* PPYA 1999; PPYA 2005. (F)

Shusterman, Neal. *Downsiders.* QP 2000; PPYA 2002. (F)

Sleator, William. *The Boxes.* QP 1999; PPYA 2001. (F)

Sones, Sonya. *One of Those Hideous Books Where the Mother Dies.* QP 2005; PPYA 2008. (F)

———. *Stop Pretending: What Happened When My Big Sister Went Crazy.* QP 2000; PPYA 2002. (F)

Stine, R. L. *Dangerous Girls.* QP 2004; PPYA 2005. (F)

Stolarz, Laurie Faria. *Blue Is for Nightmares.* QP 2005; PPYA 2007. (F)

Stratton, Allan. *Leslie's Journal.* QP 2001; PPYA 2003. (F)

Takaya, Natsuki. Fruits Basket series, vol. 1. QP 2005; PPYA 2006. (F)

Vizzini, Ned. *Be More Chill.* QP 2005; PPYA 2007. (F)

Volponi, Paul. *Black and White.* QP 2006; PPYA 2008. (F)

Wallace, Rich. *Wrestling Sturbridge.* PPYA 1999; PPYA 2008. (F)

Watson, Esther Pearl, and Mark Todd, eds. *The Pain Tree, and Other Teenage Angst-Ridden Poetry.* QP 2001; PPYA 2001. (NF)

Werlin, Nancy. *The Killer's Cousin.* QP 1999, PPYA 2003. (F)

Westerfeld, Scott. *The Secret Hour.* QP 2005; PPYA 2008. (F)

Williams, Stanley "Tookie," and Barbara Cottman Becnel. *Life in Prison.* QP 1999; PPYA 2006. (NF)

Willingham, Bill. *Legends in Exile.* QP 2004; PPYA 2005. (F)

Wilson, Daniel H. *How to Survive a Robot Uprising: Tips on Defending Yourself against the Coming Rebellion.* QP 2006; PPYA 2007. (F)

Wittlinger, Ellen. *Hard Love.* QP 2000; PPYA 2002. (F)

Yamanaka, Lois-Ann. *Name Me Nobody.* PPYA 2003; PPYA 2005. (F)

Zindel, Paul. *Rats.* QP 2000; PPYA 2002. (F)

PHOTOGRAPHS AND PHOTOGRAPHERS (NONFICTION)

Bey, Dawoud. *Class Pictures.*

Carlowicz, Michael. *The Moon.*

Handy, Roger, and Karen Elsener, eds. *Found Photos: Rear Ends.*

Kenner, Rob, and George Pitts. *VX: 10 Years of Vibe Photography.*

Oser, Bodhi. *Fuck This Book.*

Partridge, Elizabeth. *Restless Spirit: The Life and Work of Dorothea Lange.*

Pearce, Fred. *Earth Then and Now: Amazing Images of Our Changing World.*

Pilobolus Dance Theater. *Twisted Yoga.*

Pletka, Bob, ed. *My So-Called Digital Life: 2,000 Teenagers, 300 Cameras, and 30 Days to Document Their World.*

Powell, Kevin, ed. *Who Shot Ya? Three Decades of Hiphop Photography.*

Scalora, Suza. *Fairies: Photographic Evidence of the Existence of Another World.*

Schatz, Howard. *Athlete.*

Williamson, Kate T. *Hello Kitty through the Seasons: Photographs and Haiku.*

Wood, Nick. *360 Degrees New York.*

ROMANCE (FICTION)

Abbott, Hailey. *Summer Boys.*

Austen, Jane. *Pride and Prejudice.*

Bauer, Joan. *Thwonk.*

Bennett, Cherie. *The Haunted Heart.*

Bernardo, Anilu. *Loves Me, Loves Me Not.*

Bonner, Cindy. *Lily: A Love Story.*

Brownley, Margaret. *Buttons and Beaus.*

Cabot, Meggin. *The Boy Next Door.*

Castellucci, Cecil. *Beige.*

——. *Boy Proof.*

Frank, Lucy. *Oy, Joy!*

Gabaldon, Diana. *Outlander.*

Green, John. *Looking for Alaska.*

Klause, Annette Curtis. *Blood and Chocolate.*

Korman, Gordon. *Son of the Mob.*

Lane, Dakota. *Johnny Voodoo.*

Mackler, Carolyn. *Guyaholic: A Story of Finding, Flirting, Forgetting . . . and the Boy Who Changes Everything.*

——. *Love and Other Four Letter Words.*

McCants, William D. *Much Ado about Prom Night.*

McDaniel, Lurlene. *I'll Be Seeing You.*

McKinley, Robin. *Beauty: A Retelling of the Story of Beauty and the Beast.*

Meyer, Stephenie. *New Moon.*

——. *Twilight.*

Plummer, Louise. *The Unlikely Romance of Kate Bjorkman.*

Putney, Mary Jo. *One Perfect Rose.*

Shusterman, Neal. *Downsiders.*

Sones, Sonya. *What My Girlfriend Doesn't Know.*

———. *What My Mother Doesn't Know.*

Stewart, Mary. *Nine Coaches Waiting.*

Taylor, William. *The Blue Lawn.*

SCHOOL LIFE (FICTION)

Atkins, Catherine. *Alt Ed.*

Brewer, Heather. *Eighth Grade Bites.*

Carvell, Marlene. *Who Will Tell My Brother?*

Chbosky, Stephen. *The Perks of Being a Wallflower.*

de Lint, Charles. *The Blue Girl.*

Draper, Sharon M. *Darkness before Dawn.*

Flake, Sharon. *The Skin I'm In.*

Flinn, Alex. *Breaking Point.*

Foon, Dennis. *Skud.*

Frank, Hilary. *Better Than Running at Night.*

Giles, Gail. *Shattering Glass.*

Grant, Vicki. *Pigboy.*

Green, John. *Looking for Alaska.*

Grimes, Nikki. *Bronx Masquerade.*

Hartinger, Brent. *The Geography Club.*

Koertge, Ron. *The Brimstone Journals.*

Korman, Gordon. *No More Dead Dogs.*

Kyi, Tanya Lloyd. *Truth.*

Marchetta, Melina. *Saving Francesca.*

Moore, Terry. *Strangers in Paradise: High School.*

Myers, Walter Dean. *Shooter.*

Pearsall, Shelley. *All of the Above.*

Peters, Julie Anne. *Define "Normal."*

Pinkwater, Jill. *Buffalo Brenda.*

Rallison, Janette. *All's Fair in Love, War, and High School.*

Sheldon, Dyan. *Confessions of a Teenage Drama Queen.*

Strasser, Todd. *Boot Camp.*

van Diepen, Allison. *Snitch.*

Von Ziegesar, Cecily. Gossip Girl series.

SHORT STORIES (FICTION)

Appelt, Kathi. *Kissing Tennessee: And Other Stories from the Stardust.*

Block, Francesca Lia. *Girl Goddess #9: Nine Stories.*

Carlson, Lori M., ed. *American Eyes: New Asian-American Short Stories for Young Adults.*

Cart, Michael, ed. *Love and Sex: Ten Stories of Truth.*

———. *Tomorrowland: Ten Stories about the Future.*

Conford, Ellen. *Crush.*

Crutcher, Chris. *Athletic Shorts: Six Short Stories.*

Gallo, Donald R., ed. *Join In: Multiethnic Short Stories by Outstanding Writers for Young Adults.*

———. *No Easy Answers: Short Stories about Teenagers Making Tough Choices.*

———. *On the Fringe.*

———. *Ultimate Sports: Short Stories by Outstanding Writers for Young Adults.*

Galloway, Priscilla. *Truly Grim Tales.*

Greenberg, Martin, and Russell Davis, eds. *Faerie Tales.*

Howe, James, ed. *The Color of Absence: 12 Stories about Loss and Hope.*

Hughes, Monica, ed. *What If . . . ? Amazing Stories.*

Kightlinger, Laura. *Quick Shots of False Hope: A Rejection Collection.*

Lane, Dakota. *The Secret Life of It Girls.*

LeGuin, Ursula K. *The Wind's Twelve Quarters: Seventeen Stories of Fantastic Adventure.*

Mazer, Anne, ed. *Walk in My World: International Short Stories about Youth.*

———. *Working Days: Short Stories about Teenagers at Work.*

Mazer, Harry, ed. *Twelve Shots: Outstanding Short Stories about Guns.*

Moss, Steve, ed. *World's Shortest Stories: Murder, Love, Horror, and Suspense.*

Myers, Walter Dean. *145th Street: Short Stories.*

———. *What They Found: Love on 145th Street.*

Reynolds, Marilyn. *Beyond Dreams.*

Singer, Marilyn. *Stay True: Short Stories for Strong Girls.*

Smith, Charles R., Jr. *Tall Tales: Six Amazing Basketball Dreams.*

Soto, Gary. *Petty Crimes.*

Springer, Nancy, ed. *Prom Night.*

Thomas, Rob. *Doing Time: Notes from the Undergrad.*

Velez, Ivan. *Dead High Yearbook.*

Westall, Robert. *Demons and Shadows: The Ghostly Best Stories of Robert Westall.*

SKATEBOARDING (FICTION AND NONFICTION)

Boards: The Art and Design of the Skateboard. (NF)

Brisick, Jamie. *Have Board, Will Travel: The Definitive History of Surf, Skate and Snow.* (NF)

Brooke, Michael. *The Concrete Wave: The History of Skateboarding.* (NF)

Davis, James. *Skateboarding Is Not a Crime: 50 Years of Street Culture.* (NF)

Harmon, Michael. *Skate.* (F)

Hawk, Tony. *Between Boardslides and Burnout: My Notes from the Road.* (NF)

Hawk, Tony, with Sean Mortimer. *Hawk: Occupation, Skateboarder.* (NF)

Nelson, Blake. *Paranoid Park.* (F)

Skate and Destroy: The First 25 Years of "Thrasher" Magazine. (NF)

Thatcher, Kevin, ed. *"Thrasher" Presents: How to Build Skateboard Ramps, Halfpipes, Boxes, Bowls and More.* (NF)

"Thrasher": Insane Terrain. (NF)

UNSUNG HEROES (FICTION AND NONFICTION)

Brennan, Michael. *Electric Girl.* (F)

Busiek, Kurt. *Kurt Busiek's Astro City: Life in the Big City.* (F)

Dougall, Alastair. *James Bond: The Secret World of 007.* (NF)

Ellis, Warren. *Force of Nature.* (F)

Howe, Norma. *The Adventures of Blue Avenger.* (F)

Johns, Geoff. *A Kid's Game.* (F)

Kirkman, Robert. *Invincible.* (NF)

Kunkel, Mike. *The Inheritance.* (F)

Millar, Mark. *The Tomorrow People,* vol. 1. (F)

Powell, Michael. *Superhero Handbook.* (NF)

Simonson, Louise. *DC Comics Covergirls.* (NF)

Vaughan, Brian K. Runaways series. (F)

VAMPIRES (FICTION) [WEB]

Atwater-Rhodes, Amelia. *Demon in My View.*

———. *In the Forests of the Night.*

———. *Midnight Predator.*

———. *Shattered Mirror.*

Brewer, Heather. *Eighth Grade Bites.*

Cary, Kate. *Bloodline.*

Cast, P. C., and Kristin Cast. The House of Night series. Book 1, *Marked;* book 2, *Betrayed.*

de la Cruz, Melissa. *Blue Bloods.*

———. *Masquerade.*

Hahn, Mary Downing. *Look for Me by Moonlight.*

Hamilton, Laurell K. *Guilty Pleasures.*

Hirano, Kohta. Hellsing series.

Klause, Annette Curtis. *The Silver Kiss.*

Mancusi, Mari. *Boys That Bite.*

Mead, Richelle. *Vampire Academy.*

Meyer, Stephenie. *New Moon.*

———. *Twilight.*

Moore, Christopher. *Bloodsucking Fiends: A Love Story.*

Niles, Steve. *30 Days of Night.*

Petrie, Doug. *Ring of Fire.*

Rees, Douglas. *Vampire High.*

Schreiber, Ellen. *Vampire Kisses.*

Stine, R. L. *Dangerous Girls.*

Thompson, Kate. *Midnight's Choice.*

Vande Velde, Vivian. *Companions of the Night.*

Velez, Ivan. *Dead High Yearbook.*

Whedon, Joss. *Fray.*

WHO ARE THESE PEOPLE? (NONFICTION)

Baskin, Julia, et al. *The Notebook Girls: Four Friends, One Diary, Real Life.*

Beil, Karen Magnuson. *Fire in Their Eyes: Wildfires and the People Who Fight Them.*

Blais, Madeleine. *In These Girls, Hope Is a Muscle.*

Boylan, Jennifer Finney. *She's Not There: A Life in Two Genders.*

Bradley, James, and Ron Powers. *Flags of Our Fathers: Heroes of Iwo Jima.*

Chang, Pang-Mei. *Bound Feet and Western Dress: A Memoir.*

Crisp, Terri. *Out of Harm's Way: The Extraordinary True Story of One Woman's Lifelong Devotion to Animals.*

Fleischman, John. *Phineas Gage: A Gruesome but True Story about Brain Science.*

Fong-Torres, Ben. *The Rice Room: Growing Up Chinese-American; From Number Two Son to Rock 'n' Roll.*

Gantos, Jack. *Hole in My Life.*

Gottlieb, Lori. *Stick Figure: A Diary of My Former Self.*

Grealy, Lucy. *Autobiography of a Face.*

Gregory, Julia. *Sickened: The Memoir of a Munchausen by Proxy Childhood.*

Hamilton, Bethany, with Sheryl Berk and Rick Bundschuh. *Soul Surfer: A True Story of Faith, Family, and Fighting to Get Back on the Board.*

Mah, Adeline Yen. *Chinese Cinderella: The True Story of an Unwanted Daughter.*

Myers, Walter Dean. *Bad Boy: A Memoir.*

Opdyke, Irene Gut. *In My Hands: Memories of a Holocaust Rescuer.*

Partridge, Elizabeth. *Restless Spirit: The Life and Work of Dorothea Lange.*

Paulsen, Gary. *My Life in Dog Years.*

Pelzer, Dave. *A Child Called "It": One Child's Courage to Survive.*

Rodriguez, Luis J. *Always Running: La Vida Loca; Gang Days in L.A.*

Runyon, Brent. *The Burn Journals.*

Salant, James. *Leaving Dirty Jersey: A Crystal Meth Memoir.*

Sanchez, Reymundo. *My Bloody Life: The Making of a Latin King.*

Santiago, Esmeralda. *Almost a Woman.*

Satrapi, Marjane. *The Story of a Childhood.*

Shivak, Nadia. *Inside Out: Portrait of an Eating Disorder.*

Steffans, Karrine. *Confessions of a Video Vixen.*

Tarbox, Katherine. *Katie.com: My Story.*

Ung, Loung. *First They Killed My Father: A Daughter of Cambodia Remembers.*

Vizzini, Ned. *Teen Angst? Naaah . . . : A Quasi-Autobiography.*

Walls, Jeannette. *The Glass Castle: A Memoir.*

Williams, Stanley "Tookie," and Barbara Cottman Becnel. *Life in Prison.*

Winick, Judd. *Pedro and Me: Friendship, Loss, and What I Learned.*

Zailckas, Koren. *Smashed: Story of a Drunken Girlhood.*

WITCHES AND WITCHCRAFT (FICTION AND NONFICTION)

Atwater-Rhodes, Amelia. *Shattered Mirror.* (F)

Bird, Isobel. Circle of Three series. Vol. 1, *So Mote It Be;* vol. 2, *Merry Meet;* vol. 3, *Second Sight;* vol. 4, *What the Cards Said;* vol. 5, *In the Dreaming;* vol. 6, *Ring of Light;* vol. 7, *Blue Moon.* (F)

Delaney, Joseph. *Revenge of the Witch.* (F)

Gaiman, Neil, and Terry Pratchett. *Good Omens: The Nice and Accurate Prophecies of Agnes Nutter, Witch.* (F)

Manoy, Lauren. *Where to Park Your Broomstick: A Teen's Guide to Witchcraft.* (NF)

Nash, Naomi. *You Are So Cursed.* (F)

Rain, Gwinevere. *Spellcraft for Teens: A Magical Guide to Writing and Casting Spells.* (NF)

Ravenwolf, Silver. *Teen Witch: Wicca for a New Generation.* (NF)

Rees, Celia. *Witch Child.* (F)

Tiernan, Cate. Balefire series. Book 1, *A Chalice of Wind;* book 2, *A Circle of Ashes.* (F)

———. Sweep series. Book 1, *Book of Shadows;* book 2, *Coven;* book 3, *Blood Witch;* book 4, *Dark Magick;* book 5, *Awakening.* (F)

Vande Velde, Vivian. *Never Trust a Dead Man.* (F)

WOMEN IN SPORTS (NONFICTION)

Anderson, Joan. *Rookie: Tamika Whitmore's First Year in the WNBA.*

Blais, Madeleine. *In These Girls, Hope Is a Muscle.*

Colton, Larry. *Counting Coup: A True Story of Basketball and Honor on the Little Big Horn.*

Corbett, Sara. *Venus to the Hoop: A Gold Medal Year in Women's Basketball.*

Gottesman, Jane. *Game Face: What Does a Female Athlete Look Like?*

Inside Cheerleading, ed. *Cheerleading: From Tryouts to Championships.*

Laurer, Joanie, with Michael Angeli. *Chyna: If They Only Knew.*

Macy, Sue. *A Whole New Ball Game: The Story of the All-American Girls Professional Baseball League.*

———. *Winning Ways: A Photohistory of American Women in Sport.*

Macy, Sue, and Jane Gottesman. *Play like a Girl: A Celebration of Women in Sports.*

INDEX

Note: Authors, titles, and subjects are interfiled in one alphabet. Authors print in roman, titles in *italics,* and subjects in **boldface.** Annotations are indicated by **bold** page numbers.

You may also be interested in

Serving Teens through Readers' Advisory: Getting teens to read for fun is the ultimate challenge, yet research shows that it improves skills in grammar and spelling while expanding vocabularies. Readers' advisors who serve teens (or want to) now have a ready-to-use resource from an expert in teen readers' advisory. Accessible and encouraging for beginners and an informative refresher for those more experienced, this hands-on guide addresses teens' unique needs with practical tools.

Multicultural Programs for Tweens and Teens: A one-stop resource that encourages children and young adults to explore different cultures. The fifty flexible programming ideas allow you to choose a program specific to your scheduling needs, create an event that reflects a specific culture, and recommend further resources to tweens and teens interested in learning more about diverse cultures.

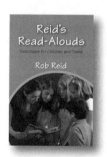

Reid's Read-Alouds: Best-selling author Rob Reid makes reading aloud to teens easy by selecting titles in high-interest topics published between 2000 and 2008. Providing context to spotlight great passages, Reid makes reading fun and exciting with read-aloud passages from 200 titles, advice on how to prepare for a read-aloud, subject and grade-level indexes to make program planning easier, and a bibliography of included titles.

Best Books for Young Adults: Covering forty years of the best in young adult literature, plus background on the history, committee procedures, and current issues facing the BBYA Committee, this book is relevant to anyone working with teens. Perfect for readers' advisory and collection development, this resource includes a recap of the trends in teen literature as reflected in the past decade of BBYA lists, twenty-seven themed and annotated reproducible book lists, and indexed, annotated lists extending back to 1966.

For more information, please visit www.alastore.ala.org.